Microsoft Silverlight 5 and Windows Azure Enterprise Integration

A step-by-step guide to creating and running scalable Silverlight Enterprise Applications on the Windows Azure platform

David Burela

[PACKT] enterprise

PUBLISHING

professional expertise distilled

BIRMINGHAM - MUMBAI

Microsoft Silverlight 5 and Windows Azure Enterprise Integration

First published: March 2012

Production Reference: 1120312

Published by Packt Publishing Ltd.
Livery Place
35 Livery Street
Birmingham B3 2PB, UK.

ISBN 978-1-84968-312-8

www.packtpub.com

Cover Image by Anvar Khodzhaev (cbetah@yahoo.com)

Credits

Author
David Burela

Reviewers
Alex Mackey

Nick Randolph

William Tulloch

Acquisition Editor
Kerry George

Development Editor
Hyacintha D'Souza

Technical Editors
Ameya Sawant

Azharuddin Sheikh

Copy Editor
Laxmi Subramanian

Project Coordinator
Michelle Quadros

Proofreader
Julie Jackson

Indexers
Monica Ajmera Mehta

Rekha Nair

Graphics
Manu Joseph

Production Coordinator
Aparna Bhagat

Cover Work
Aparna Bhagat

About the Author

David Burela works full time as a Senior .Net consultant for the Australian consulting firm Hazaa (http://Hazaa.com.au).

He also holds Microsoft certifications, making him an Azure Microsoft Certified Professional Developer (MCPD) and a Silverlight Microsoft Certified Technology Specialist (MCTS). At university, he did a Bachelors in Computer Science, a Masters in Computer Science, and an MBA (Masters of Business Administration). He uses this unique mixture of technical and business skills to help the clients he consults for.

David loves researching the latest cutting-edge technologies and frameworks, and has heavily invested in Windows Azure, Silverlight, and Windows Phone 7. This passion for researching and learning sees him helping out the developer community. He ran a local .Net user group for three years, and currently runs the Melbourne Silverlight User Group. While running user groups is enjoyable, presenting at them is more fun. He keeps his presentation skills sharp by delivering talks every few months on a variety of topics.

David has been recognized for his abilities and contributions with numerous awards. In 2007, David was acknowledged for his contributions to the community and was a state finalist for the "Young Australian of the Year" award of the Australian Government.

In 2008, David entered into a global programming competition run by Microsoft and competed against winning teams from over 80 different countries. David and his team won the global competition with their cloud-based agriculture system that would assist farmers and growers in drought-stricken regions. In 2010, David entered into another Microsoft programming competition, this time for Windows Phone 7, and came runner-up for his submission. The phone application notified the residents of Sydney, Australia of the safety of swimming at the local beaches for the current day.

Acknowledgement

I would like to thank my employers, past and present, for all the opportunities that have helped me in writing this book. Without their support and trust in allowing me to research the cutting-edge technologies, I would never have made it to this point.

A big thank you to my friends, for understanding why I have missed out on many social events during the writing of this book.

But no acknowledgement is complete without thanking my family, and my loving partner YanLi Shen. Thanks YanLi for cooking so many dinners for me while I tried to concentrate on the book.

About the Reviewers

William Tulloch lives and works in Australia and is currently a Senior Consultant with Readify. He has been actively involved in software and web development for over 19 years and is as enthusiastic about coding as he was when he started.

Having been involved with .Net since 2002, William has a broad working knowledge of the various .Net technologies. His current interests are in the areas of Azure, federated identity with a focus on Windows Identity Foundation, ALM, and Silverlight or XAML development. He is also active in the user community, speaking regularly at the user groups and events, such as "Developer Developer Developer".

Alex Mackey specializes in web development and works for the Australian .Net consultancy Readify. He is a Microsoft Most Valuable Professional (MVP) in Internet Explorer development and an author (Introducing .Net 4.0 with Visual Studio 2010, Apress). Alex has spoken at a number of technical conferences (TechEd Remix, Australian ALM), and organizes the community conference DDD Melbourne.

Nick Randolph currently runs Built To Roam, which focuses on building rich mobile applications. Previously, Nick was a co-founder and Development Manager for Nsquared Solutions where he led a team of developers to build inspirational software using next-wave technology. Prior to Nsquared, Nick was the lead developer at Intilecta Corporation Limited where he was integrally involved in designing and building their application framework.

After graduating from a combined engineering (Information Technology) and commerce degree, Nick went on to be nominated as a Microsoft MVP in recognition of his work with the Perth .Net user group, and his focus on mobile devices. He is still an active contributor in the device application development space through his blog at http://nicksnettravels.builttoroam.com, Visual Studio Magazine (http://visualstudiomagazine.com/Articles/List/Mobile-Corner.aspx), and BuildMobile (http://buildmobile.com/category/windows/).

Nick has been invited to present at a variety of events including TechEd Australia and New Zealand, MEDC, and Code Camp. He has also authored articles for MSDN Magazine (ANZ edition) for four books, with the latest being Professional Visual Studio 2010 and Professional Development for Windows Phone, and helped in judging the 2004, 2005, 2007, 2008, 2010, and 2011 world finals for the Imagine Cup.

www.PacktPub.com

Support files, eBooks, discount offers and more

You might want to visit www.PacktPub.com for support files and downloads related to your book.

Did you know that Packt offers e-book versions of every published book, with PDF and epub files available? You can upgrade to the e-book version at www.PacktPub.com and as a print book customer, you are entitled to a discount on the e-Book copy. Get in touch with us at service@packtpub.com for more details.

At www.PacktPub.com, you can also read a collection of free technical articles, sign up for a range of free newsletters, and receive exclusive discounts and offers on Packt books and e-books.

http://PacktLib.PacktPub.com

Do you need instant solutions to your IT questions? PacktLib is online digital book library of Packt. Here, you can access, read, and search across the entire library of Packt books.

Why Subscribe?

- Fully searchable across every book published by Packt
- Copy and paste, print and bookmark content
- On-demand and accessible through web browser

Free Access for Packt account holders

If you have an account with Packt at www.PacktPub.com, you can use this to access PacktLib today, and view nine free books entirely. Simply use your login credentials for immediate access.

Instant Updates on New Packt Books

Get notified! Find out when new books are published by following @PacktEnterprise on Twitter, or the *Packt Enterprise* Facebook page.

Table of Contents

Preface

Integrating **Silverlight** and **Windows Azure** can be difficult without guidance. This book will take you through all the steps to create and run a Silverlight Enterprise application on the Windows Azure platform. It starts by providing the steps required to set up the development environment, providing an overview of Azure. The book then dives deep into topics such as hosting Silverlight applications in Azure, using Azure Queues in Silverlight, storing data in Azure Table storage from Silverlight, accessing Azure Blob storage from Silverlight, relational data with SQL Azure and RIA, and manipulating data with RIA services among others.

What this book covers

Chapter 1, Getting Started, shows how to set up your development environment. It covers the basics of ensuring that Visual Studio 2010, the Silverlight Software Development Kit (SDK), and the Azure SDK are installed. The tools that can be of assistance will be mentioned, such as Expression Blend, LINQPad to SQL Azure, and the Azure Storage explorer.

Chapter 2, Introduction to Azure, gives an overview of Windows Azure. It covers what Azure is, how Microsoft abstracts away the entire infrastructure worries so that the business can just focus on creating the business logic instead.

Chapter 3, Hosting Silverlight Applications in Azure, teaches how to create a Visual Studio solution that contains both the Silverlight and the Azure Project. The basics of how to consume a Windows Communication Foundation (WCF) service, hosted on Azure from within Silverlight is shown, as well as the basics of creating an Azure account and deploying it.

Chapter 4, Using Azure Queues with Silverlight, introduces the Azure storage service and the role it has within the Azure platform. The rest of the chapter then focuses on introducing the Azure Queue service. A Silverlight application is built that uses queues to indicate that widgets should be built.

Chapter 5, Accessing Azure Blob Storage from Silverlight, explains Azure Blob storage. A Silverlight application is built that can interact with the Blob storage to display the photos. It introduces the Azure CDN (Content Delivery Network) and how it can be used to increase the application performance.

Chapter 6, Storing Data in Azure Table Storage from Silverlight, introduces Azure Table storage and how it compares to the relational databases. Concepts such as how to partition your data for scalability are introduced. A Silverlight application is built that uses Azure Table storage to publish news stories.

Chapter 7, Relational Data with SQL Azure and Entity Framework, introduces SQL Azure and how it can be accessed through Entity Framework. You will learn the basics of querying and selecting data from an SQL Azure, and how to expose this data through WCF services.

Chapter 8, RIA Services and SQL Azure, explains how SQL Azure and RIA Services are combined. Rather than writing WCF methods by hand, RIA Services will be utilized to simplify the application development. You will learn how to modify and create data from within Silverlight.

Chapter 9, Exposing OData to Silverlight Applications, explains how OData is an open standard for exposing data. Data exposed in this way is queryable across a number of platforms, such as Silverlight, JavaScript, iPhones, and so on.

Chapter 10, Web-scale considerations, discusses breaking your application into asynchronous components that assists with the scaling of your architecture. Techniques for globalizing your application by hosting in multiple datacenters around the world are also shown.

Chapter 11, Application Authentication, focuses on how to get standard ASP.Net authentication and roles working with an Azure application by storing it in SQL Azure. The Azure Access Control System is also introduced as well as the Federated Authentication.

Chapter 12, Using Azure AppFabric Caching to Improve Performance, explores what data caching is and how it can improve the performance of your application.

What you need for this book

No prior knowledge of Windows Azure is assumed. However, a basic background in Silverlight is expected. The chapters and exercises have been written to allow completion regardless of current skills.

The first chapter will take you through configuring your computer to allow you to complete the rest of the book. As long as you have an Internet connection and a copy of Windows (Vista or later), you will be able to obtain everything you require.

Who this book is for

This book would primarily be aimed at application developers who want to build and run Silverlight Enterprise applications using Azure Storage, WCF Services, RIA services, and SQL Azure. A working knowledge of Silverlight and Expression Blend would be required. However, knowledge of Azure would not necessarily be required since the book would be covering how to integrate the two technologies in detail.

Conventions

In this book, you will find a number of styles of text that distinguish different kinds of information. Here are some examples of these styles, and an explanation of their meaning.

A block of code is set as follows:

```
using System.ServiceModel;

namespace WebRole1
{
  [ServiceContract]
  public interface IHelloWorldService
  {
    [OperationContract]
    string GenerateHelloWorldGreeting();
  }
}
```

When we wish to draw your attention to a particular part of a code block, the relevant lines or items are set in bold:

```
using System;
using Microsoft.WindowsAzure.ServiceRuntime;

namespace WebRole1
{
  public class HelloWorldService : IHelloWorldService
  {
    public string GenerateHelloWorldGreeting()
```

```
    {
        var currentTime = DateTime.Now.ToLongTimeString();
        var instanceId = RoleEnvironment.CurrentRoleInstance.Id;

        return string.Format("Hello World! The server time is {0}.
                    Processed by {1}", currentTime, instanceId);
    }
  }
 }
}
```

New terms and **important words** are shown in bold. Words that you see on the screen, in menus, or dialog boxes for example, appear in the text like this: "Right-click on the Silverlight project **HelloWorldSilverlightProject** and select **Add Service Reference**. Click on **Discover** to allow Visual Studio to automatically detect the WCF service in the solution".

Warnings or important notes appear in a box like this.

Tips and tricks appear like this.

Reader feedback

Feedback from our readers is always welcome. Let us know what you think about this book—what you liked or may have disliked. Reader feedback is important for us to develop titles that you really get the most out of.

To send us general feedback, simply send an e-mail to feedback@packtpub.com, and mention the book title in the subject line of your message.

If there is a topic that you have expertise in and you are interested in either writing or contributing to a book, see our author guide on www.packtpub.com/authors.

Customer support

Now that you are the proud owner of a Packt book, we have a number of things to help you to get the most from your purchase.

Downloading the example code

You can download the example code files for all Packt books you have purchased from your account at http://www.packtpub.com. If you purchased this book elsewhere, you can visit http://www.packtpub.com/support and register to have the files e-mailed directly to you.

Errata

Although we have taken every care to ensure the accuracy of our content, mistakes do happen. If you find a mistake in one of our books—maybe a mistake in the text or the code—we would be grateful if you would report this to us. By doing so, you can save other readers from frustration and help us improve subsequent versions of this book. If you find any errata, please report them by visiting http://www.packtpub.com/support, selecting your book, clicking on the **errata submission form** link, and entering the details of your errata. Once your errata are verified, your submission will be accepted and the errata will be uploaded to our website, or added to any list of existing errata, under the **Errata** section of that title.

Piracy

Piracy of copyright material on the Internet is an ongoing problem across all media. At Packt, we take the protection of our copyright and licenses very seriously. If you come across any illegal copies of our works, in any form, on the Internet, please provide us with the location address or website name immediately so that we can pursue a remedy.

Please contact us at copyright@packtpub.com with a link to the suspected pirated material.

We appreciate your help in protecting our authors, and our ability to bring you valuable content.

Questions

You can contact us at questions@packtpub.com if you are having a problem with any aspect of the book, and we will do our best to address it.

1
Getting Started

This chapter will cover how to configure a development environment that is ready for both **Silverlight** and **Windows Azure** development.

While this book assumes a basic knowledge of Silverlight, setting up a development environment to support the Azure development requires a few additional tools and Software Development Kits (SDKs) to be installed.

It is possible to develop Windows Azure applications that are developed entirely on a developer's machine and are never deployed to the Windows Azure servers. To utilize Windows Azure, you will eventually need to deploy your application onto the Windows Azure servers. This chapter will cover how to create an Azure account and deploy directly to it with **Visual Studio 2010**.

In this chapter, we will discuss the following topics:

- How to prepare a system for Azure and Silverlight developments
- Useful tools to assist with the development
- How to deploy applications onto the Azure platform

Installation

Getting your system ready for the development with Silverlight and Windows Azure can be tricky, as there can be a lot of service packs, tools, SDKs, and SDK toolkits that need to be installed. Microsoft has a page dedicated to getting your system ready for the Silverlight development (http://www.silverlight.net/getstarted/) and another for setting up Windows Azure (http://www.microsoft.com/windowsazure/getstarted/).

As it can be difficult to keep a track of which versions of which tools need to be installed, the recommended setup method is to use the automated **Microsoft Web Platform Installer**.

Visual Studio 2010

Azure and Silverlight developments can be done with both the free Visual Studio 2010 Express Web Edition (http://www.microsoft.com/express/Web) and the full versions of Visual Studio 2010 (Professional, Premium, and Ultimate). There is a system requirement of **IIS 7**, which requires that your development machine should be Windows Vista or above (Windows Server 2008, Windows 7, Windows 8, and so on).

This book will assume that the reader is using a full version of Visual Studio 2010, but most features should still be available in both the versions. If the reader does wish to use Visual Studio 2010 Express Web Edition, then it can be installed automatically at the same time with the Microsoft Web Platform Installer.

Web platform installer

Once Visual Studio 2010 has been installed on your computer, the recommended way for installing the required tools and SDKs is with the **Microsoft Web Platform Installer** (http://www.microsoft.com/web/downloads/). The web platform installer always lists the latest versions of the tools and SDKs, which save your time, trying to track them down. The web platform installer will also download and install any required prerequisites. The steps are as follows:

1. Download and install the web platform installer from http://www.microsoft.com/web/downloads/.

2. Open the Microsoft Web Platform Installer from the start menu by clicking on **Start** | **All Programs** | **Microsoft Web Platform Installer**.

3. In the search window, type **Visual Studio 2010 service pack** and select the latest service pack. In the following screenshot, *Service Pack 1*(**SP1**) was the latest available:

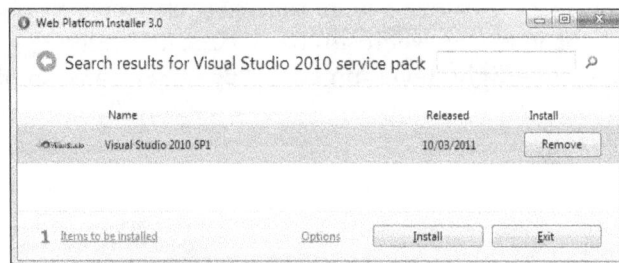

4. Search for **Silverlight 5** and select **Silverlight 5 Tools for Visual Studio 2010**, as shown in the following screenshot:

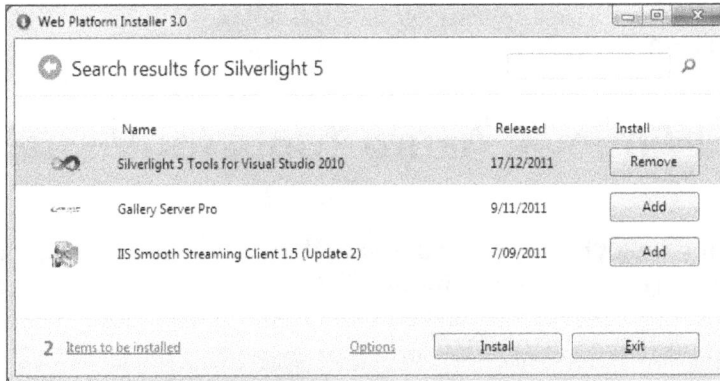

5. Search for **RIA Services Toolkit** and select the latest version of the **WCF RIA Services Toolkit.**

6. Search for **Azure** and select the latest versions of:
   ○ **Windows Azure SDK for .Net**
   ○ **Windows Azure Libraries for .Net**

7. In order to connect to SQL Azure, the *2008 R2 version* of **SQL Management Studio** is required. The free express version is available to be installed. Search for **SQL Server Express 2008 R2** and install the following:
   ○ **SQL Server Express 2008 R2 Management Studio Express with SP1**
   ○ **SQL Server Express 2008 R2**

> **Frequently updated tools**
>
> The tools available to be installed can change frequently. Use the list as a guide to what should be installed on your PC. An easy rule of thumb is to select any option that mentions **Silverlight RIA Services** or **Azure**.

8. Once all the components have been selected and installed, the web platform installer should show those components as **Installed** and unable to be selected again for installation.

Useful tools

There are many tools available to assist you with the development of Silverlight and Windows Azure enterprise applications. The following is a short list of tools that may be useful while progressing through this book.

Official Windows Azure Tools for Visual Studio

The best tool for deploying to and diagnosing Windows Azure is the official **Microsoft Azure Tools for Visual Studio**. These tools enable you to manage your Windows Azure services while you work with Visual Studio. Some of the functionalities provided are as follows:

- The ability to deploy directly to Azure from within the Visual Studio
- IntelliTrace debugging of your deployed instances
- Azure storage services access through the **Visual Studio Server Explorer**

The following screenshot shows the **Server Explorer** being used to browse the contents of the **Blob** storage. It can be accessed from Visual Studio from the menu bar by selecting **View | Server Explorer**. New accounts can then be added by right-clicking on the **Windows Azure Storage** node and selecting **Add new storage account**:

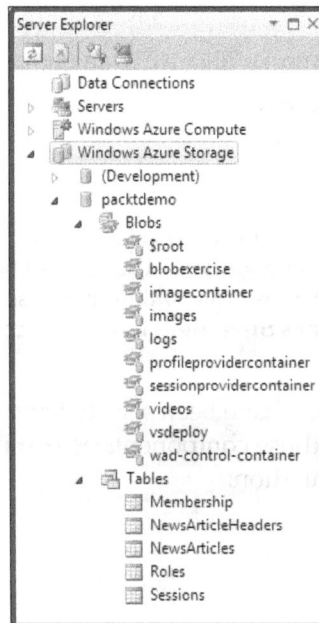

Azure Storage Explorer

The Windows Azure Tools for Visual Studio provide a basic support for browsing storage accounts to assist with debugging. However, the functionality of the built-in tools can be lacking if you are trying to upload new files or modify the metadata.

The **Azure Storage Explorer** (`http://azurestorageexplorer.codeplex.com`) is a GUI tool for viewing and modifying the data in a blob, queue, and table storage within the Windows Azure Storage. The tool is useful for quickly creating folders and uploading files such as media, or for downloading log files for viewing. It is also valuable for debugging the messages waiting to be processed in a queue, or whichever data is present in a table.

The tool is free and open source and is a good first choice when looking for a way to view the contents of your storage accounts. The following screenshot demonstrates the **Azure Storage Explorer** being used to browse and open an image of a Tulip from the **Blob** storage:

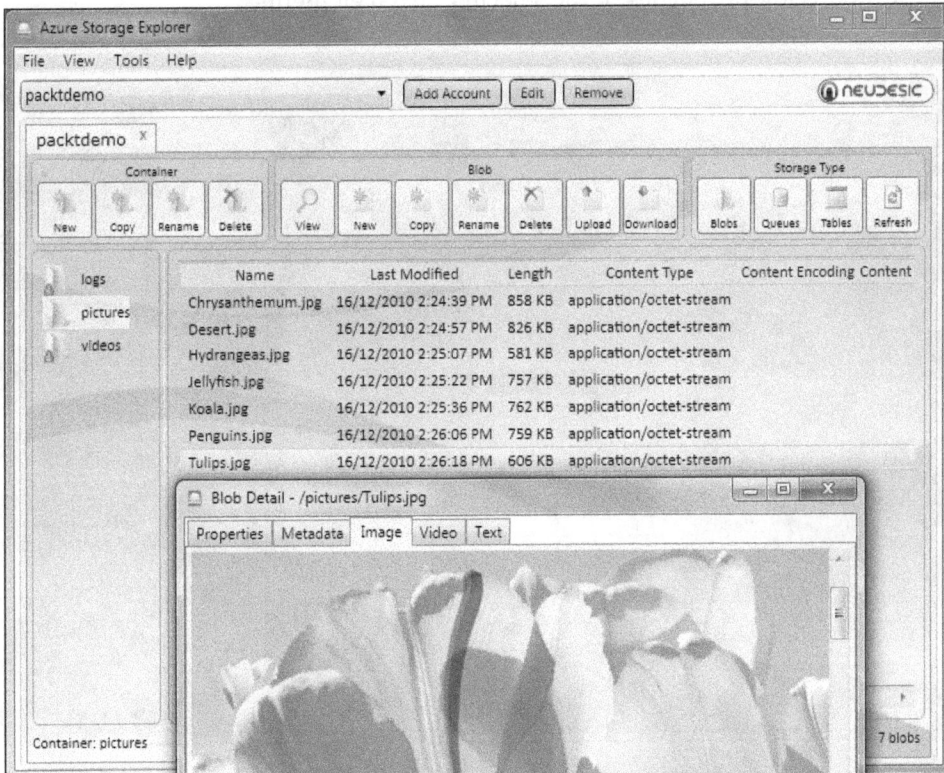

Expression Blend

If you plan to perform any serious UI work on a Silverlight application, then **Expression Blend** (http://www.microsoft.com/expression/products/Blend_Overview.aspx) is an essential tool. Expression Blend is a tool for designers to create XAML-based user interfaces. While it is designer focused, anyone who is creating serious Silverlight applications should be using it over the built-in designer tools within Visual Studio 2010. Expression Blend offers a rich experience while designing screens and has a number of useful features, such as design-time data (sample data while designing a screen), or the ability to create keyframe-based animations.

Expression Blend and Visual Studio 2010 integrate well together, both applications have the ability to work simultaneously with the same solution. As Expression Blend works with the same solution files, all the design work can be kept in a source control, side-by-side with the code. The following screenshot shows a Visual Studio 2010 solution that has been opened with Expression Blend. The tabs on the left-hand side are for selecting files within the project, while the tabs on the right-hand side are used for modifying properties of the selected visual elements:

Expression Blend is not a free product and must be purchased in the same way as Visual Studio 2010. If you are in a possession of an **MSDN** account, then you may find that it is already included in your subscription.

Silverlight Toolkit

Silverlight comes with a basic set of UI controls that can be used to create simple screens for your application. However, most applications will require additional controls. The **Silverlight Toolkit** (http://silverlight.codeplex.com/) provides a range of extra controls that can be used in your applications for free. These are the basic set of additional controls that your application should be using.

Two controls that are useful for working with data are the **Data Grid** and **Data Grid Pager**. Silverlight does not come with controls to display tabled data, making these controls useful for *data heavy applications*.

The Silverlight Toolkit also gives support for themes, allowing you to change the look and feel of all controls in your application with ease.

Other useful controls available in the toolkit include the following:

- Charting
  - Bar chart
  - Line chart
  - Pie chart
  - Bubble chart
- Calendar control / date picker
- Busy indicator
- Dock panel

Telerik Silverlight controls

The Silverlight Toolkit is a minimum set of additional controls that all projects should take advantage of, but it is highly recommended that you purchase a commercial control set.

> I have personally used a number of different control packs from different vendors, but I consistently come back to using the Telerik controls (http://www.telerik.com/products/silverlight.aspx). Their controls have a wide range of functionality, are updated frequently, and the technical support is exceptional. Any issues I have had with implementing the controls in my applications have been promptly addressed every time.

A short list of the available controls includes:

- Advanced charting
- High performance datagrids
- Sparklines
- Windows that can be docked and tabbed

The controls can be pricey, but the amounts of time they will save a development team quickly recover the costs.

Silverlight Spy

Silverlight Spy (`http://firstfloorsoftware.com/silverlightspy/`) is a runtime inspection tool useful for debugging Silverlight applications. Silverlight Spy allows you to explore the visual hierarchy of your screens at runtime, which can assist when you are trying to discover why a control is missing a border, or is on the wrong side of the screen.

There are many other functions that the tool allows, such as the ability to inspect the isolated storage of the application, real-time performance metrics of your Silverlight application, and event monitor for watching in real time as events are raised.

The application is not free, but it may be worth the purchase if you find yourself in a tricky debugging situation.

LINQPad

LINQPad (`http://www.linqpad.net/`) acts as a scratchpad that allows you to quickly compile and execute short snippets of C#, VB.Net, or F# code. It may not have any direct impact on your Azure development, but it is a useful tool to be stored in your collection.

The main use of LINQPad is to quickly write and execute LINQ statements against data sources. This quick execution cycle allows you to tweak and modify your LINQ queries quicker than trying to recompile and execute an entire application.

The power of LINQPad is its ability to query against a variety of data sources directly. A few of the supported sources include:

- LINQ to SQL (SQL Server)
- LINQ to XML
- SQL Azure

- Azure tables
- OData endpoints
- WCF data services endpoints

The ability to query against OData endpoints directly can help develop applications against data from other sources. The following screenshot demonstrates the ability to query against the **Netflix** endpoint at `http://odata.netflix.com/v1/Catalog/`. Using LINQPad, you are able to construct a standard LINQ query to retrieve all movie titles that were released in the year 1990 and have an average rating over three stars:

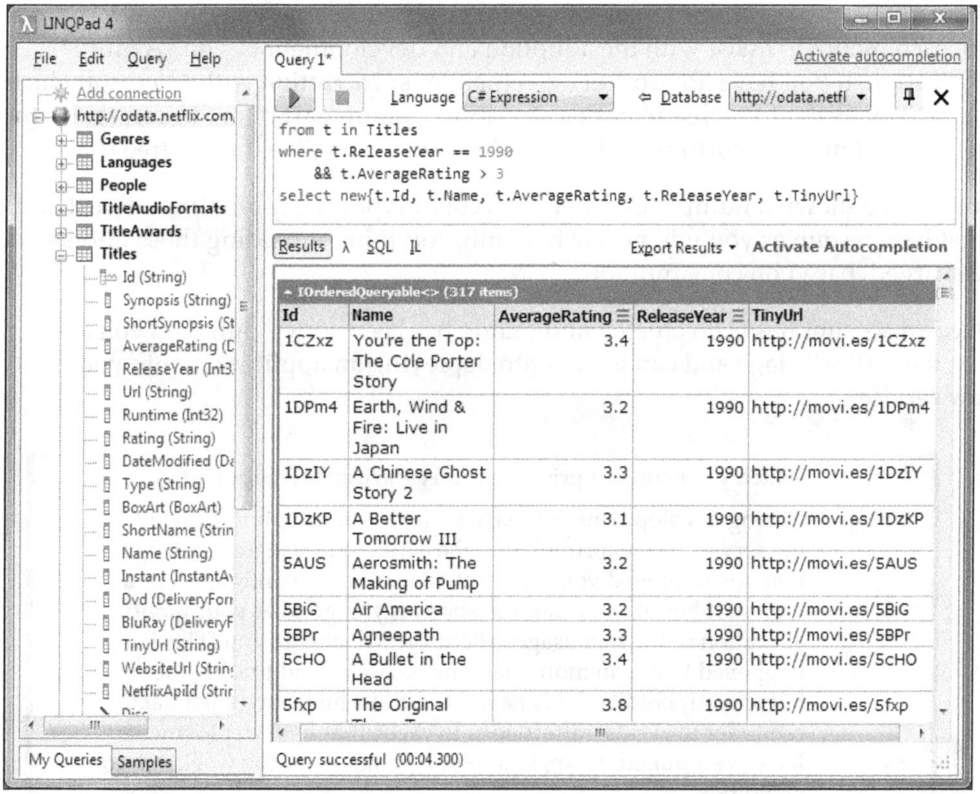

Creating a Windows Azure account

Signing up for a Windows Azure account is a relatively easy process. Go to `http://azure.com/` and click on **Sign up** to begin the sign up process.

Windows Azure is a consumption-based hosting service that requires you to pay for the resources that you consume. Microsoft charges for the usage of each distinct service that they offer, based on the consumption of that individual resource or service, for example, CPU hours, Internet bandwidth, storage, AppFabric, or SQL Azure. The various components of Windows Azure will be explored further in *Chapter 2, Introduction to Windows Azure*.

Microsoft has many promotional offers that give you a certain amount of resources free each month to assist with the adoption and development of your Azure application. If you have any sort of agreement or subscription with Microsoft (such as a MSDN, BizSpark, DreamSpark subscription, or are part of the Microsoft Partner Network), it may be worth checking whether you are eligible for any free trials.

You will be shown a number of different account types. They all differ by cost and what base resources you will get each month. Anything exceeding those quotas will be charged, based on consumption.

Once an account has been created and billing has been sorted out, then you are past the difficult stage and can move onto deploying an application onto your new service.

> **Watch your consumption carefully during development**
>
> During development, it is easy to deploy your application onto the servers to see it running in the cloud. It is also easy to forget that you deployed your application and had it configured for a high number of computer instances. If you go over your monthly allocation of the free usage, Microsoft will charge you. This has happened to me on more than one occasion, and finding the bill on your credit card is never a good feeling. Set a calendar reminder for Friday afternoons to check that your deployments have been pulled down, before you go home for the weekend, to avoid this.

Deploying to Windows Azure from Visual Studio 2010

In order to be able to deploy a Windows Azure application onto the Windows Azure servers, you will be required to create an **hosted service** that will host and execute your code and a **storage account** that will hold the packaged Azure application before the deployment. Deploying an Azure application onto the hosted service from Visual Studio 2010 will require setting up **certificates**.

The next section will explain the entire process of deployment end-to-end. Later chapters in the book will describe how to run and debug applications on the local developer machine.

Creating the hosting service

In order to create the hosting service, you will need to complete the following steps:

1. Log on to the **Windows Azure Management Portal** at `https://windows.azure.com`.

2. Go to the **Hosted Services, Storage Accounts & CDN** section and click on **Create a New Hosted Service**.

3. Give the hosted service a friendly name for you to keep track of and also a suitable URL prefix. The URL prefix is public, so it must be globally unique. In this example, the complete URL `https://packtdemoapp.cloudapp.net` has been used.

4. Select the option to **Create a New Affinity Group**. On the next screen, when asked about the location where your services should be hosted, select one that is close to your physical location. For this example, **South Central US** has been selected. Creating a new affinity group allows you to group your services together at the same physical location. This is useful for making sure that the servers hosting and executing the Azure application are in the same data center as the storage accounts:

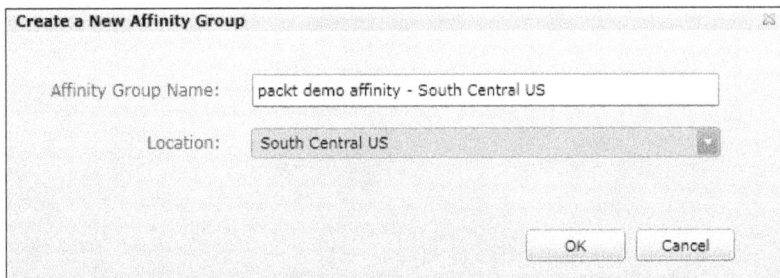

> **Affinity groups**
>
> Ensure that while deploying an Azure application, the hosted service and the storage account are hosted in the same data center by using affinity groups. Having your services hosted in different data centers can cause a lot of latency in your application, as well as potentially cause you to be charged with bandwidth costs between data centers.
>
> Just selecting a location for your service, without setting an affinity group does not guarantee that your services will be in the same data center in that location. Confirm that the affinity group is set on your services to avoid this.

5. If you had an Azure application already packaged, you could select to immediately upload and deploy the application on this screen. In this example, we are deploying to Azure directly from Visual Studio 2010, so select **Do not deploy**.

6. Click on **OK** to create the hosted service, which will be ready for us to deploy an Azure application, as shown in the following screenshot:

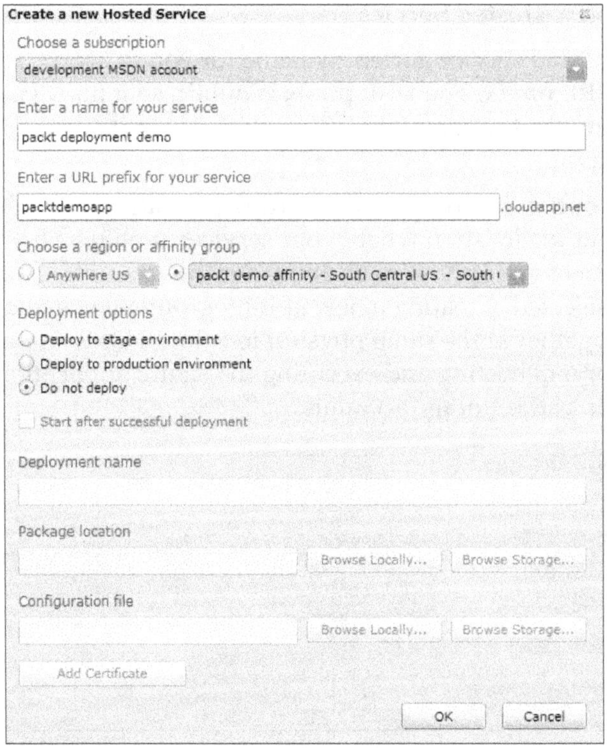

Creating the storage account

When the Windows Azure Management Portal is used to deploy your Azure application, you can directly upload your packaged Azure application onto the Azure servers. However, when deploying from Visual Studio 2010, the packaged application needs to be stored in the Azure Storage, so that it can be deployed onto the Azure servers from there.

Instead of the Windows Azure Management Portal, create a storage account and again give it a suitable endpoint name. The following screenshot shows an endpoint being created within the **South Central US** affinity group with the endpoint name **packtdemo**:

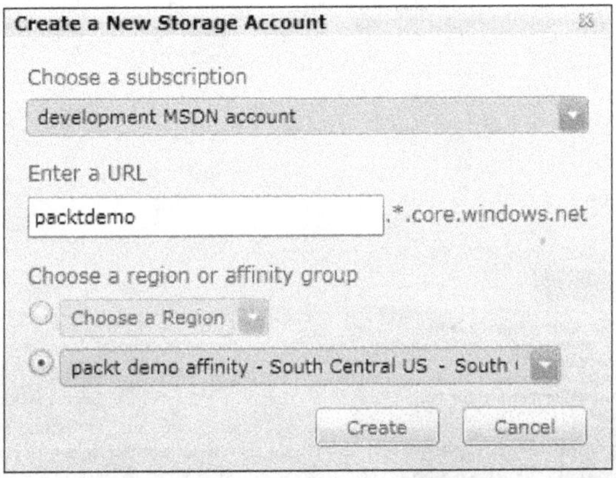

Deploying applications onto Azure servers

In order to be able to deploy an application onto Azure servers, you will first need an application to deploy. Next, you will create a new Azure project that will be used as our example:

1. Open Visual Studio 2010, create a new **Windows Azure Project**, and give the project a suitable name, such as **PacktAzureDeploymentDemo**, as shown in the following screenshot:

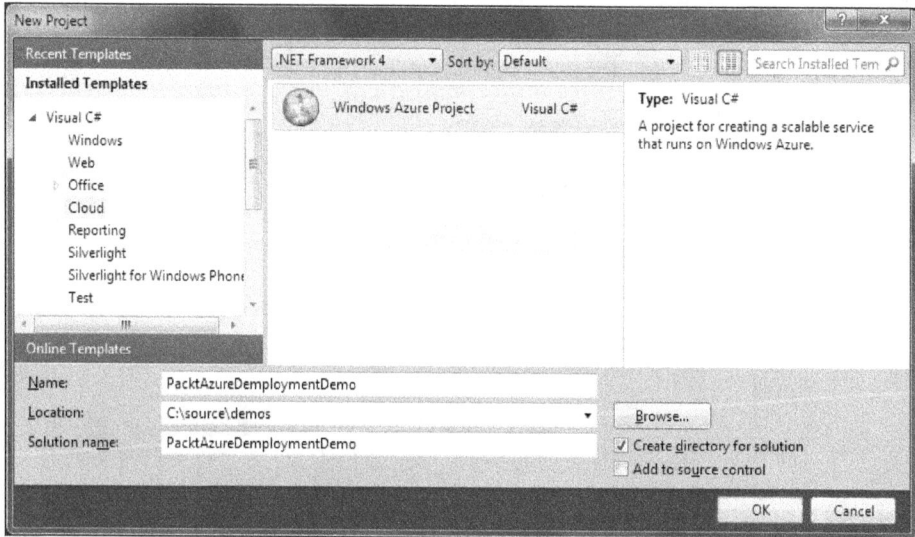

2. Add a single **ASP.NET Web Role** into the project. An Azure solution with a single web role added to it can be seen in the following screenshot. Other roles are visible and selectable, but this exercise will only be utilizing the web role:

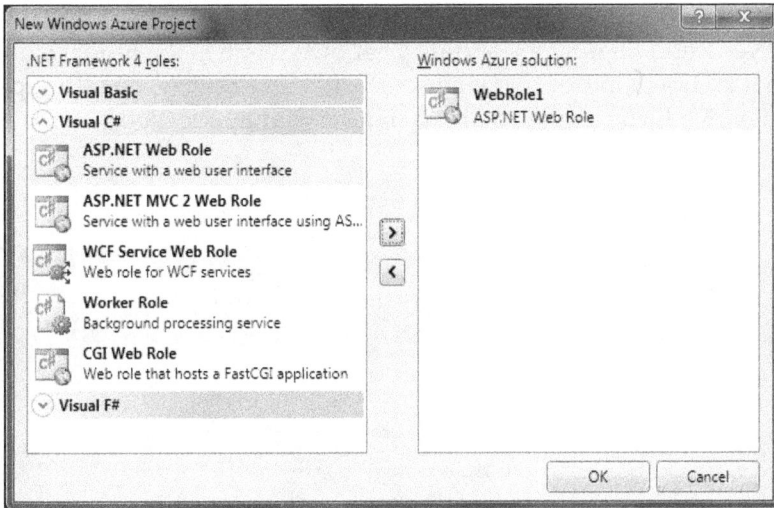

3. Visual Studio will create the solution with two projects as can be seen in the following screenshot. The first project **PacktAzureDeploymentDemo** is the Azure project that defines the metadata for all of the roles and instances that will be created when deployed onto Azure servers. The second project **WebRole1** is a standard ASP.Net project, where all the logic of your project will reside:

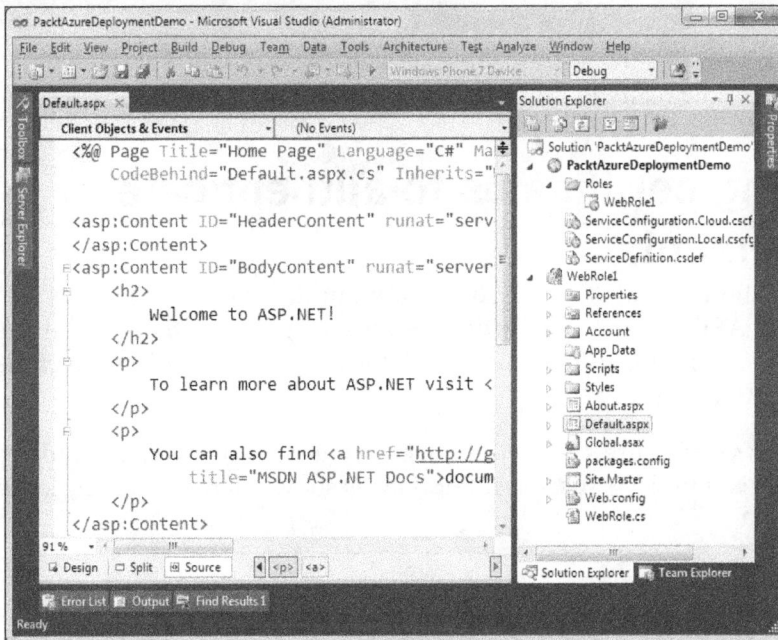

4. Once the project has been created, feel free to modify the `Default.aspx` file in **WebRole1** slightly, by adding your own name to the header similar to what is shown in the following screenshot. In this way, once the application is deployed, you can see that it is indeed your application:

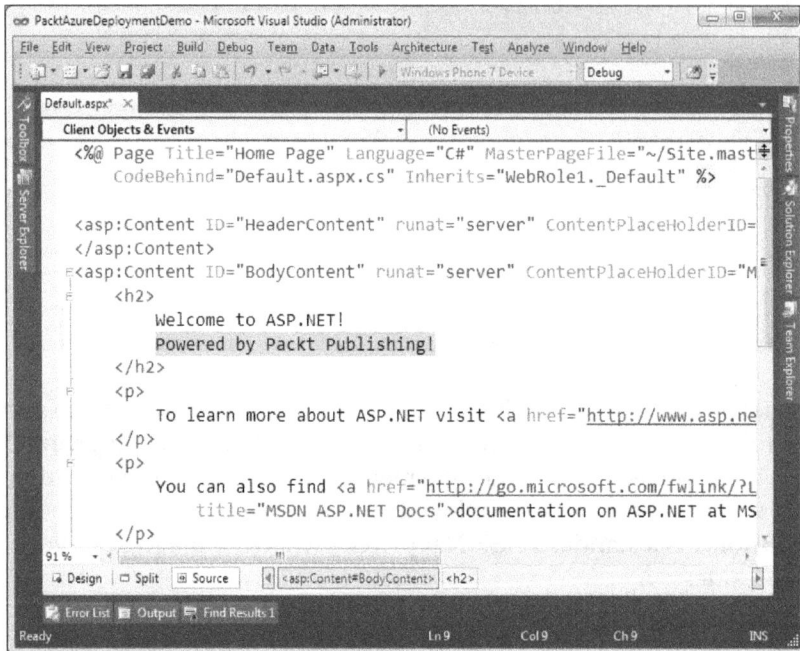

The project is now ready to be deployed onto the Azure servers.

Creating certificates to authenticate deployment

In order to allow Visual Studio 2010 to communicate with the Windows Azure deployment API, management certificates are required to authenticate the requests. Visual Studio has a wizard that helps with the creation and uploading of the required certificates:

1. With your Azure solution still open, right-click on the Azure project (not the ASP.Net project) and select **Publish**, as shown in the following screenshot:

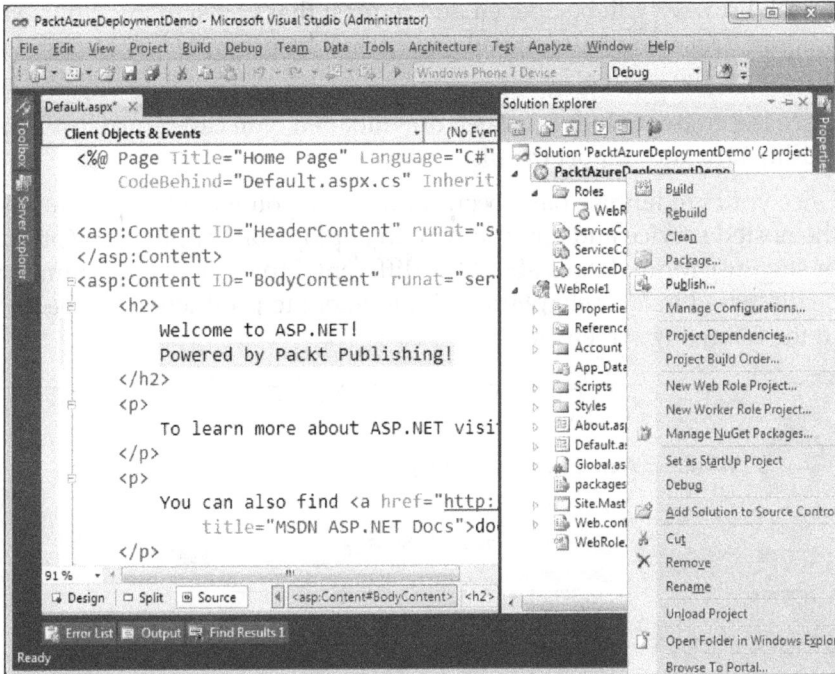

2. This will bring up a new **Publish Windows Azure Application** dialog box as shown in the following screenshot. If you had previously configured your credentials, you could select them here. As this is the first time you are opening this dialog box, you will be required to configure your credentials. Click on **Sign in to download credentials** to begin the process:

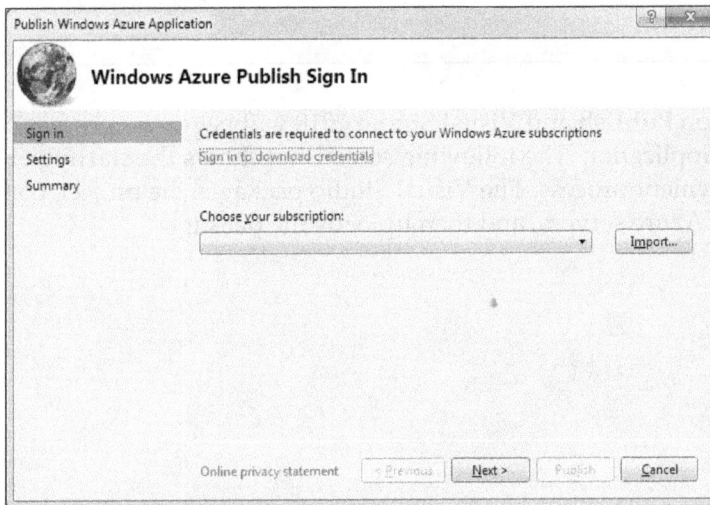

3. A web browser will be opened and request that you sign into your Azure account. Once you have signed in, you will be prompted by the browser to download the **credential file**.

4. Once the credential file has been downloaded, you can return to Visual Studio 2010 and import the file.

5. Once your credentials have been configured, you will now be able to select the hosted service and environment to deploy your application (production or staging). More details about the different deployment environments will be discussed in later chapters. A deployment to production has been chosen in the following screenshot:

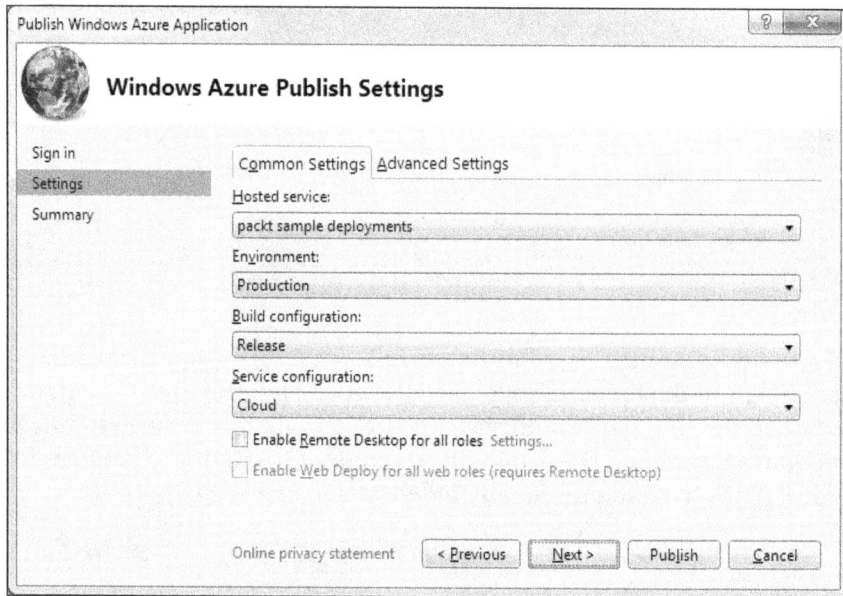

6. Click on **Publish** and Visual Studio 2010 will begin the process of deploying your application. The following screenshot shows the starting of the deployment process. The Visual Studio packages the project, connects to the Azure servers, and then uploads the package:

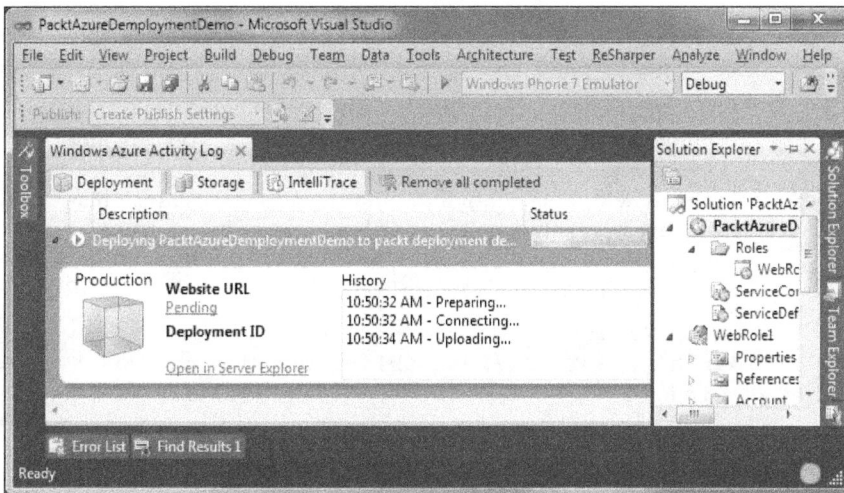

7. The deployment process has been completed in the following screenshot. The package was successfully uploaded and the web role was initialized and brought online, ready to service user requests. Be aware that the first deployment to your instances can take a long time, sometimes up to 15 minutes before they are fully running. There are ways to shorten the deployment time during the development by using **web deployment** after the initial deployment:

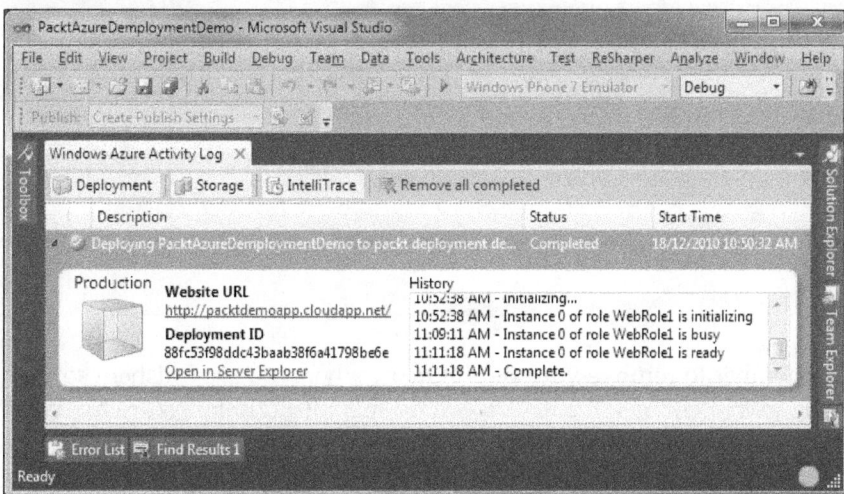

> **Web deployment**
>
> To shorten the development cycle, it is possible to use web deployment to update an existing deployment. You can only have a single compute instance running and the changes made are only temporary until the compute instance restarts. This is a development enhancer and should never be used on a production deployment. More details about this feature can be found on the Windows Azure Tools blog at the following URL:
>
> ```
> http://blogs.msdn.com/b/cloud/
> archive/2011/04/19/enabling-web-deploy-for-
> windows-azure-web-roles-with-visual-studio.aspx
> ```

8. Once Visual Studio 2010 has completed the deployment and the servers have reported back that the service has started successfully, you will finally be able to view your application.

9. Click on the website URL in the **Windows Azure Activity Log** window to browse to the site, this will be the URL you configured when creating the hosted service. If all goes well, you should see your website running with your modifications, similar to the following screenshot:

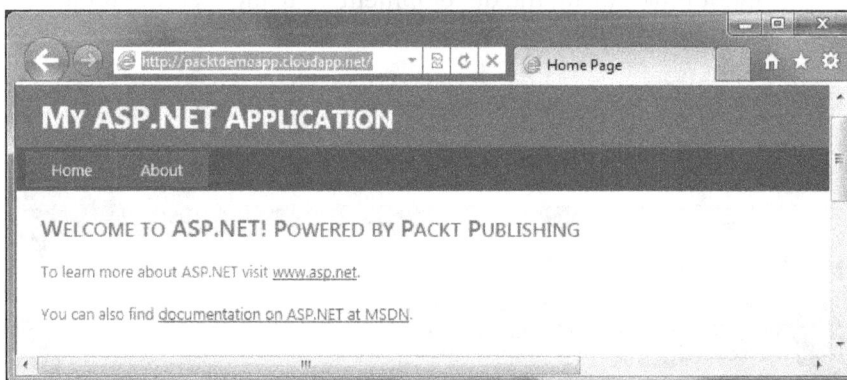

10. Remember to remove your deployment when you are finished, so that you are not charged for it. You can do this through the Azure Management Portal. You can also do it quickly from within the Visual Studio by right-clicking on **Deployment** in the **Windows Azure Activity Log** window and selecting **Delete**.

Summary

You have now seen how to prepare your system for development with Silverlight and Windows Azure. Previously, setting up a machine could be difficult, but it has been made simpler with the release of the Microsoft Web Platform Installer.

There are also a wide range of tools that can be utilized to assist the development of applications. Explore the options available to you and see what helps to speed your own development times.

In the next chapter, a more detailed introduction to the Windows Azure Platform will be provided.

2
Introduction to Windows Azure

The Windows Azure platform comprises a number of services that can be used independently or combined together to create cloud-enabled applications. In order to create scalable solutions, it is important to understand how all the pieces of a platform relate to each other.

In this chapter, we will discuss the following topics:

- Windows Azure
- Developing applications locally
- Resourcing issues within the enterprises

Windows Azure

Windows Azure is a set of services that enables the enterprises to create scalable, fault-tolerant web applications that are hosted within the owned **datacenters** and operated by Microsoft. Microsoft abstracts the infrastructure for hosting the applications, so that you can focus on your application and features. The Windows Azure platform provides on-demand compute, storage, and middleware services that can be used to host, scale, and manage web applications.

The web applications hosted by Azure can be public-facing websites, secured enterprise applications, or any other standard application that would be hosted in a datacenter. Microsoft hosts datacenters at different strategic locations around the world. Offering a range of hosted datacenters across the world allows the enterprises to deploy their applications to geolocations that are physically close to their expected users, lowering **latency**.

Windows Azure automates the allocation and usage of the underlying hardware resources (servers for computation, storage units for data persistence). By abstracting the underlying hardware and focusing on automation, an enterprise no longer requires a team of IT staff to worry about allocating servers, configuring load balancers, and other routine tasks. In the same way, you would expect a **Desktop Operating System** to handle the allocation of CPU resources to execute applications, Windows Azure automates the allocation of servers to execute an application that is deployed on it.

The mechanism that Windows Azure uses to allocate and monitor these base resources is called the **Windows Azure Fabric**. It is a controller that monitors the health of the hardware in a datacenter and can automatically reboot machines that appear faulty, or have hung due to an application error. It is also able to redeploy an application to a new host if a machine continues to be faulty.

> **Windows Azure Fabric**
>
> The Windows Azure Fabric monitors the health of hardware in a datacenter.

The abstraction from the administration and management of physical servers and towards "computational resources" takes the burden away from enterprises. Enterprises can now focus on defining and developing business logic that is specific to their business. More time can be spent on developing features that will enhance the value of an enterprise, instead of worrying about how to develop a robust, fault-tolerant environment for their application.

> **Fault tolerance**
>
> Windows Azure will detect any hardware that is faulty and will automatically reboot machines if necessary. If a machine continues to fail, then the Windows Azure Fabric will take the machine offline and redeploy the applications onto a different server in the datacenter.

Main components of Windows Azure

Windows Azure is a collection of services that can be consumed independently, and billed based on consumption. This allows an enterprise to selectively use and pay for the components they require, rather than being charged for the complete platform which they may not be utilizing.

The Windows Azure platform can be roughly divided into the following three groups of functionalities:

- Computation as follows:
    - Windows Azure compute services (hosting websites, processing data)
    - Custom virtual machine hosting

- Persistence as follows:
    - Windows Azure storage services (files, queues, and non-relational tables)
    - SQL Azure (Relational database)

- Supporting services through Windows Azure AppFabric as follows:
    - Service bus (secure connectivity and messaging)
    - Access control (identity management and access control)
    - Integration (legacy application orchestration)
    - Composite application (using metrics to automate deployment and management of Azure applications)

Each component of the Azure platform can be consumed independently. There is no need to use everything in a single application. An enterprise can scale the usage of each component up and down individually as needed, for example, scaling the storage service when more file storage is required, but maintaining the same level of computing resources. The billing will again be based on consumption. So, there will be an additional charge for the storage services, but the compute service charges will remain constant.

The following diagram shows how these major components relate to each other within the Azure platform:

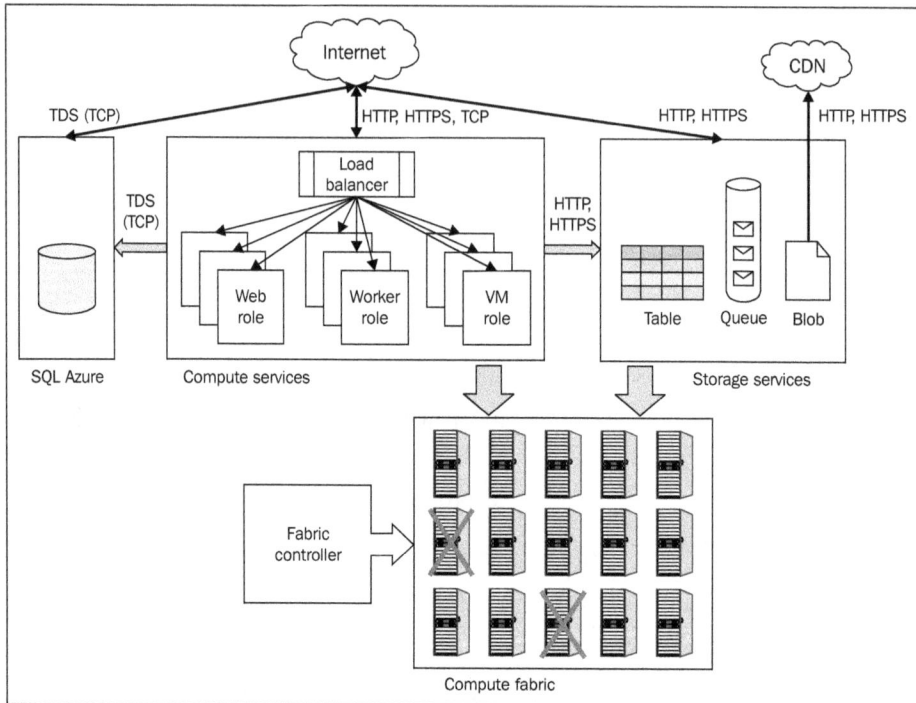

- The Windows compute fabric is made up of hundreds of physical machines. These machines are housed in massive datacenters all around the world.

- The fabric controller monitors the health of the compute fabric. It is in charge of allocating the machines to handle requests for resources. When the fabric controller detects that a machine is not responding, it will reboot the machine. If a machine is too faulty, then the fabric controller will de-provision the machine and assign a new machine to the task.

- Compute services sit on top of the compute fabric. When an application is deployed, the compute service looks at the number of roles, as well as the number of instances requested within the package manifest. Compute services will then request the appropriate resources from the compute fabric.

- Compute services employ a load balancer to distribute requests over the deployed instances of a role.

- Deployed applications running inside compute services are able to access storage services and SQL Azure.

- Storage services use the resources of the physical machine to provide data storage services. Behind the scenes, the storage services is made up of hundreds of deployments of a special storage service role available only to Microsoft.

- Storage services have the option of exposing the blob data through the Azure **Content Delivery Network**.

By factoring out the common management tasks related to managing servers and applications, Microsoft has provided an **application-centric** model of development. You provide your application code and metadata about the service and Microsoft worries about the rest.

Fabric naming convention

Be cautious while using the word *fabric* with Windows Azure. The **Windows Azure Compute Fabric** and **Windows Azure AppFabric** are separate technologies. The terms can be easily confused.

Windows Azure compute services

The unit of deployment to the Azure compute services is the **role**. Azure applications comprise one or more roles, with each role handling an aspect of the application logic. One-to-many Azure compute instances can be run to execute the code defined in a role. A role can be thought of as a specific logic that can be executed and scaled independently of other roles within the same application. By focusing on roles and instances, the compute service abstracts you away from the need to know about individual servers.

Role types

Each role in an application needs to be based on one of the three role types offered by the compute services:

- **Web role**: It is the **virtual machines** that are preconfigured with **IIS**. They are most useful for hosting ASP.Net, WCF services, PHP, and other web technologies.

- **Worker role**: It is meant for applications that do not require IIS. It is mostly used in an application code that processes requests asynchronously (generating reports, video processing, periodic calculations).

- **VM role**: Enterprises can supply their own **Windows Server 2008 R2** image that is used while provisioning the instances of this role. Be aware that doing this requires you to keep the image updated with the latest security patches.

> **Operating system updates**
>
> It is recommended that the web role and worker role are used wherever possible. Microsoft periodically updates the base images of these roles with the latest security updates, ensuring you stay protected. While using the VM role, the responsibility of deploying security updates rests with you.

Azure projects contain a metadata file that defines the number of roles in your application, what type of role they are (web/worker), and how many instances of each role should be initialized. Developers can combine a number of different role types into a single application. All roles in an application are not required to be of the same role type.

Example usage of roles

A hypothetical application could be created for a video website that contains three roles. This application is a website that allows people to upload videos which are then processed into a smaller format. Once the video has been processed, an e-mail is sent to all people who have subscribed to the website. The application will comprise:

- **A web role to host the website**: Users can log on and upload videos. The load generated to serve web pages is low: two instances of this role are enough.

- **A worker role to process videos**: Video processing is very resource-intensive. It can take any time from ten minutes to an hour to fully convert each video. Due to the high load it creates, four instances of this role are required.

- **A worker role to send a notification to subscribed users**: This is a simple service that waits for an event indicating that a video has been processed. An e-mail is then generated and sent to the subscribed users. Only one instance is required. However, as discussed in the following section, *Things to be aware of when working with role instances*, Microsoft requires a minimum of two instances to support their SLA regarding downtime. The developers can take an informed decision if they are satisfied that a single instance without an SLA will meet their requirements. As it is a low-priority process, send a few e-mails each hour, one instance may be acceptable.

The following diagram conceptually shows what the application would look like when deployed onto the Windows Azure servers. The instances of each role would be deployed on top of the Windows Azure Fabric. The load balancer would then distribute requests among the instances within each role:

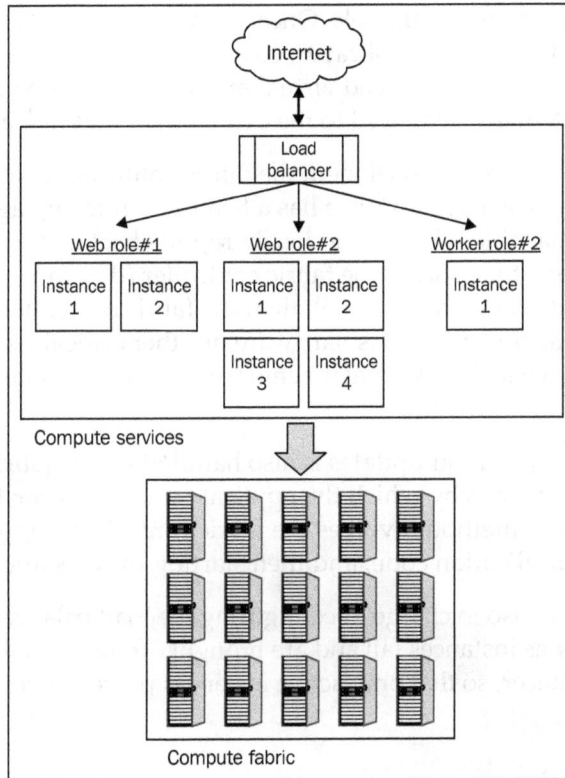

Compute fabric

All running instances are provisioned within the **compute fabric**. The compute fabric provides a soup of processing capabilities that your application can consume. When an application comes under heavy load and requires more resources, the application can request more resources (by spawning more instances) and can be charged accordingly.

Under the covers, each role instance is actually a virtual machine that has been provisioned and is dedicated to running that single instance. These virtual machines that make up the compute fabric are provisioned on top of the Windows Azure Fabric. The underlying mechanism that handles the deployment and allocation of individual instances within the compute fabric is called the **Azure fabric controller**.

When a Windows Azure application is published, the Windows Azure fabric controller ensures that the resources for the application are configured and initializes each instance to start the execution. The fabric controller inspects the metadata file of the deployed application and provisions, based on the contents. The role type defines the base on which the virtual machine image should be used. A fresh virtual machine is provisioned for each instance of the role. Once a virtual machine has been provisioned, the fabric controller deploys the application code onto that virtual machine and then begins the execution. Each provisioned virtual machine is allocated resources (CPU and Memory) that are dedicated to the execution of that role instance.

After each instance has been provisioned, the fabric controller continues to monitor the health of the instance. Each instance has a health monitoring agent running inside each virtual machine which periodically reports back to the fabric controller. If the health agent fails to report to the fabric controller (due to the virtual machine crashing, or other software related issue), then the fabric controller can automatically reboot the virtual machine. If there is hardware or other critical issues, the fabric controller can de-provision the virtual machine and provision a new instance on another set of physical hardware.

The deployment of application updates is also handled by the fabric controller. There are a number of ways by which the application updates can be pushed to the instances. The simplest method involves the fabric controller stopping each instance, deploying the new application code, and then starting the execution again.

The fabric controller is also in charge of configuring the load balancer. As new instances are brought online or as instances fail and are brought offline, the fabric controller updates the load balancer, so that only active instances process incoming requests.

Instance counts

The fabric controller is not aware of the optimal number of instances for your application by itself. It is up to the developer to notify the fabric controller whether the instance count should be increased or decreased.

The number of instances can be adjusted manually by logging into the **Windows Azure Management Portal**, by using AppFabric Composite Application, or by making calls to the **Windows Azure service API**. A developer can write application business logic to determine when the application is over- or underutilized, and make calls to the service API to adjust the number of instances.

More information on the Azure management API can be found at the following URL:

http://msdn.microsoft.com/en-us/library/windowsazure/ee460799.aspx

Things to be aware of when working with role instances

It is important to realize that individual instances can be lost at any time due to application or hardware failures. Rolling out updates can also result in instances being restarted or replaced. When an instance is lost, this will result in a loss of all the volatile states that were inside the instance (session state, application state), as well as all the requests that were currently being handled for a client.

> It is expected that all the compute instances will at some stage be lost or rebooted due to failures or upgrades. Always persist critical data to a durable store such as the Azure storage or SQL Azure.

Microsoft recommends that you always deploy at least two instances of each role to help in maintaining the uptime. The **SLA (Service Level Agreement)** on the Azure website (http://www.windowsazure.com/en-us/support/sla/) states that:

For compute, we guarantee that when you deploy two or more role instances in different fault and upgrade domains, your Internet facing roles will have external connectivity at least 99.95% of the time.

Applications are scaled on Windows Azure by distributing the work over multiple role instances. Anything kept by an instance in the memory locally will not be accessible by other instances. It is important to remember this while developing applications that handle sequential requests from a single user.

In an example scenario, a user is adding items to a shopping cart. When adding the products to the shopping cart, instance #1 handled the requests and stored the cart items in the memory. The user then clicks to checkout which items are handled by instance #2. Instance #2 has no knowledge of the items in the shopping cart as that information is still stored in instance #1. The user is then confused at the time when the website returns, showing that their shopping cart is empty.

> **Session state**
>
> User requests are load balanced across multiple instances of your roles. This means that applications cannot rely on the server-side session state. Two simultaneous requests from a single user may be processed by different role instances. Store the information in a central place, so that all the instances can access the same, such as the Azure storage (table and blob) or SQL Azure.

Compute instance sizes

Compute instances are all provisioned as virtual machines. Due to the virtual nature of the instances, enterprises can choose what magnitude of resources should be allocated, based on the application resource requirements. Applications that are not much resource-intensive (such as a company blog) could be hosted with small instances. Applications that require a lot of processing and are in the memory caching of data may require the use of large instances for the large increase in allocated CPU and memory resources.

With the exception of the extra small instance (which is a special low-cost size), each increase in instance size gives roughly twice the resources of the size below it, that is, a medium-sized instance has roughly twice the resources of a small instance. The base pricing of instances may vary over time, but a general rule of thumb is that each increase in the instance size is a doubling of the hourly rate as follows:

Compute Instance Size	CPU	Memory	Instance Storage	I/O Performance
Extra Small	Shared	768 MB	20 GB	Low
Small	1.6 GHz	1.75 GB	225 GB	Moderate
Medium	2 x 1.6 GHz	3.5 GB	490 GB	High
Large	4 x 1.6 GHz	7 GB	1,000 GB	High
Extra large	8 x 1.6 GHz	14 GB	2,040 GB	High

Further details on pricing and instance size specifications can be found on the following Azure website:

http://www.windowsazure.com/en-us/home/tour/compute

Windows Azure storage services

The **Windows Azure storage service** provides a scalable and durable way to persist data. The compute service is volatile and will lose all the data stored within an instance. This makes the storage service a good way of maintaining an application state or hosting files for the users to download.

Storage services provide three main ways to store data:

- **Blob storage**: It includes the storage of binary files (images, videos, documents, Silverlight files, and so on)

- **Queues**: It has asynchronous messaging between roles and role instances in an application

- **Table storage**: It comprises NoSQL-style data storage, non-relational, and simple table storage

All storage service operations can be done through a **REST-based API**. On being exposed as a REST service, it allows the developers to consume the storage service APIs with Silverlight, ASP.Net, JavaScript, and other technologies. To assist with the consumption of these APIs within the .Net code, Microsoft has provided a storage client library that simplifies development.

RESTful services

REST (Representational State Transfer) is used as a standard for using the **HTTP protocol** to interact with resources on a web server. The URL is used to define which object on the server is being acted upon, while the HTTP verb (GET/PUT/POST/DELETE) is used to define the operation being invoked. In this way, resources can be queried, created, edited, and deleted. If a service implements this style of interaction, it can be named a RESTful service. More information can be found on Wikipedia at the following URL:

```
http://en.wikipedia.org/wiki/Representational_
State_Transfer
```

A storage services subscription can be created and **scaled independently** of a compute services subscription and the other Azure components. It is possible to use the storage service without using any other part of Windows Azure. A storage services account could be created and used as a cheap way of hosting files to distribute to the users.

Microsoft charges for the consumption of storage services in three ways: the total amount of storage space used, data transfer in or out of the datacenter, and storage transactions, for example, querying table storage or deleting a message from a queue. Due to the volume of transactions that can be expected for a typical application, Microsoft charges storage transactions in blocks — $0.01 per 10,000 transactions (pricing can vary). The transaction fee is used as a deterrent to discourage developers from writing inefficient code, or polling too often.

All data stored within the Azure storage services (blobs, queues, and table storage) is saved multiple times for redundancy. Each piece of data is replicated at least three times over different fault-tolerant zones, so that in the event of a hardware failure, data is not lost. Under the covers, the Azure storage service is actually just a special Azure application deployed onto the Azure Fabric by Microsoft.

SQL Azure

The Azure storage service provides simple non-relational table storage. Table storage is cheap, fast, and scalable, but it does have drawbacks. The tables have no defined schema, making it possible for a table to hold multiple entities, each having different properties. The querying API can be restrictive, and operations such as sorting are not available.

To oversimplify SQL Azure, it can be thought of as *SQL Server hosted in the cloud*. You can take an existing .Net application that uses an SQL client and a technology, such as **LINQ to SQL** or **Entity Framework**, change the connection string to point to the SQL Azure server, and the application will continue to run. This is an oversimplification of what is happening under the covers, but Microsoft has put much effort into making SQL Azure as compatible as possible for the existing .Net development patterns.

A developer would choose SQL Azure over Windows Azure Table storage when there is a need for a relational data store. Azure applications that use Entity Framework for their data access will work seamlessly with SQL Azure, making it the first choice for developers building their first applications on the Windows Azure platform.

It is important to realize that SQL Azure is not able to scale indefinitely. Having a single database that holds 50 gigabytes while being hammered with transactions from 80 Azure compute instances simultaneously is going to result in performance issues. To scale relational data, it is important to think of the ways by which the data can be logically segregated, be it by a customer ID or other key. SQL Azure offers ways to automatically share application data across multiple databases with a feature named **SQL Azure Federation**.

Most features of Microsoft SQL Server are directly available on SQL Azure (such as reporting), but it is important to trace those few features that are not available due to the distributed scaling nature of **cloud computing**. Stored procedures, file streams, and direct access of the database files are examples of operations that are not available. Security and cross database queries are other features that act differently. Be sure to read the whitepapers from the SQL Azure website for best practices to create an application that will require using it.

Windows Azure AppFabric

Windows Azure AppFabric is a collection of middleware services that help to reduce the complexities of building the cloud applications. The services are **interoperable**, and **consumable** by Azure applications and other development environments.

The services can be standalone or combined together as follows:

- **Caching**: It is a distributed memory application caching system. It can improve application performance by regularly caching used information, for example, application code rather than fetching it repeatedly from a slower data source.

- **Access control**: It provides identity and access control to your applications. User authentication is federated to other identity services (Active Directory, Windows Live ID, Facebook, Google, Yahoo, and so on) allowing users to use their existing identities to log into your application.

- **Service Bus**: It is used as a communication intermediary between applications. It is useful for connecting applications that are not able to directly communicate with each other due to firewalls, for example, two organizations wanting to connect their on-premise applications.

- **Integration**: It can be simplified as "Microsoft BizTalk in the cloud". Pipelines, converters, adapters, and rule engines can be used to integrate the existing legacy applications.

- **Composite application**: It automates the deployment and management of an Azure application. Performance metrics can be defined that determine when resources need to be scaled up or down.

Each of the AppFabric services can be consumed independently. Consumption pricing for each service varies greatly. So, be sure to consult the pricing pages on the following Azure website: http://www.azure.com.

Developing applications locally

Microsoft has made it easy for the developers to develop Windows Azure applications on their local machines. When the Windows Azure SDK and tools are installed, a basic simulation of the Azure compute and storage services is included. This gives the developers the ability to run and debug Azure applications locally.

The compute service is simulated by spawning multiple instances of the role, rather than provisioning multiple virtual machines. The system is still limited by the resources of the development machine. So, creating 20 instances of a role would result in a degraded performance.

Storage services are simulated by creating REST endpoints on the local development machine. While developing applications, the endpoint URL just needs to be set to the local endpoint. These endpoints are only accessible from the local machine and are not exposed on the network.

SQL Azure is not directly simulated, but can be done by connecting it to a local **Microsoft SQL Server 2008 Instance** (Express or Full version).

> **Debugging issues in production**
>
> In order to assist in keeping track of the production issues, it can be useful to debug an application on the local developer machine, but make sure to connect it to the online data services. This can be done easily by changing the storage service endpoint in the configuration file, or by changing the SQL connection string to the SQL Azure.

Summary

The Windows Azure platform can help enterprises to be more agile by enabling them to quickly deploy new applications or scale as the demand changes. There are many components offered by the Windows Azure and it is important to be aware of the role that each plays.

Splitting a large complex application into discrete roles can help to lower the complexity of an application and allow each piece to be scaled independently. However, also remember that scaling a single role over multiple instances brings new development challenges while trying to share the state between machines.

In the next chapter, we will explore how Windows Azure and Silverlight can be used together within the same application. We will also see techniques for scaling WCF services over multiple Azure instances.

3
Hosting Silverlight Applications in Azure

It can be difficult to combine multiple different frameworks into the same solution while working with new technologies. This chapter will focus on how to combine Silverlight 4, Windows Azure, and a **WCF 4.0 (Windows Communication Foundation)** service together.

In this chapter, we will discuss the following topics:

- Combining Silverlight and Windows Azure projects
- Consuming an Azure-hosted WCF service within a Silverlight application
- Configuring the number of web roles

Combining Silverlight and Windows Azure projects

Standard Silverlight applications require that they be hosted on HTML pages, so that they can be loaded in a browser. Developers who work with the .Net framework will usually host this page within an ASP.Net website.

The easiest way to host a Silverlight application on Azure is to create a single web role that contains an ASP.Net application to host the Silverlight application. Hosting the Silverlight application in this way enables you, as a developer, to take advantage of the full .Net framework to support your Silverlight application. Supporting functionalities can be provided such as hosting WCF services, RIA services, Entity Framework, and so on.

In the upcoming chapters, we will explore ways by which RIA services, OData, Entity Framework, and a few other technologies can be used together. For the rest of this chapter, we will focus on the basics of hosting a Silverlight application within Azure and integrating a hosted WCF service.

Creating a Silverlight or Azure solution

Your system should already be fully configured with all Silverlight and Azure tools. If your system has not been prepared, then please refer to *Chapter 1, Getting Started* for information on preparing your system.

In this section, we are going to create a simple Silverlight application that is hosted inside an Azure web role. This will be the basic template that is used throughout the book as we explore different ways in which we can integrate the technologies together:

1. Start Visual Studio as an administrator. You can do this by opening the Start Menu and finding Visual Studio, then right-clicking on it, and selecting **Run as Administrator**. This is required for the Azure compute emulator to run successfully.

2. Create a new Windows Azure Cloud Service. The solution name used in the following example screenshot is **Chapter3Exercise1**:

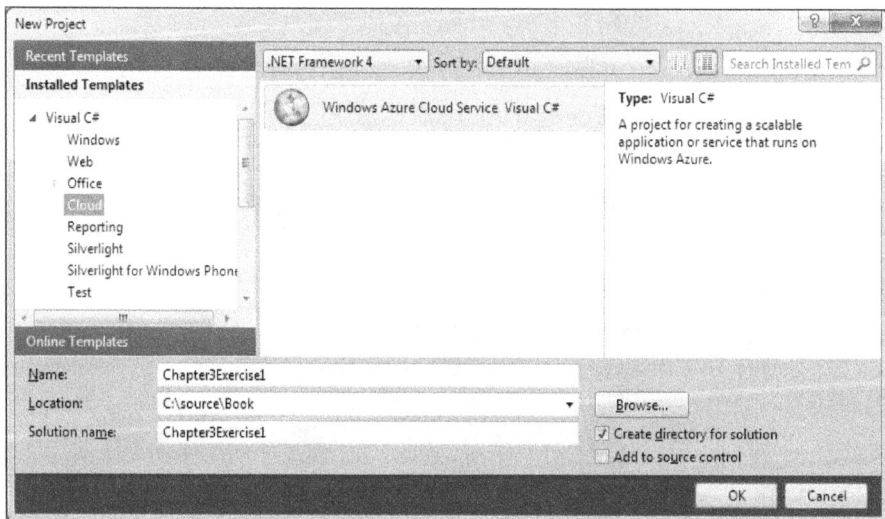

3. Add a single **ASP.Net Web Role** as shown in the following screenshot. For this exercise, the default name of **WebRole1** will be used. The name of the role can be changed by clicking on the pencil icon next to the **WebRole1** name:

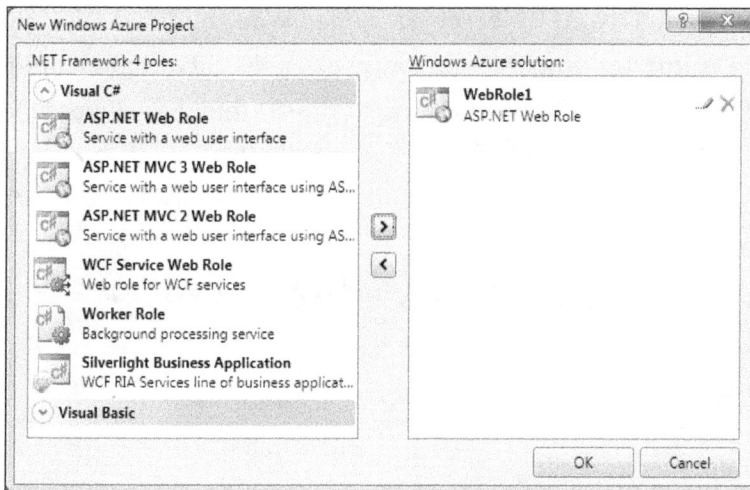

4. Visual Studio should now be loaded with a single Azure project and an ASP. Net project. In the following screenshot, you can see that Visual Studio is opened with a solution named **Chapter3Exercise1**. The solution contains a Windows Azure Cloud project, also called **Chapter3Exercise1**. Finally, the ASP.Net project can be seen named as **WebRole1**:

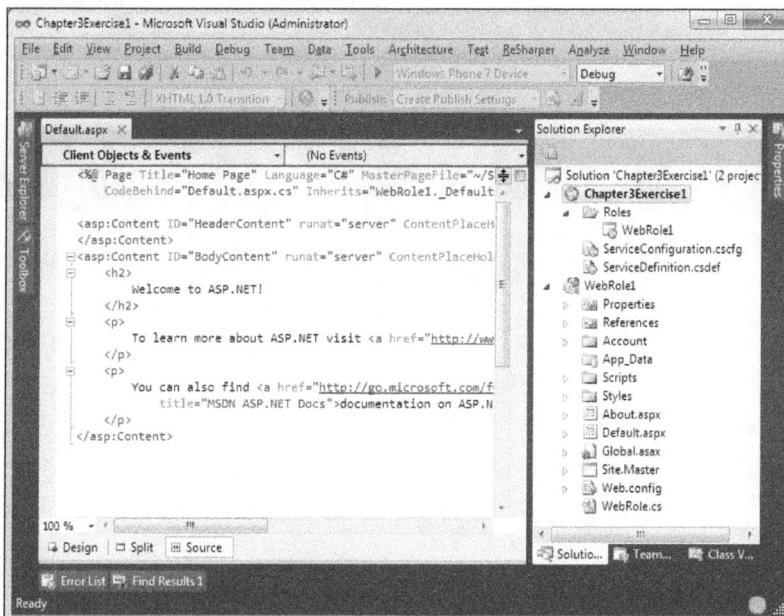

5. Right-click on the ASP.Net project named **WebRole1** and select **Properties**.

6. In the **WebRole1** properties screen, click on the **Silverlight Applications** tab.

7. Click on **Add** to add a new Silverlight project into the solution. The **Add** button has been highlighted in the following screenshot:

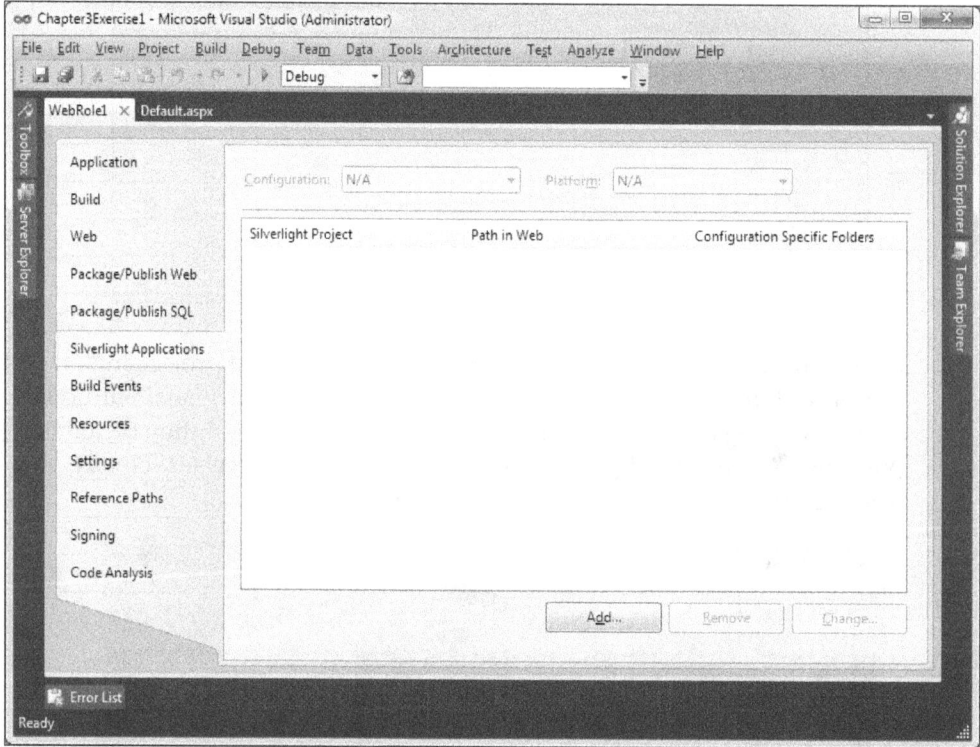

8. For this exercise, rename the project to **HelloWorldSilverlightProject**. Click on **Add** to create the Silverlight project. The rest of the options can be left to their default settings, as shown in the following screenshot. Later chapters utilize the **Enable WCF RIA Services** option to assist you in the development of applications:

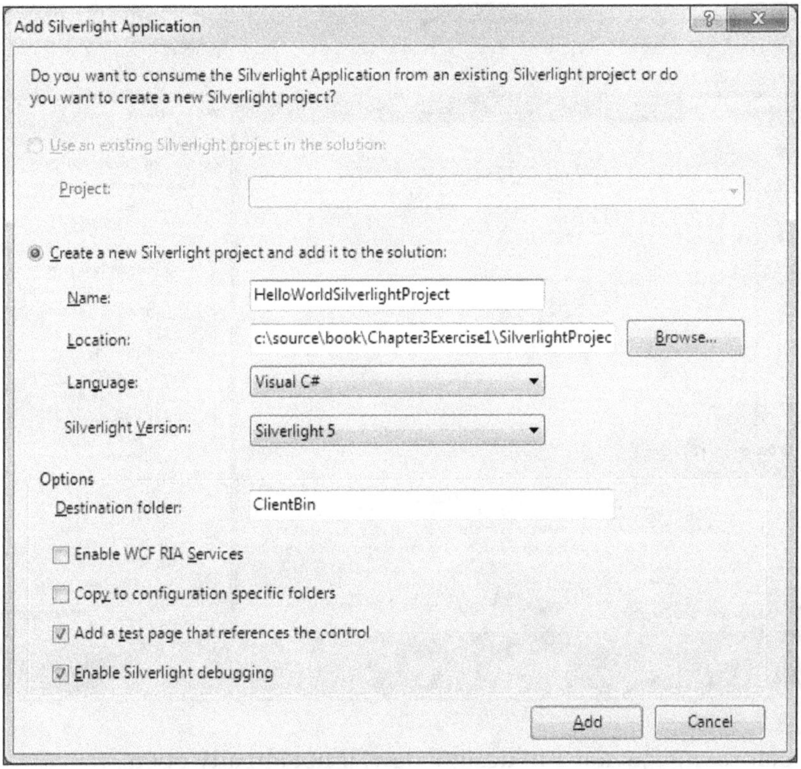

9. Visual Studio will now create the Silverlight project and add it to the solution. The resulting solution should now have three projects as shown in the following screenshot. These include the original Azure project, **Chapter3Exercise1**; the ASP.Net web role, **WebRole1**; and the third new project **HelloWorldSilverlightProject**:

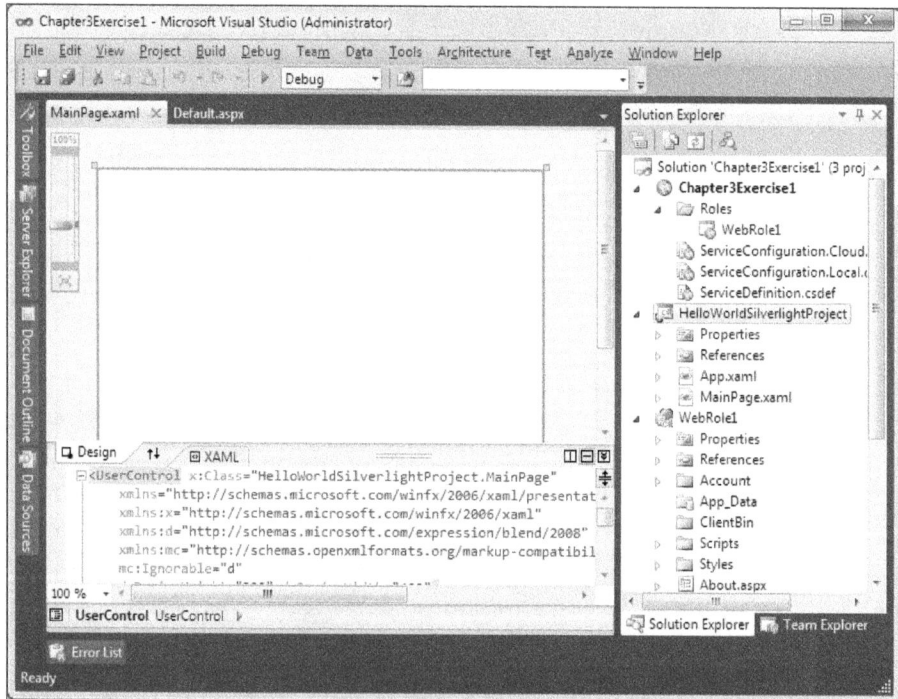

10. Open `MainPage.xaml` in design view, if not already open.

11. Change the grid to a `StackPanel`.

12. Inside the `StackPanel`, add a button named `button1` with a height of 40 and a content that displays `Click me!`.

13. Inside the `StackPanel`, underneath `button1`, add a text block named `textBlock1` with a height of 20.

14. The final XAML should look similar to this code snippet:

```
<UserControl>
    <StackPanel x:Name="LayoutRoot" Background="White">
        <Button x:Name="button1" Height="40"
                Content="Click me!" />
```

```
        <TextBlock x:Name="textBlock1" Height="20" />
    </StackPanel>
</UserControl>
```

15. Double-click on `button1` in the designer to have Visual Studio automatically create a click event. The final XAML in the designer should look similar to the following screenshot:

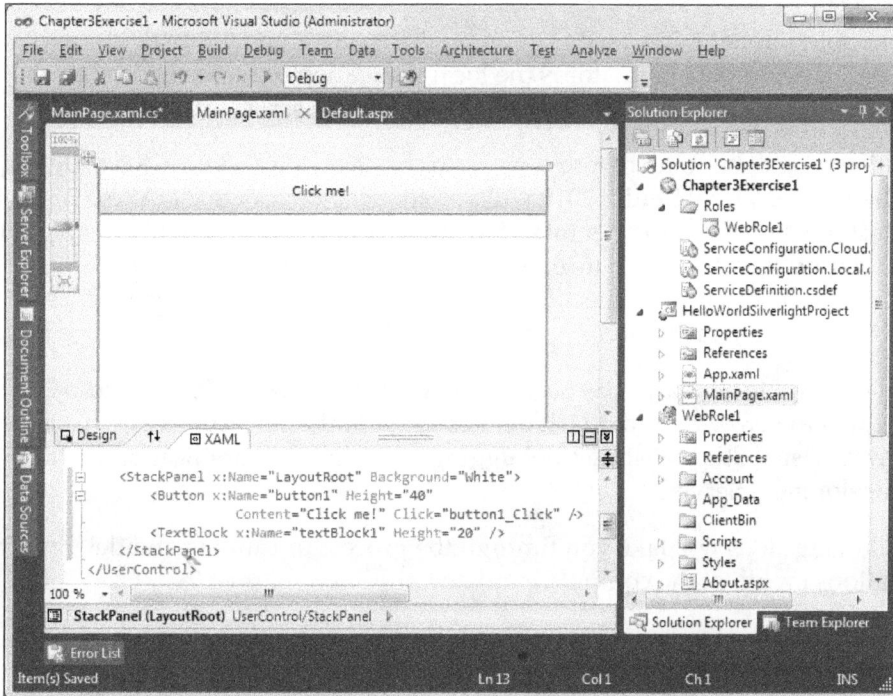

16. Open the `MainPage.xaml.cs` code behind the file and find the `button1_ Click` method. Add a code that will update `textBlock1` to display `Hello World` and the current time as follows:

```csharp
private void button1_Click(object sender, RoutedEventArgs e)
{
    textBlock1.Text = "Hello World at " +
        DateTime.Now.ToLongTimeString();
}
```

17. Build the project to ensure that everything compiles correctly.

Now that the solution has been built, it is ready to be run and debugged within the Windows Azure compute emulator. The next section will explore what happens while running an Azure application on the compute emulator.

Running an Azure application on the Azure compute emulator

With the solution built, it is ready to run on the Azure simulation: the **compute emulator**. The compute emulator is the local simulation of the **Windows Azure compute emulator** which Microsoft runs on the Azure servers it hosts.

When you start debugging by pressing *F5* (or by selecting **Debug | Start Debugging** from the menu), Visual Studio 2010 will automatically package the Azure project, then start the Azure compute emulator simulation. The package will be copied to a local folder used by the compute emulator. The compute emulator will then start a Windows process to host or execute the roles, one of which will be started as per the instance request for each role.

Once the compute emulator has been successfully initialized, Visual Studio 2010 will then launch the browser and attach the debugger to the correct places. This is similar to the way Visual Studio handles debugging of an ASP.Net application with the ASP. Net Development Server.

The following steps will take you through the process of running and debugging applications on top of the compute emulator:

1. In **Solution Explorer**, inside the **HelloWorldSilverlightProject**, right-click on **HelloWorldSilverlightProjectTestPage.aspx**, and select **Set as startup page**.

2. Ensure that the Azure project (**Chapter3Exercise1**) is still set as the start-up project.

3. In Visual Studio 2010, press *F5* to start debugging (or from the menu select **Debug | Start Debugging**). Visual Studio will compile the project, and if successful, begins to launch the Azure compute emulator as shown in the following screenshot:

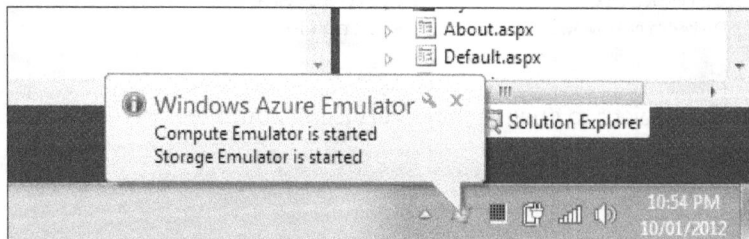

4. Once the compute emulator has been started and the Azure package deployed to it, Visual Studio 2010 will launch Internet Explorer. Internet Explorer will display the page set as the start-up page (which was set to in an earlier step `HelloWorldSilverlightProjectTestPage.aspx`).

5. Once the Silverlight application has been loaded, click on the **Click me!** button. The `TextBlock` should be updated with the current time, as shown in the following screenshot:

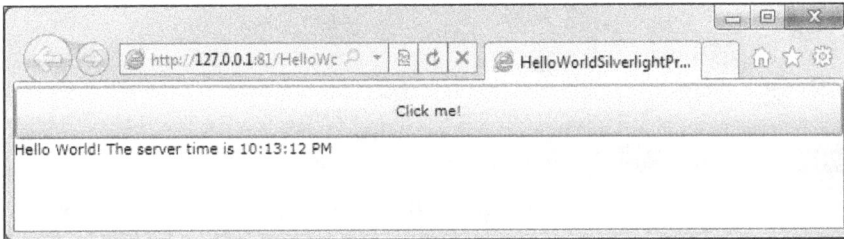

Upon this completion, you should now have successfully deployed a Silverlight application on top of the Windows Azure compute emulator. You can now use this base project to build more advanced features and integration with other services.

Consuming an Azure-hosted WCF service within a Silverlight application

A standalone Silverlight application will not be able to do much by itself. Most applications will require that they consume data from a data source, such as to get a list of products or customer orders. A common way to send data between .Net applications is through **WCF Services**.

The following steps will explore how to add a WCF service to your Azure web role, and then consume it from within the Silverlight application:

1. In Visual Studio, right-click on the ASP.Net web role project (**WebRole1**) and click on **Add | New Item**.

2. Add a new WCF service named **HelloWorldService.svc** as shown in the following screenshot:

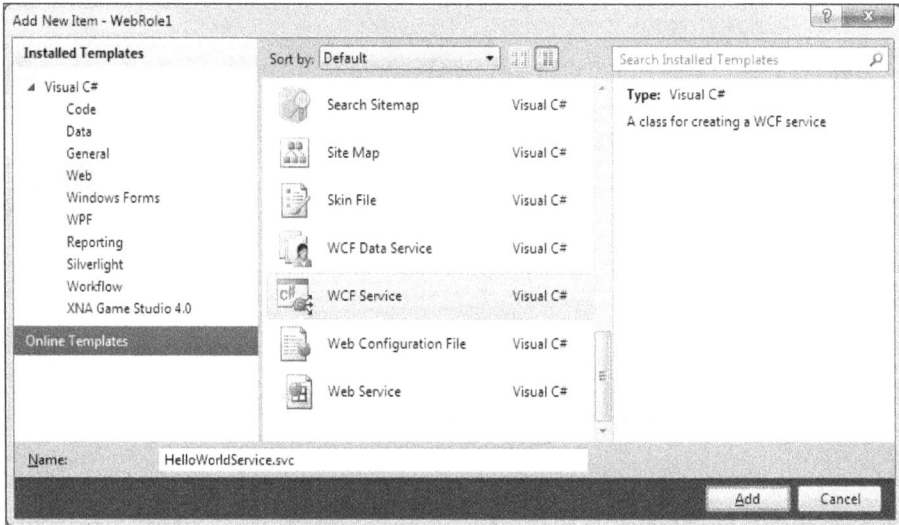

3. Once the WCF service has been added into the project, three new files will be added to the project: `IHelloWorldService.cs`, `HelloWorldService.svc`, and `HelloWorldService.svc.cs`.

4. Open `IHelloWorldService.cs` and change the interface, so that it defines a single method named `GenerateHelloWorldGreeting` that takes no parameters and returns a string. The entire file should look similar to the following code snippet:

```
using System.ServiceModel;

namespace WebRole1
{
  [ServiceContract]
  public interface IHelloWorldService
  {
    [OperationContract]
    string GenerateHelloWorldGreeting();
  }
}
```

5. Open `HelloWorldService.svc.cs` and modify the code, so that it implements the `GenerateHelloWorldGreeting` method as follows (the method in the code snippet returns `Hello World`, as well as the current server time):

```
using System;

namespace WebRole1
{
  public class HelloWorldService : IHelloWorldService
  {
    public string GenerateHelloWorldGreeting()
    {
      var currentTime = DateTime.Now.ToLongTimeString();

      return "Hello World! The server time is " + currentTime;
    }
  }
}
```

6. Add a **breakpoint** on the line of code that returns the "Hello world" message. This breakpoint will be used in a later step.

7. Build the solution to ensure there are no syntax errors. If the solution does not build, then runtime errors can occur when trying to add the service reference.

8. Right-click on the Silverlight project **HelloWorldSilverlightProject** and select **Add Service Reference**. Click on **Discover** to allow Visual Studio to automatically detect the WCF service in the solution. Select the service and name the reference `HelloWorldServiceReference`, as shown in the screenshot, and click on **OK**:

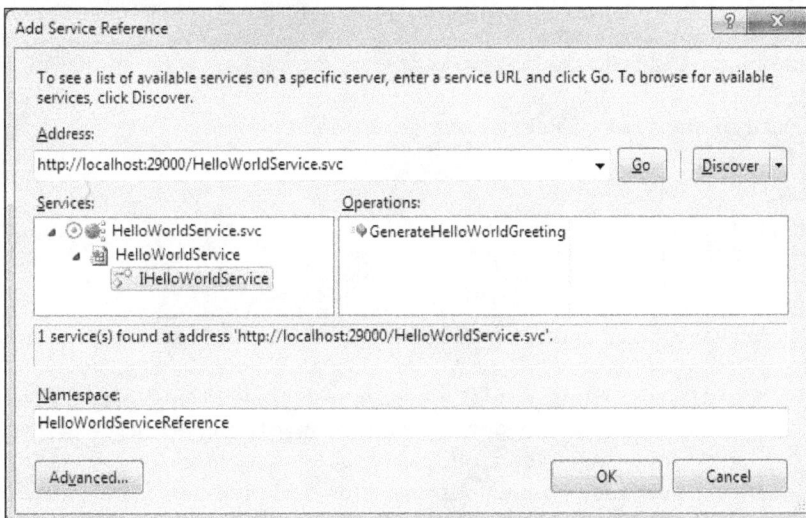

9. With the WCF service reference added to the Silverlight application, we will change the functionality of the `Click me!` button. Currently when clicked, the event handler will update the `TextBlock` with a "Hello world" message and the current time on the client side. This will be changed, so that clicking on the button will cause the Silverlight application to call the WCF service and have the "Hello world" message generated on the server side. In Visual Studio 2010, within the Silverlight project, open `MainPage.xaml.cs`.

10. Modify the `button1_Click` method, so that it calls the WCF service and updates `textBlock1` with the returned value. Due to the dynamic nature of developing with Azure, the address of the service endpoint can change many times through the development lifecycle. Each time Visual Studio 2010 deploys the project onto the compute emulator, a different port number can be assigned if the previous deployment has not been de-provisioned yet. Deploying to the Windows Azure staging environment will also give it a new address, while deploying to production will provide yet another endpoint address. The following code shows one technique to automatically handle the Silverlight application being hosted at different addresses. The Silverlight application invokes the WCF service by accessing it relative to where the Silverlight application is currently being hosted. This is in contrast to the usual behavior of calling WCF services which require an absolute address that would need to be updated with each deployment.

```
using System;
using System.ServiceModel;
using System.Windows;
using System.Windows.Controls;
using HelloWorldSilverlightProject.HelloWorldServiceReference;

namespace HelloWorldSilverlightProject
{
  public partial class MainPage : UserControl
  {
    public MainPage()
    {
      InitializeComponent();
    }

    private void button1_Click(object sender, RoutedEventArgs e)
    {
      //Find the URL for the current Silverlight .xap file. Go up
          one level to get to the root of the site.
      var url = Application.Current.Host.Source.OriginalString;
      var urlBase = url.Substring(0, url.IndexOf("/ClientBin",
        StringComparison.InvariantCultureIgnoreCase));
```

```
//Create a proxy object for the WCF service. Use the root
    path of the site and append the service name
var proxy = new HelloWorldServiceClient();
proxy.Endpoint.Address = new EndpointAddress(urlBase +
    "/HelloWorldService.svc");

proxy.GenerateHelloWorldGreetingCompleted +=
    proxy_GenerateHelloWorldGreetingCompleted;
proxy.GenerateHelloWorldGreetingAsync();
}

void proxy_GenerateHelloWorldGreetingCompleted(object sender,
    GenerateHelloWorldGreetingCompletedEventArgs e)
{
    textBlock1.Text = e.Result;
}
}
}
```

Relative WCF services

The code in the code snippet shows a technique for calling WCF services relative to the currently executing Silverlight application. This technique means that the Silverlight application is not dependent on the service address being updated for each deployment. This allows the whole ASP.Net application to be hosted and deployed on a number of environments without configuration changes, such as the ASP.Net development server, Azure compute emulator, Azure staging or production environments, or on any other IIS host.

11. Compile the application to check that there are no syntax errors.

12. Press *F5* to run the whole application in a debug mode. The Azure compute emulator should start up and Internet Explorer should be launched again with the Silverlight application.

13. Click on the **Click me!** button. The Silverlight client will call the WCF service causing Visual Studio to hit the breakpoint that was set earlier inside the WCF service. This shows that even though we are running and debugging a Silverlight application, we are still able to debug WCF services that are being hosted inside the Azure compute emulator.

14. Remove the breakpoint and continue the execution. Click on the button a few more times to watch the `TextBlock` update itself. The results should look similar to the following screenshot. Be sure to keep the browser open for the next steps:

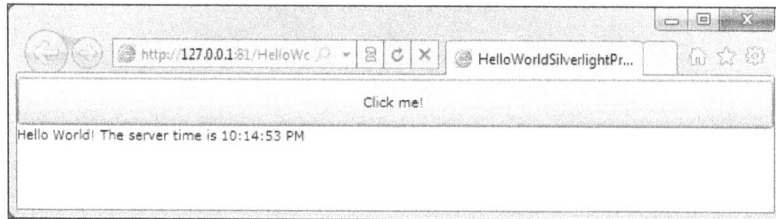

15. Open the Azure compute emulator. Do this by right-clicking on the Azure icon in the system tray, and then clicking on **Show Compute Emulator UI**.

16. The compute emulator UI should now be open and look similar to the following screenshot. In the screenshot, you can see that there is a single deployment (the 29th one that has been deployed to the compute emulator). The deployment has one Azure project named **Chapter3Exercise1**. This Azure project has a single web role named **WebRole1**, which is currently executing a single instance. Clicking on the instance will show the output terminal of that instance. Here the trance information can be seen, being an output to the window:

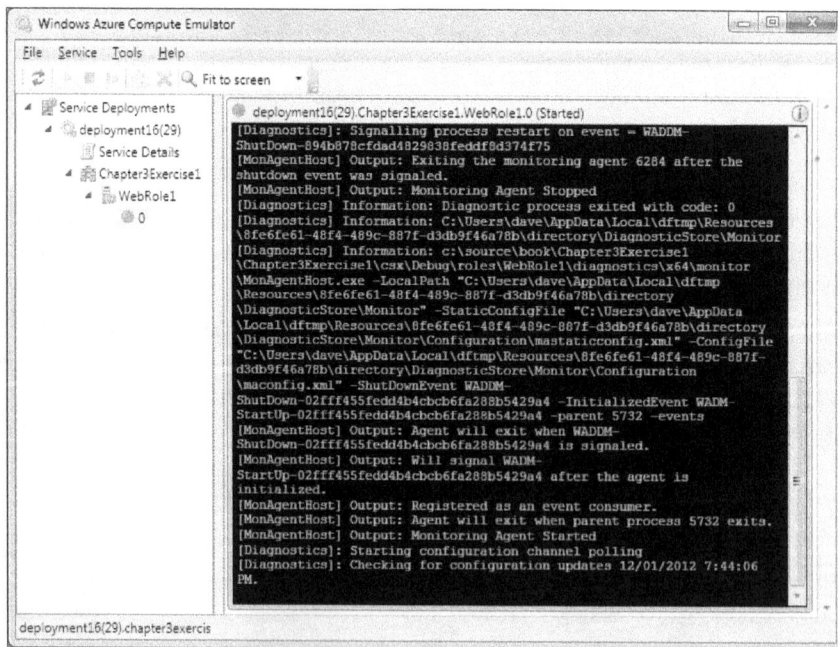

Configuring the number of web roles

The power in Azure comes from running multiple instances of a single role and distributing the computational load. It is important to understand how to configure the size and number of instances of a role that should be initialized.

The following steps will explain how this can be done within the Visual Studio 2010:

1. Stop debugging the application and return to Visual Studio 2010.
2. Inside the Azure project **Chapter3Exercise1**, right-click on **WebRole1**, and select **Properties**.

The role properties window is used to specify both the size of the instances that should be used, as well as the number of instances that should be used.

The **VM size** has no effect on the compute emulator, as you are still constrained by the local development machine. The **VM size** setting is used when the package is deployed onto the Windows Azure servers. It defines the number of CPUs and amounts of RAM allocated to each instance. These settings determine the charges Microsoft will accrue to your account.

In the earlier stages of development, it can be useful to set the **VM size** to extra small to save consumption costs. This can be done in situations where performance is not a high requirement, such as when a few developers are testing their deployments.

> **Extra small instances**
>
> The extra small instances are great while developing as they are much cheaper instances to deploy. However, they are low-resourced and also have bandwidth restrictions enforced on them. They are not recommended for use in a high performance production environment.

The **Instance count** is used to specify the number of instances of the role that should be created. Creating multiple instances of a role can assist in testing concurrency while working with the compute emulator. Be aware that you are still constrained by the local development box, setting this to a very large number can lower the performance of your machine:

1. Set the **Instance count** to **4** as shown in the following screenshot. If you are planning to deploy the application to the Windows Azure servers, it is a good idea to set the **VM size** to **Extra Small** while testing:

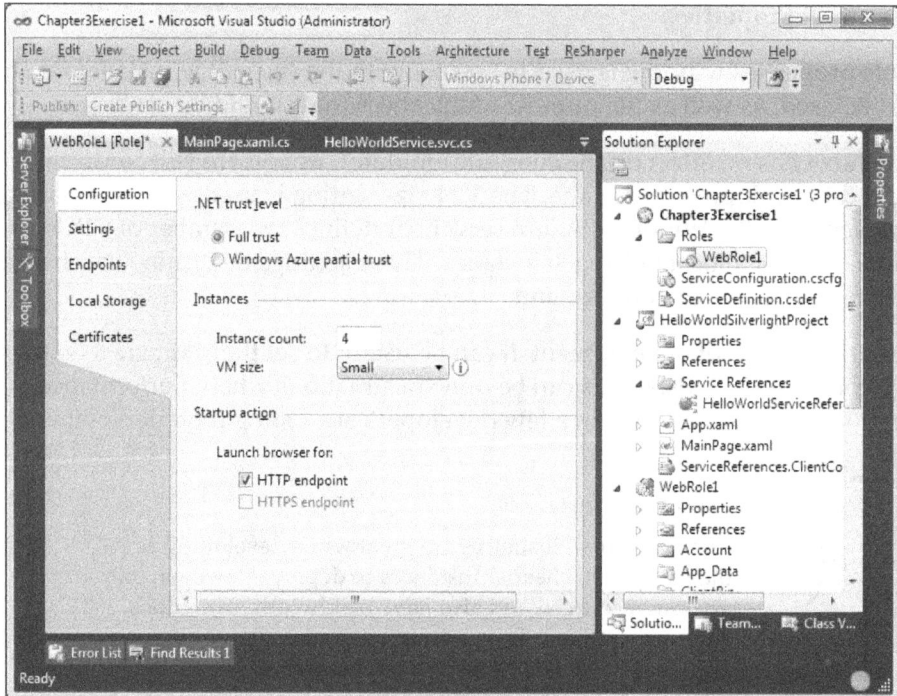

2. Open `HelloWorldService.svc.cs` and modify the service implementation. The service will now use the Windows Azure SDK to retrieve instance ID that is currently handling the request:

```
using System;
using Microsoft.WindowsAzure.ServiceRuntime;

namespace WebRole1
{
  public class HelloWorldService : IHelloWorldService
  {
    public string GenerateHelloWorldGreeting()
```

```
    {
        var currentTime = DateTime.Now.ToLongTimeString();
        var instanceId = RoleEnvironment.CurrentRoleInstance.Id;

        return string.Format("Hello World! The server time is {0}.
                        Processed by {1}", currentTime, instanceId);
    }
  }
}
```

3. Press *F5* to debug the project again.

4. Open the Azure compute emulator UI. There should now be four instances handling the request.

5. In Internet Explorer, click on the **Click me!** button multiple times. The text will update with the server time and the instance that handled the request. The following screenshot shows that instance 1 was handling the request. If the instance ID does not change after multiple clicks, try to launch a second browser, and click again. Sometimes, affinity can cause a request to get sticky and stay with a single instance:

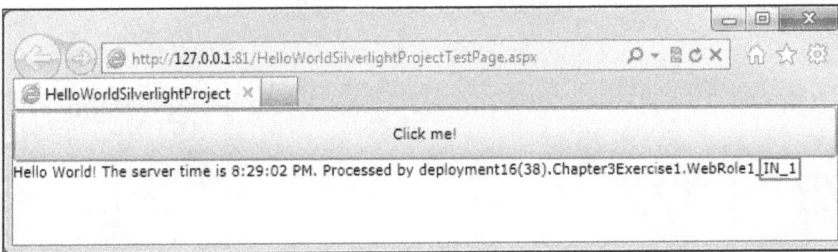

This exercise demonstrated requests for a WCF service being load balanced over a number of Azure instances. The following diagram shows that as requests from the Silverlight client come in, the load balancer will distribute the requests across the instances. It is important to keep this in mind while developing Azure services and develop each role to be **stateless services** when working with multiple instances. Each request may be handled by a different instance each time, requiring you to not keep any session state inside an instance:

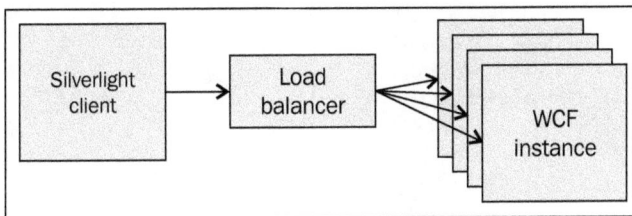

Summary

In this chapter, we created a new Silverlight application that was hosted with an Azure project. We then created a WCF service that was also hosted within the Azure project, and consumed it from the Silverlight application. The WCF service was then scaled to 4 instances to demonstrate how WCF requests can be load balanced across multiple instances. A technique was also shown to allow a WCF service to be consumed through a relative path, allowing the website to be hosted anywhere without the service address needing to be changed for each deployment.

In the next chapter, we begin the introduction of the Azure Storage by looking at the Azure Queue Service.

4
Using Azure Queues with Silverlight

The Windows Azure storage service is focused on the durable storage of persistent data and comprises three distinct services: blob, queue, and table.

We will begin this chapter by covering the fundamentals of Windows Azure storage, and then diving into the specifics of Azure Queue services.

Most introductions to Azure storage services begin with Azure Blob storage and continue from there. However, out of the three services (blob, queue, and table), Blob storage contains the most new concepts that need to be introduced simultaneously. There are enough fundamentals being introduced while using the Azure storage service with Silverlight for the additional Blob storage specific functions to complicate things. For this reason, we will first cover the **Azure Queue service** which has a simpler interaction model. Later chapters will then focus on Blob storage and finally Table storage.

In this chapter, we will discuss the following topics:

- Fundamentals of Windows Azure storage services
- Azure Storage Queue service
- Using queues for application scalability
- Queuing work from a Silverlight application
- Handling poison messages (a message that repeatedly fails to process)

Fundamentals of Azure storage services

The **Windows Azure storage service** provides a scalable and durable way to persist data. It is recommended to store your data and "application state" in the Azure Storage, separated from your Azure compute instances. Each of the operations that are performed in the compute instances should be **stateless**, with the final state stored in a non-volatile store. Although it is possible to store data locally in the compute service instances, it is not a good idea as all the data stored inside an instance can be lost if an instance is taken offline.

All the operations of storage services can be done through a **REST-based API**. On being exposed as a REST service, it allows developers to consume the storage service APIs with Silverlight, ASP.Net, JavaScript, and other technologies.

> **RESTful services**
>
> REST (**RE**presentational **S**tate Transfer) is used as a standard way of using the **HTTP protocol** to interact with the resources on a web server. The URL is used to define the object on the server that is being acted upon, while the HTTP verb (GET/PUT/POST/DELETE) is used to define the operation being invoked. In this way, resources can be queried, created, edited, and deleted. If a service implements this style of interaction, it can be said to be a RESTful service. More information can be found on Wikipedia at the following URL:
>
> ```
> http://en.wikipedia.org/wiki/Representational_State_
> Transfer
> ```

Microsoft stores all the data within the Azure storage services (blobs, queues, and table storage) multiple times across their data farm for **redundancy**. Each piece of data is replicated at least three times, so that in the event of a hardware failure, there is no data loss. Under the covers, Azure storage services is actually just a special Azure application deployed onto the Azure Fabric by Microsoft.

It is possible to do the majority of these exercises with the **local storage emulator** and most exercises target the same. However, if you want to attempt the exercises by developing against the Azure servers directly, then you need to create an account. If you have not created a storage account yet, please refer to *Chapter 1, Getting Started*, for instructions on how to provision one. Both methods will work equally well for the exercises. So feel free to use whichever is more convenient to you. However, be aware that there may be differences between the storage emulator and the online version. So please consult **MSDN** for a list of differences at the following URL:

```
http://msdn.microsoft.com/en-us/library/windowsazure/gg432968.aspx
```

Windows Azure storage can be accessed and consumed in two supported ways:

- Using the REST service
- Using the Azure storage client library

Accessing storage services through REST APIs

Microsoft enabled a cross-platform way of programmatically accessing the Windows Azure storage service. It achieved this by exposing all the operations as a HTTP REST service. This is great for the development against the storage service as it means that all the web-enabled development platforms are virtually able to consume the service (such as ASP.Net, Java, Silverlight, iPhones, and so on). For public services, all that is needed to make a call to a REST service is to construct the URL, make a HTTP request, and then parse the response. Services can also require that the clients authenticate themselves by requiring the *certificates* and *keys* attached to the **HTTP request header**. One potential weakness of REST calls can be the difficulty to construct the calls under advanced scenarios. As the complexity of an operation increases (by adding additional filters and sorts to the request), the corresponding URL length grows with it. You can combine this with the fact that most operations performed against the Windows Azure storage REST service require the call to be authenticated, which can eventually lead to a lot of manual coding.

To simplify programing against the Windows Azure storage service, this book recommends the use of the Windows Azure storage client library. The client library greatly simplifies the construction of HTTP requests to the REST service.

Accessing storage services with storage client library

For .Net developers, it makes a lot more sense to use the Windows Azure storage client library, rather than manually creating REST requests. The storage client is a .Net library that Microsoft ships to simplify development against the Azure storage service. It strongly provides **typed access** to Azure Storage, and streamlines most of the underlying complexity. The exercises throughout this book will rely heavily on the use of the storage client library.

The storage client library provides classes that map to each of the logical structures of the Azure storage service such as queues, messages, blobs, containers, tables, and so on. Methods are then exposed to each of the class that maps to the associated REST methods. It also helps to make the authentication easier by just requiring you to add the **shared key** as a *string*, and it will take care of all the underlying details of attaching it to the request.

The storage client library is usable only in the full .Net framework (ASP.Net) and is not available for Silverlight. This is by design, as the shared key is required for a majority of operations, and it is not secure to put the shared key into an application that will be sent to end users. While accessing the storage service, it should **always** be done through an Azure compute instance. By doing so, the shared key is stored on the server and need not be revealed to the client. There is one exception to this rule when it comes to **shared access signatures** with Blob storage, but this will be discussed in a later chapter.

Using shared keys to access storage services

The shared key is a 512-bit **symmetric key** that is used to sign the requests sent to the REST service. The key is the "shared secret" that the storage service and your application use to communicate to each other. A symmetric key is used because it is very fast to encrypt and decrypt data. If the key is kept secret with only those two machines knowing it, then both the parties can be assured that the request or response did not come from a third party trying to intercept.

The Azure storage service provides you with two keys: a *primary key* and a *secondary key*. These two keys are provided to help you with the revocation of keys. If the primary key is compromised, then your applications can be informed to use the secondary key. The primary key can then be regenerated, restricting the compromised use of it. Without these two keys, your application would stop working until you deploy the application again with the new key.

The following screenshot shows where the primary and secondary keys are located within the Azure Management Portal:

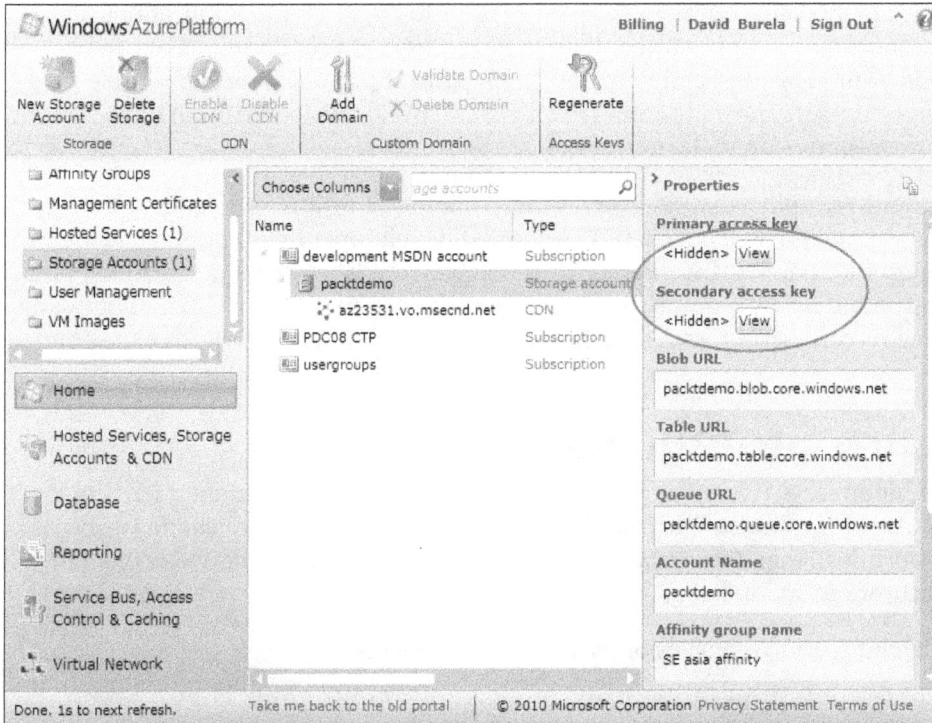

Collocation of storage and computer services

As discussed in *Chapter 1, Getting Started*, it is important to place both your **compute instances** and **storage service** in the same datacenter. Having both services collocated within the same datacenter reduces latency and prevents you from being charged for data transfer fees between the datacenters.

> **Affinity groups**
>
> Affinity groups allow you to specify a datacenter region that your collection of services should be collocated. If you are servicing North Europe, for example, you could create an affinity group for that region and provision services (storage, compute, and so on) that would be collocated in the same datacenter for maximum performance.

Local storage emulator

The **local storage emulator** combined with the **compute fabric** gives a complete local developmental environment that can be used to create Azure applications. Once the storage emulator is started, there will be three local endpoints that can be used within your local application to develop against it (one each for Blob, Table, and Queue storage). The endpoints are only available locally and cannot be accessed by other computers on your network.

In order to simplify the exercises in this book to follow and self-contain, the local storage emulator will be used. A supported development methodology is used to develop the code locally, but you should have your development machine point to the online Azure storage service. This can be useful as it helps to highlight any **timing** or **connection issues** that are not apparent while using the storage emulator.

Azure Storage Queue service

The Queue service is a way of sending reliable messages to different parts of your Azure application. If you have multiple roles in your application (web and worker roles), then there is a need to be able to communicate between them in an asynchronous manner.

The Queue service consists of two main components:

- **Queue**: Holds the individual messages within itself
- **Message**: The packet of information that is stored inside of the queue

Queues are private and are held with a storage account. A storage account may have an unlimited number of message queues, as long as each are named uniquely. The name of the queue only needs to be unique within the storage account and not globally unique as it is specific to an account.

Messages in a queue have no **fixed schema**, so it is possible to put many different message types within a single queue , for example, data for cats that need to be identified and also dogs. Be aware that putting many different message types into a single queue can result in a complicated code to handle each differing message. There are no limits on the number of queues that can be created and you pay for the total amount of storage used, not the number of queues in use. To simplify development, a queue should be created for each message type or the functional area of your code that needs to communicate within your Azure application. This helps to keep the different parts of your system separated and helps to debug issues.

There are no limits imposed on the number of messages that can be held within a queue. Each message can be up to a maximum size of 8 KB. If more than 8 KB is needed (such as adding a large file to the queue), then a **common pattern** is used to store the data into the Blob storage and add the URL to the data into the message.

To access a queue through the REST service, the URL is constructed as follows:

```
http://<StorageAccount>.queue.core.windows.net/<QueueName>
```

Breaking down into its components, we can see that the **subdomain** is the name of your storage account, and the **specific queue nam**e is being accessed within the storage account.

The following diagram shows the conceptual layout of the Queue service. An account has multiple queues, with each queue holding a number of messages:

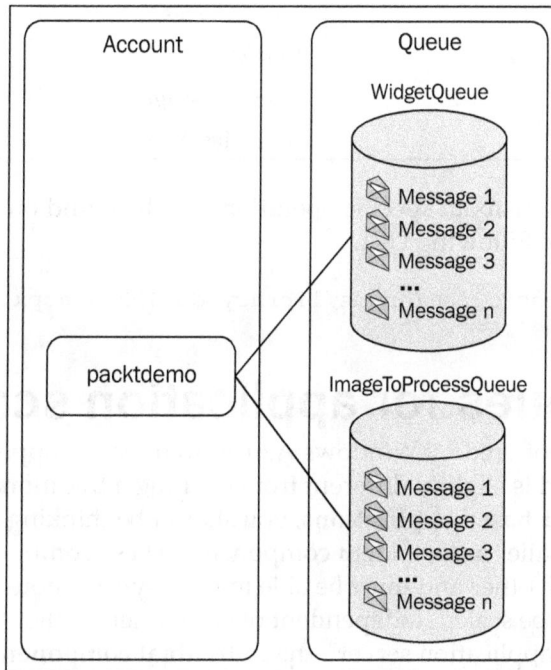

Queue service operations

The Queue REST API exposes a number of methods around the creation, or listing, or reading, or deletion of queues and messages within the storage service. The following table groups the available service operations with the object they interact with:

	Operation name
Queues	List Queues
	Create Queues
	Delete Queues
Queue Metadata	Get Queue Metadata
	Set Queue Metadata
Messages	Put Message
	Get Messages
	Peek Messages
	Delete Messages
	Clear Messages

Additional information about specific operations can be found online in the MSDN documentation at the following URL:

```
http://msdn.microsoft.com/en-us/library/dd179363.aspx
```

Using queues for application scalability

Due to the elasticity offered by Windows Azure, architecting applications that can scale in the cloud is slightly different from creating a traditional application. When creating **cloud-based applications**, you should be thinking about breaking your system into smaller independent components. These components need to be decoupled from each other and must be able to run asynchronously. Once separated, the components can be scaled, independent of each other. Rather than a very coarse level of "scaling the application server", the **individual components** of the system that are creating the **bottlenecks** can be scaled.

If the system is to do any useful work, then these decoupled components should be able to message and communicate with each other. Queues are the ones that facilitate the communication between different areas of the application. Queues provide two main benefits: **durable asynchronous messaging** and the ability to **buffer** work to be done.

Asynchronous messaging allows the different parts of a system to continue working while waiting for something else to complete. Rather than the component **A** making a request of component **B,** and then sitting there, waiting for a response, component **A** can continue working on something else instead. This prevents component **A** from being **blocked**.

Queues also give an application the ability to **buffer** the work to be done. Work can continue to accumulate in the queue, and a worker process can process each message one at a time as it is able to. Rather than requiring enough instances online to handle all the messages instantly, and sitting there idle for the rest of the time, buffering messages allow the smooth processing of the **bursts of work** over a period of time.

To give a more in-depth look at how queues can be used within the architecture of a cloud application, we will investigate a fictitious website named **Azure Tube**. Azure Tube is a website that allows the users to upload the video content, and gets it hosted online. When the users upload the video content, the video needs to be re-encoded into different codecs and bit rates.

If the video uploading was to be done with a traditional website, then the file may be uploaded directly to the server, and the same server would process it correctly at that time. This would be **synchronous execution** and would bring severe scalability issues with it. In this model, as more and more users upload videos to be processed, the server would become overloaded quickly. Scaling would become an issue as the application would be constrained by how many servers you currently have online, trying to handle the user load. Any lack of resources here would be noticeable instantly. The following diagram shows what traditional website architecture and a user load may look like:

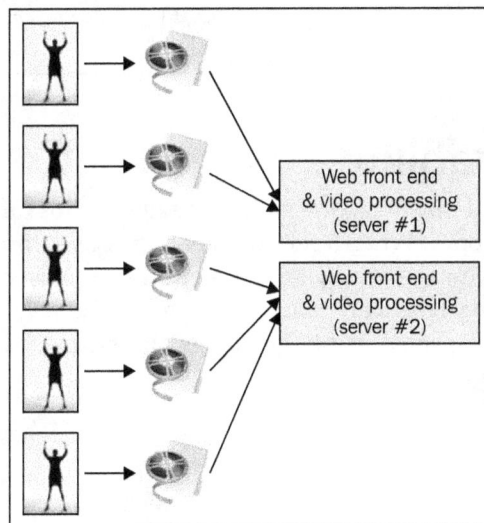

Azure Tube does not suffer from the limitations of a traditional website. It uses queues to buffer the workload. The web frontend takes each uploaded video, stores it in a temporary location in the Blob storage, and adds a message to the queue. The user is instantly told that the video is in the queue to be processed and will be notified by an e-mail once the video has been processed. In this way, the web frontend has asynchronously messaged a second part of the system to process the video when it is able to. Worker roles can then be used to go through the queue and process each message or video one at a time. The other benefit of this system is the ability to scale the processing resources up and down. If the queue starts becoming too long during a peak period, then the extra work roles can be brought online to process the videos. Once the queue has come down to a reasonable level, the additional worker roles can be deprovisioned again. The following diagram shows what the architecture of Azure Tube would look like:

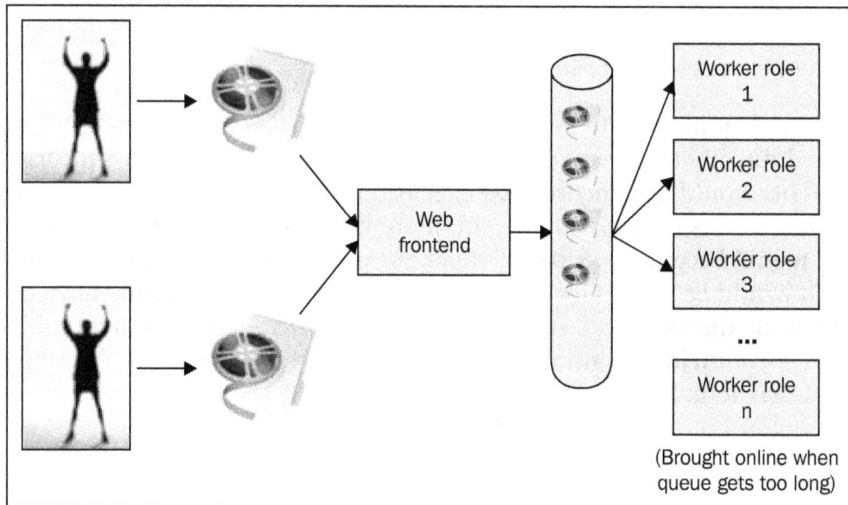

Message durability

Messages that are placed into an Azure storage queue are **durable**, and are guaranteed to be processed at least once. When a server takes a message from the queue and begins processing the message, it may fail for a number of reasons such as application error, server taken offline, hardware failure, and so on. The way Azure Queues operate helps to ensure that a message does not get lost in an unexpected condition.

When a message is read from the queue, the message is not deleted from the queue, instead the message is hidden for a set amount of time. The consumer of the queue should grab a message, process it, and once processing is done, he/she should delete the message from the queue. This provides a way to ensure that each message is processed at least once. If a server begins to process a message, but then fails due to an error, then the message will become visible after the timeout has expired and another consumer will pick up the message and process it.

However, you need to be aware that it is possible for a message to be processed more than once. A server could process the message fully, but can be taken offline just as it is about to delete the message from the queue. This can cause issues in a banking system where processing a message to deduct $100 from an account would cause $200 to be deducted instead. It is important to internally track the transaction IDs while processing the messages, so that if a second consumer attempts to process the message for a second time, it will detect the money transfer that has already been processed.

Queuing work from a Silverlight application

To help in exploring the Azure Storage Queue service, we will use a fictitious scenario, for example, a factory creates widgets to be sold to the customers. People can submit their orders for a batch of widgets and they will be manufactured on request.

The application that will support this is a simple **Silverlight client** that can submit an order for the widgets that should be manufactured. Each of these orders will be sent from the Silverlight client and eventually be added to the queue. A worker role will then process each of the orders on the queue and manufacture these widgets.

Silverlight is not able to interact directly against the API (due to the limitations of requiring the shared key). Instead for this exercise, the Silverlight application will call a WCF service, hosted in an Azure web role, and request it to place the widget order into the queue.

The following diagram shows what the architecture of this exercise looks like. The Silverlight client will submit orders through the WCF to the Azure web role. The web role will place the message onto the queue. The worker role will then pick the message from the queue, and process it:

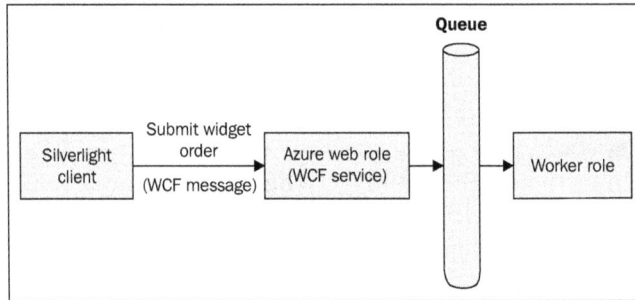

We will start this exercise by creating the WCF service that will take a widget order and add it to the queue, ready for processing:

1. In **Visual Studio 2010,** create a new **Windows Azure Project** named **QueueExercise1** as shown in the following screenshot:

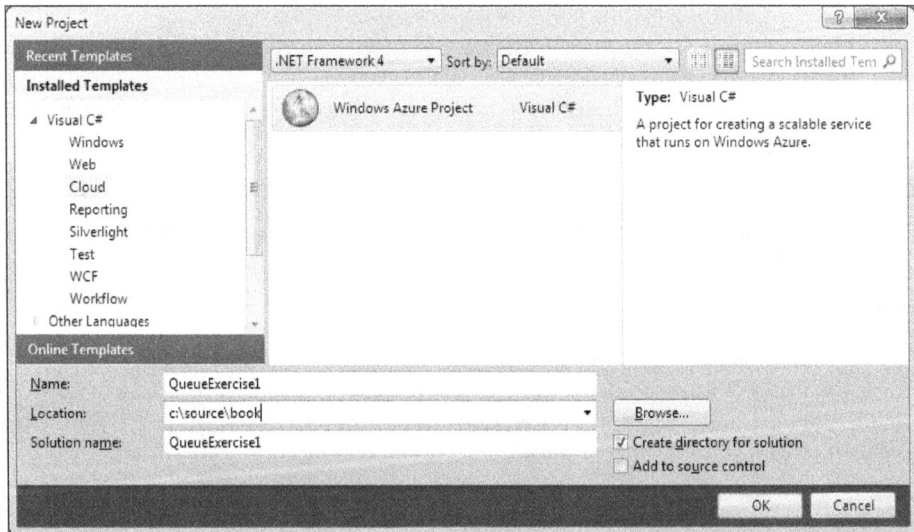

2. Add a **WCF Service Web Role** and a **Worker Role** to the project. Rename them to **WcfServiceWebRole** and **WidgetFactoryWorkerRole** as shown in the following screenshot. Click on **OK** to create the application:

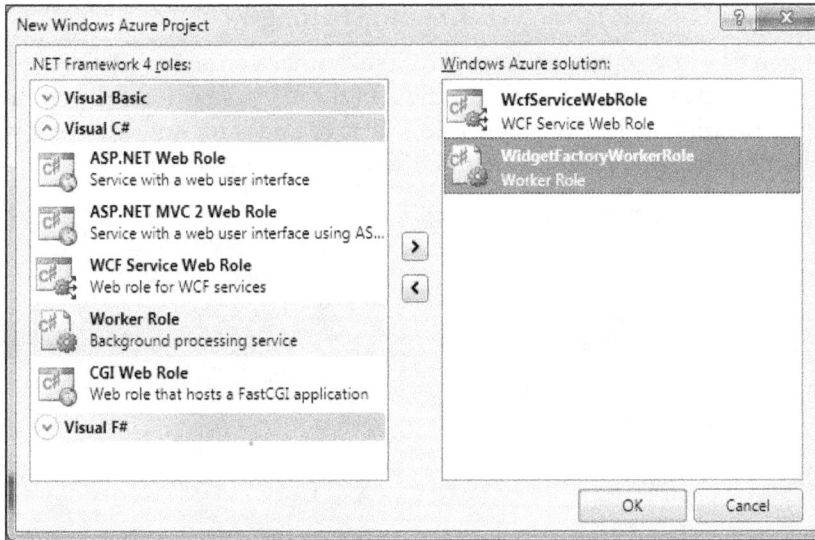

3. Once Visual Studio 2010 has finished creating the solution, expand the **QueueExercise1** cloud project, expand the `Roles` folder, right-click on **WcfServiceWebRole**, and select **Properties**. As shown in the following screenshot, this is the role definition file and not the web role project:

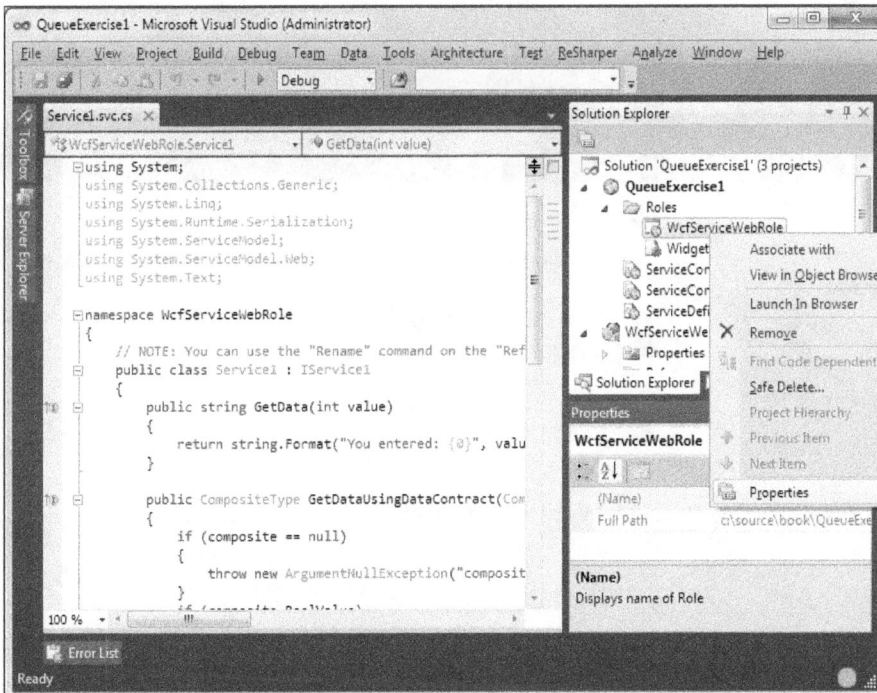

4. Go to the **Settings** tab and click on **Add Setting**.

5. Name the new setting as **AzureStorageConnectionString**, change it to **Connection String**, and then click on the ellipsis button to open the configuration. Select **Use the Azure storage emulator** and click on **OK**. The final result should look similar to the following screenshot:

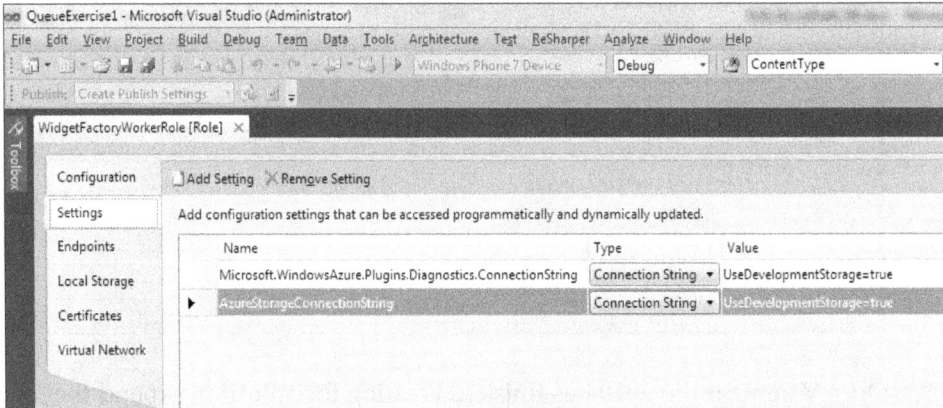

6. Repeat the preceding steps to add a connection string to the **WcfServiceWebRole**. The result will appear as shown in the following screenshot:

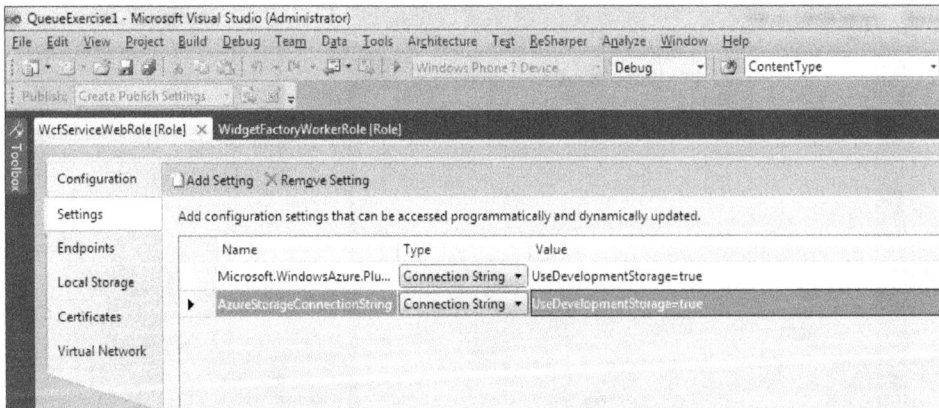

7. From the **WcfServiceWebRole** project, open **IService.cs**.

8. Modify the interface, so that it has a single method named
   SubmitWidgetOrder that takes the number of orders that should be submitted:

```
using System.ServiceModel;

namespace WcfServiceWebRole
{
  [ServiceContract]
  public interface IService1
  {
    [OperationContract]
    void SubmitWidgetOrder(int numberOfWidgets);
  }
}
```

9. Open **Service1.cs** to implement the service. The following code
   does three distinct things. First, it retrieves the connection string
   AzureStorageConnectionString from the service configuration file and
   creates a cloud storage account object that is held in the storageAccount
   variable. Next, the storageAccount is used to access the queue storage and
   gets a handle to a queue named widgetqueue. The code verifies that the
   queue has been created, and creates it if it does not exist. Finally, now that
   the code has a handle to the widgetqueue, it is able to add a message to the
   queue. In this instance, it is adding the number of widgets to be created
   as a message:

```
using Microsoft.WindowsAzure;
using Microsoft.WindowsAzure.ServiceRuntime;
using Microsoft.WindowsAzure.StorageClient;

namespace WcfServiceWebRole
{
  public class Service1 : IService1
  {
    public void SubmitWidgetOrder(int numberOfWidgets)
    {
      // retrieve the account settings from the configuration file
      var storageAccount = CloudStorageAccount.Parse
        (RoleEnvironment.GetConfigurationSettingValue
        ("AzureStorageConnectionString"));
      var queueClient = storageAccount.CreateCloudQueueClient();

      // get a handle to a widget queue and create it if it does
        not exist
      var queue = queueClient.GetQueueReference("widgetqueue");
      queue.CreateIfNotExist();
```

```
        // add the widget order as a message to the queue
        var msg = new CloudQueueMessage(numberOfWidgets.ToString());
        queue.AddMessage(msg);
    }
  }
}
```

With the WCF service created and ready to accept the messages, the Silverlight application will be implemented. The Silverlight application will allow the user to enter the number of widgets that should be ordered, and submit the order to the WCF service.

10. Add a new Silverlight project to the solution. Do this by right-clicking on the **WcfServiceWebRole** project and selecting **Properties**. Go to the **Silverlight Applications** tab, then click on **Add**. Name the Silverlight application as WidgetSubmissionSilverlightProject.

11. Right-click on **WidgetSubmissionSilverlightProjectTestPage.aspx** in the web role and select **Set as start page**.

12. Be sure to build the project to ensure that the WCF service is compiled.

13. Right-click on the Silverlight project, and then click on **Add Service Reference**.

14. Click on **Discover**. Select **Service1.svc** and rename the service reference to **WidgetServiceReference** as shown in the following screenshot:

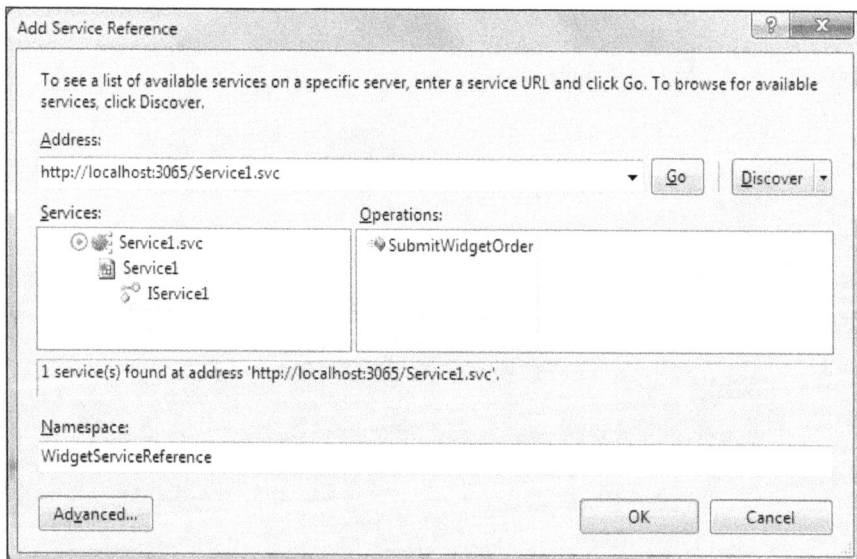

15. Open **MainPage.xaml**. A `TextBox`, `TextBlock`, and a `Button` will be added to the screen, so that the user can enter the number of widgets that should be added to the order. The following code shows the XAML:

```
<UserControl>
  <StackPanel x:Name="LayoutRoot" Background="White">
    <TextBlock Text="Number of widgets to create"/>
    <TextBox x:Name="widgetNumberTextBlock" Height="30" />
    <Button Content="Submit order" Height="50"
      Click="ButtonClick"/>
  </StackPanel>
</UserControl>
```

16. Open **MainPage.xaml.cs**. The code to submit an order to the WCF service will be added. First, the code checks that the text entered into the text box is actually a number. If it does not parse correctly, then the user is prompted to enter a number. Next, the code calls the WCF service relative to the location of the XAP file. This code is taken from an earlier chapter, and allows the WCF call to be executed without the need to change the connection strings between developing locally and deploying it into production:

```
private void ButtonClick(object sender, RoutedEventArgs e)
{
  int numberOfWidgets;
  if(int.TryParse(widgetNumberTextBlock.Text,
      out numberOfWidgets) == false)
  {
    MessageBox.Show("Please enter a number");
    return;
  }

  // This is the same code from Chapter 3. To allow this code to
  //   work locally and in the production, find the URL for the
  //   current Silverlight XAP file. Go up one level to get to the
  //   root of the site.
  var url = Application.Current.Host.Source.OriginalString;
  var urlBase = url.Substring(0, url.IndexOf("/ClientBin",
    StringComparison.InvariantCultureIgnoreCase));

  // Create a proxy object for the WCF service. Use the root path
  //   of the site and append the service name
  var proxy = new WidgetServiceReference.Service1Client();
  proxy.Endpoint.Address = new
    System.ServiceModel.EndpointAddress(urlBase +
                                         "/Service1.svc");

  proxy.SubmitWidgetOrderAsync(numberOfWidgets);
}
```

17. Press *F5* to compile and run the application. The Silverlight application should launch and look similar to the following screenshot:

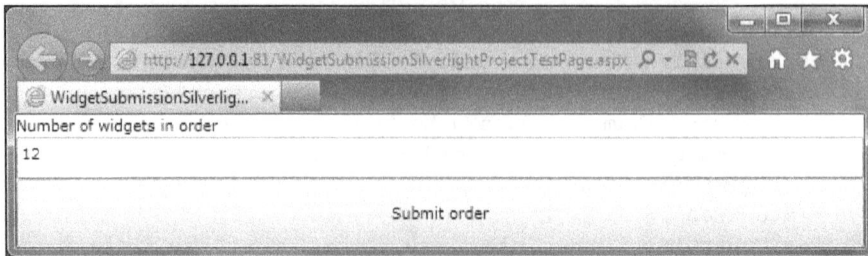

18. Submit a few orders for widgets.

19. Open the **Azure Storage Explorer** and browse to the local queue storage. You should see a number of messages waiting in the **widgetqueue** to be processed as shown in the following screenshot:

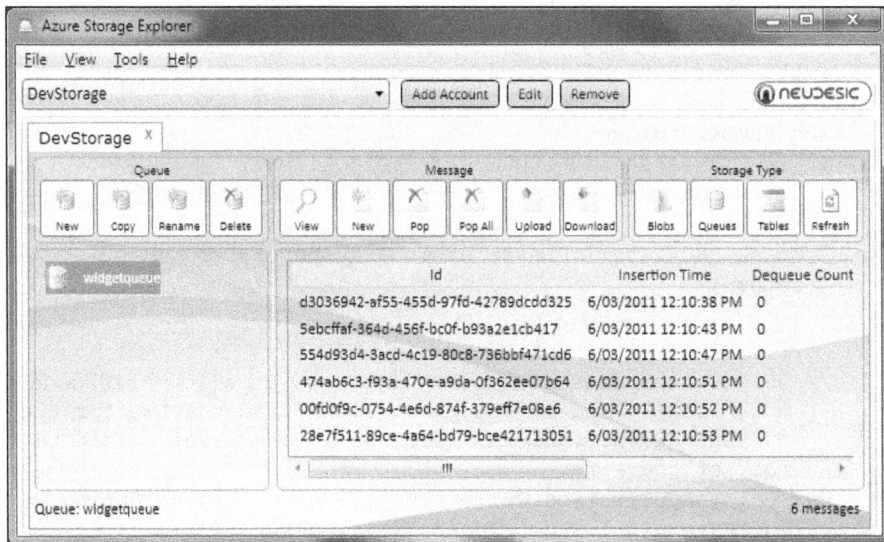

20. With the messages being queued up and ready to be processed, the worker role will now be implemented to process the messages. Open **WorkerRole.cs** from the **WidgetFactoryWorkerRole** project.

21. In **WorkerRole.cs**, replace the Run method with the following code. The Run method will first use the **trace** to write a diagnostic message to the console for us to view. Next the code retrieves the account settings from the configuration file, gets a handle on the widgetqueue, and creates the queue if it does not exist. Once set up, the Run method goes into an infinite loop where it waits for a message to appear on the queue, and retries every five seconds:

```
public override void Run()
{
  Trace.WriteLine("WidgetFactoryWorkerRole entry point called",
    "Information");

  // retrieve the account settings from the configuration file
  varstorageAccount = CloudStorageAccount.Parse
  (RoleEnvironment.GetConfigurationSettingValue
  ("AzureStorageConnectionString"));
  varqueueClient = storageAccount.CreateCloudQueueClient();

  // get a handle to a widget queue and create it if
    it does not exist
  var queue = queueClient.GetQueueReference("widgetqueue");
  queue.CreateIfNotExist();

  // keep trying to process widgets, sleep for five seconds before
    retrying
  while(true)
  {
    ProcessWidgetOrder(queue);
    Thread.Sleep(TimeSpan.FromSeconds(5));
  }
}
```

Polling costs

Microsoft charges for Azure Storage based on the total size of the storage used, bandwidth, and also for the number of transactions performed. In the development, while using the local storage emulator, it is acceptable to have a high polling frequency. However, in the production, the number of transactions should be reduced to lower the amount you are charged. One popular technique is to use an **exponential back off polling algorithm**. While the system is busy, it will poll at a higher frequency, but during quiet times, the frequency is reduced.

22. Implement the `ProcessWidgetOrder` method. The method attempts to get a message from the queue, and sets an increased visibility timeout on the message. The increased timeout is needed as processing widgets can take a while. If a message was retrieved, the code then tries to parse the message and pulls the number of widgets in the order. A loop is then used to process each widget. To simulate the worker role that takes time to process the widgets, the code simply sleeps for five seconds per widget. With the order fully processed, a method is then called to delete the message:

```
private void ProcessWidgetOrder(CloudQueue queue)
{
  // get a message, and hide it for one minute before becoming
    visible again. Widgets can take a while to process!
  var message = queue.GetMessage(new TimeSpan(0, 0, 1, 0));
  if(message != null)
  {
    int widgetsToProcess;
    if(int.TryParse(message.AsString, out widgetsToProcess))
    {
      Trace.WriteLine("Processing order #" + message.Id,
        "Information");
      for(int i = 1; i<= widgetsToProcess; i++)
      {
        Trace.WriteLine("Creatingwidget #" + i, "Information");
        // simulate the time it takes to process a widget
        Thread.Sleep(TimeSpan.FromSeconds(5));
      }
      Trace.WriteLine("Finished processing #" + message.Id,
        "Information");
      // There is some extra logic around deleting messages
      TryAndDeleteMessage(queue, message);
    }
  }
}
```

23. Due to the behavior of the messages to reappear after their visibility timeout expires, extra care needs to be taken while deleting them. A widget order may take more than a minute to process, which means that the message will become visible again and another worker role may begin to process the same message. The first worker role will delete the message, later the second worker role will attempt to delete the message, and an exception will be thrown. The following code implements the `TryAndDeleteMessage` method. A try or a catch block wraps the call to `DeleteMessage`, and logs an error if it was a message that was deleted already, or throws an exception if another exception occurred:

```
private void TryAndDeleteMessage(CloudQueue queue,
  CloudQueueMessage message)
{
  try
  {
    queue.DeleteMessage(message);
  }
  catch(StorageClientException ex)
  {
    if(ex.ExtendedErrorInformation.ErrorCode ==
        "MessageNotFound")
    {
      // The worker role took too long to process the message, the
        message became visible again and another worker role
        deleted it.
      // Log the error so that the visibility timeout can be
        tweaked later
      Trace.WriteLine("Widget processing completed for order #" +
        message.Id, "Error");
    }
    else
    {
      // another type of error occurred, throw it
      throw;
    }
  }
}
```

24. A special **trace listener** now needs to be added to the project. This trace listener will print out to the compute emulator, allowing you to watch what is happening. Open the web.

25. Press *F5* to compile and run the application.

26. Open the compute emulator, and look at the console window of the worker role. You should see the worker role processing each of the messages that were put into the queue earlier.

27. Stop debugging.

28. In Visual Studio 2010, open the role information **WidgetFactoryWorkerRole** by double-clicking on it under the `Roles` folder of the **QueueExercise1** project.

29. Change the number of instances of the worker role to **2**.

30. Press *F5* to start the application again. Open the Silverlight application, and submit a few more widget orders of different sizes. This time the compute emulator will show two worker roles, each taking jobs off the queue. The following screenshot shows an example of two worker roles processing orders:

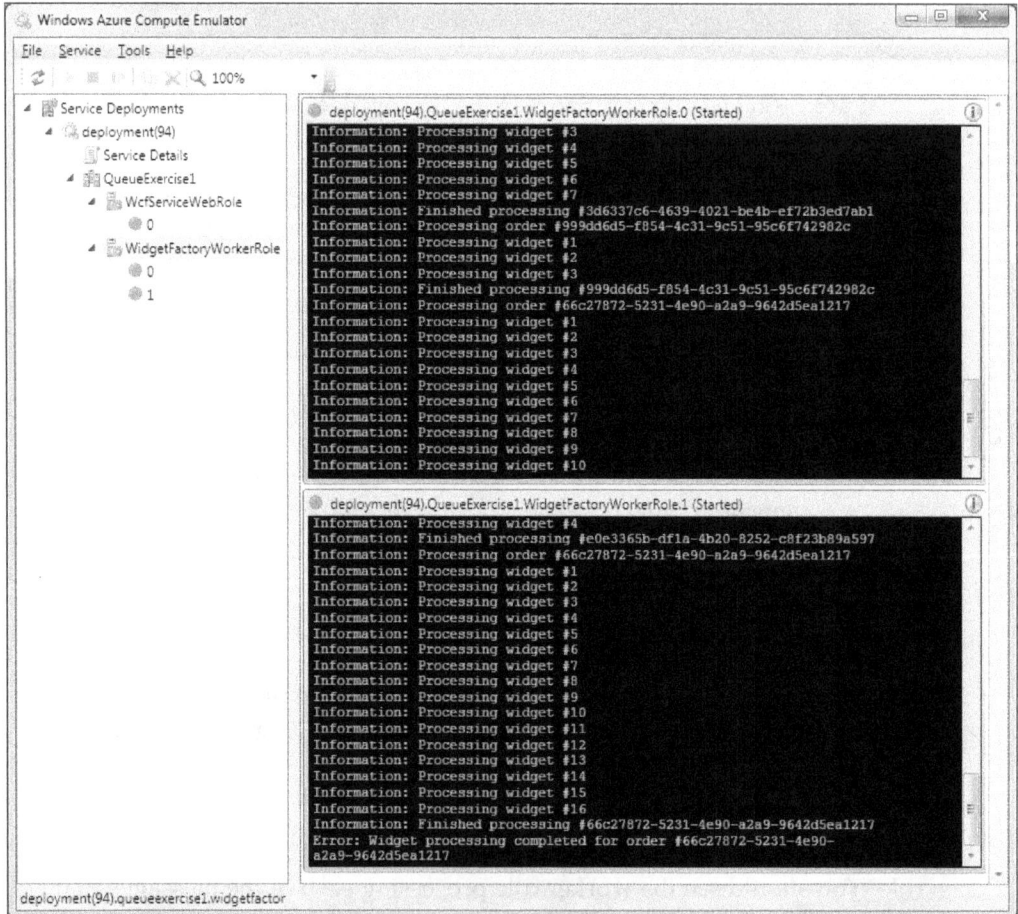

Handling poison messages

Despite taking all the care to write bug-free code, there are always circumstances that can cause the processing of a message to fail. The cause of the failure could be due to an error in the code which causes the server to throw an exception. Message processing could also fail due to a configuration issue, or reliance on an external resource which is unavailable at that moment.

In the event of a failure, the message will not be deleted from the queue as the application logic was not able to get that far. As the message was not deleted, it will eventually become visible again, and dequeued by another consumer which will attempt to process the message. If the cause of the failure was an intermittent one, then the message will be processed fine at a later time when retried. However, the issue may be persistent if it is an error with the message payload, the application code, or the configuration. These messages will be continuously dequeued, then processed by an instance, and eventually can cause the instance to crash.

Messages that are stuck in the queue, unable to be processed, are called "poison messages" and are needed to be taken care of. Each time a message is dequeued, the dequeued property will be incremented. Once a message hits a threshold for being dequeued (for example, five times), the message should be removed from the main queue and placed into a separate queue to hold poison messages.

Later when there has been a code or configuration fixation, or the required resources are brought online, then the poison messages can be inserted back into the original queue to be retried.

Summary

This chapter explained the fundamentals of the Windows Azure storage service. Concepts such as shared keys, accessing the service through the REST API, using the storage client library, and the importance of the collocation of services were all covered to give a good grounding knowledge of the service.

The Queue service was introduced as a way to allow asynchronous communication between the components of your application, and to allow your work to be buffered. The exercise in this chapter demonstrated how to submit your work from a Silverlight application into a queue, so that the work is buffered and queued up, allowing the worker roles to process messages asynchronously as they got to them.

In the next chapter, we will look at how the Azure Blob storage can be used to save files and documents in a durable persistent store, and how sending files to the users can be made faster by using **Content Distribution Networks (CDN)**.

5
Accessing Azure Blob Storage from Silverlight

Blobs are "binary large objects", which is another way of saying "any arbitrary file". There are many concepts that need to be covered in this chapter as the Blob storage API can be called directly from Silverlight, whereas the Queue and Table APIs are callable only from an Azure Role.

In this chapter, we will discuss the following topics:

- Azure Blob storage
- Creating, listing, and displaying files with Silverlight
- Using the **shared access signatures** to upload from Silverlight
- The Azure Content Delivery Network (CDN)

Azure Blob storage

Azure Blob storage is a way to persistently store data in the cloud in which files can be uploaded and retrieved at any time. Files uploaded onto the Blob storage can be held in **containers**, the accessibility of these containers can be set as public or private as follows:

- **Public**: These are files which you want to access freely over the Internet to distribute to the users (such as images, videos, and documents) that are placed into a container and made public.
- **Private**: Windows Azure computer instances may need to store persistent data (such as logs, or private user files). This is a good use of the Blob storage as private.

The ability to make Blob containers public or private differs from the way the Queue and Table services are used. The Queue and Table storage accounts are always hidden, and require the use of the **shared key** of the storage account to access it. Accessing a private Blob storage container still requires the use of the shared key, but there is a greater level of flexibility in the way temporary permissions can be granted, which will be explored later in this chapter.

Once files have been stored into the Blob storage and made public, they can be accessed through a simple URL. The URL format for a photo of a Koala uploaded onto the Blob storage would look similar to the one in the following URL:

```
http://packtdemo.blob.core.windows.net/images/Koala.jpg
```

Breaking the URL into its components, we can see that it has a defined structure shown as follows:

http://**<account>**.blob.core.windows.net/**<container>**/**<blob name>**

- **Account**: It is the name of the Azure storage account that was created in the Azure Management Portal.
- **Container**: It is a logical grouping of blobs. Containers can be independently flagged as public or private.
- **Blob name**: It is the name of the file being stored.

The following diagram visualizes the structure and relationship between the components of the URL:

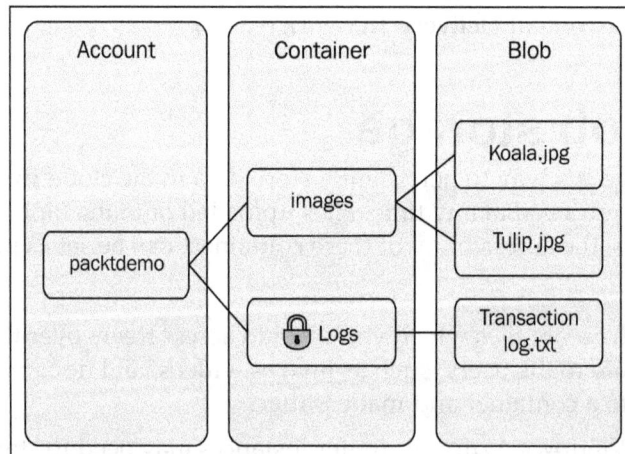

Within a single storage account, it can make sense to create multiple containers to hold different groupings of files. One container could be used to store public images used within a web application, another container could hold public marketing materials (PDFs, white papers, and so on), and a third private container could be used to store the transaction logs of the application. **Segmenting** files into different containers allows you to control the access rights to multiple sets of files independently.

Available commands

The commands in the following table are used for working with the Azure Blob storage directly. These commands allow you to list or create or delete the blobs and the containers programmatically in which they are stored:

	Operation name
Blobs	List Blobs
	Put Blob
	Get Blob
	Delete Blob
	Get Blob Properties
	Set Blob Properties
Blob metadata	Get Blob Metadata
	Set Blob Metadata
Containers	List Containers
	Create Container
	Get Container Properties
	Get Container Metadata
	Set Container Metadata
	Get Container ACL
	Set Container ACL
	Delete Container

Additional information about specific operations can be found online in the MSDN documentation at the following URL:

```
http://msdn.microsoft.com/en-us/library/dd135733.aspx
```

The Blob storage API commands are directly accessible through the REST API, or through the storage client library. Be aware that most of these commands require the use of the shared access key of the storage account which means that an Azure Role should call the commands on behalf of a Silverlight client. The Silverlight client should not call the REST API directly with the key, as it would be easy for anyone to disassemble the Silverlight application and gain access to the key.

Later in the chapter, strategies for allowing the Silverlight client to access the REST API through a **shared access signature** will be shown which helps you to get around this issue.

> **Never store the shared access key in Silverlight**
>
> Any secured connection string or access key should never be stored within a Silverlight application. It is relatively easy for a hacker to gain access to anything sensitive within the Silverlight application with a disassembly tool such as **Net Reflector** (http://www.red-gate.com) or **IL Spy** (http://ilspy.net).

Behind the scenes

Within the Azure Blob storage, each file that is stored is actually broken into many pieces in the server. There are two different ways in which the Azure Blob storage can split the files:

- **Blocks**: They are optimized for streaming data and are suitable for all types of files offered for download.
- **Pages**: They are optimized to read or write the data randomly, as well as having the ability to write to a range of bytes.

Throughout this book, we will be using only blocks. Pages will not be mentioned as this is a specialized form of Blob storage, suitable for the random input or output writes such as a **virtual hard drive**.

Block storage allows you to upload files that are up to 64 MB into the Table storage directly, which Azure will then chunk up into smaller blocks behind the scenes for storage. There are techniques that allow you to upload files larger than 64 MB (up to 1 TB-sized files).

More details about the differences between the blocks and the pages can be found within the MSDN documentation at the following URL:

http://msdn.microsoft.com/en-us/library/windowsazure/ee691964.aspx

The following diagram shows how Blob storage looks when the concept of blocks and pages are involved:

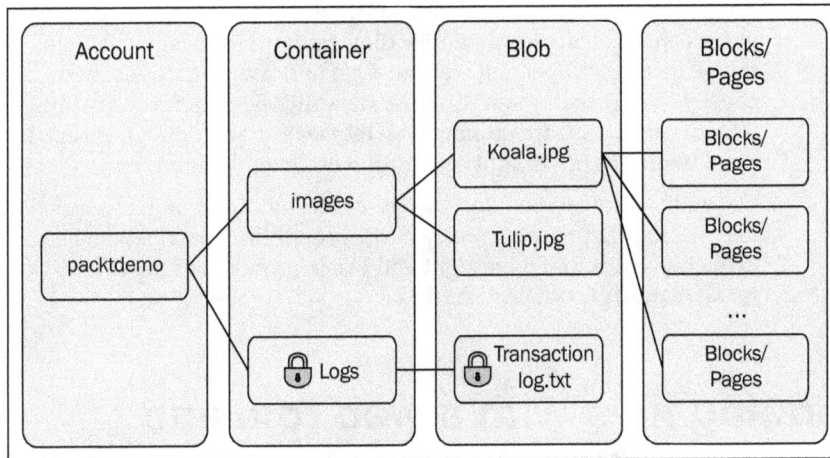

Creating, listing, and displaying files with Silverlight

In this section, a Silverlight application will retrieve files that are being held within the Azure Blob storage. These files will be initially generated and uploaded by a web role. Later, the Silverlight application will be expanded, so that the files can be uploaded and the contents of the container are listed.

There are two very important things to realize about this exercise.

Firstly, Silverlight has a restriction that prevents it from making requests to domains other than the domain it is currently being hosted on. In order to lift this restriction, we will have to place a special **client access policy** file in the root of the storage account. This is because the domain on which the Silverlight application is hosted (`http://packtdemo.cloudapp.net`) is different from the Azure storage account in which an attempt is made to retrieve the data (`http://packtdemo.blob.core.windows.net`).

Secondly, there is a known issue that prevents Silverlight from accessing the client access policy within the local storage emulator. For this reason, it is required that this exercise is developed only against a real online storage account. This exercise will fail if you try to use the local storage emulator.

Silverlight cross-domain requests

Microsoft placed certain restrictions on the Silverlight API, to help in preventing a Silverlight application from performing malicious things to an unsuspecting website. One of those restrictions is the concept of "cross-domain" calls. By default, Microsoft prevents the Silverlight client from making web requests to any domain except for the domain the Silverlight application is currently being hosted on.

This restriction can be lifted by having the administrator of a website to place the client access policy in the root of the domain, which explicitly states that Silverlight and Flash applications are able to make requests for their resources.

Generating files with a web role and displaying in Silverlight

For this exercise, an Azure web role will be used to generate a set of test files, ready for a Silverlight client to retrieve them. These files will be .txt files filled with sample data so that they do not require much code:

1. Open Visual Studio 2010 and create a new Windows Azure project named **BlobExercise1**.

2. Add a single ASP.Net web role, and rename it as **BlobExerciseWebRole**.

3. Click on **OK** and Visual Studio 2010 will create the project.

4. In the solution explorer, under the Azure project **BlobExercise1**, in the `Roles` folder, right-click on **BlobExerciseWebRole** and click on **Properties**.

5. Click on the **Settings** tab.

6. Click on the **Add Setting** button.

7. Change the name to `AzureStorageConnectionString`.

8. Click on the **...** in the value column. It has been circled in the following screenshot:

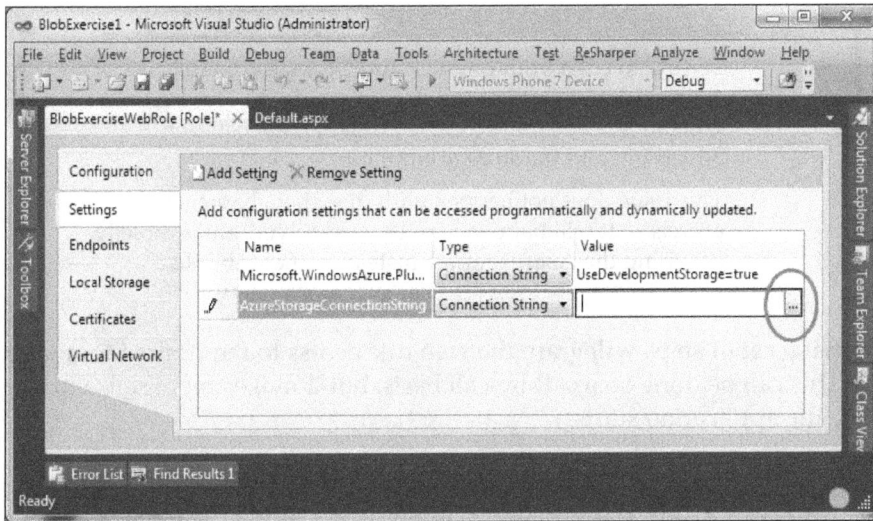

9. Do not select the storage emulator like the other chapters. Instead, select **Enter storage account credentials**. Log into the Azure Management Portal, take a note of the storage account name, and enter it in the Visual Studio 2010 dialog. Then, copy the primary access key onto the clipboard, and paste it in Visual Studio 2010. The connection string window should look similar to the following screenshot:

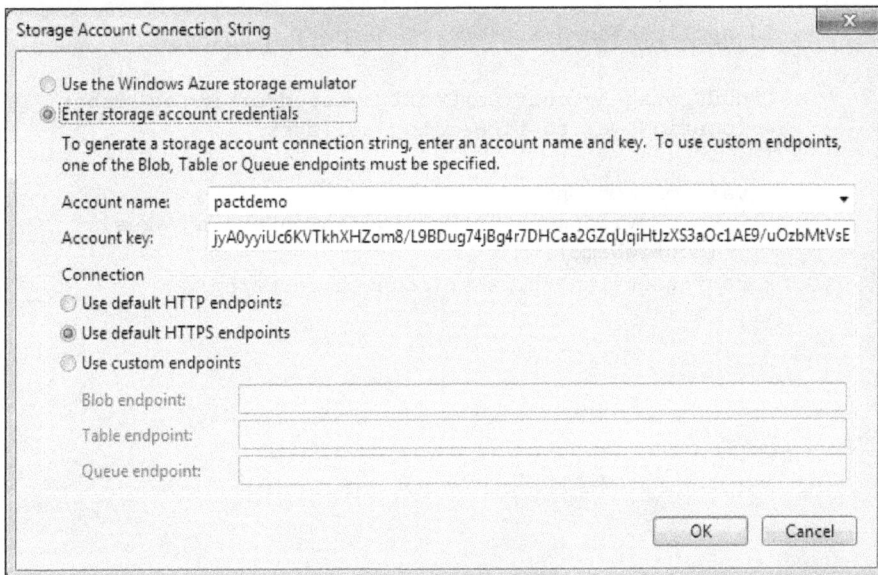

> Be sure to enter your online Azure Storage account
> credentials. Do not use the storage emulator. This exercise
> will fail due to a known cross-domain issue between
> Silverlight and the storage emulator.
>
> This issue does not happen with the other chapters or
> exercises. It will happen here because Silverlight is directly
> accessing the Azure Storage instead of the web role.

The following set of steps will grant the web role access to the Azure Storage
account. This can be done on a call-by-call basis, but it makes more sense to set
it up once the application starts:

1. In the **BlobExerciseWebRole** project, open the `Global.asax.cs` file.

2. Within the **Application_Start(...)** method, insert the following code to give
   the web role easy access to Azure Storage:

```
using System;
using Microsoft.WindowsAzure;
using Microsoft.WindowsAzure.ServiceRuntime;
namespace BlobExerciseWebRole
{
  public class Global : System.Web.HttpApplication
  {
    void Application_Start(object sender, EventArgs e)
    {
      CloudStorageAccount.SetConfigurationSettingPublisher(
        (configName, configSettingPublisher) =>
      {
        var connectionString =
          RoleEnvironment.GetConfigurationSettingValue
          (configName);
        configSettingPublisher(connectionString);
      });
    }
  }
}
```

These following steps will add the Silverlight client to the project, and also allow the web role to create the initial TXT files on which the Silverlight client will be displayed. This exercise requires the use of an ASP.Net code behind the file. So, we will be creating a new host page rather than using the default host page in this exercise as follows:

1. Right-click on the **BlobExerciseWebRole** ASP.Net project and click on **Properties**.

2. Go to the **Silverlight Applications,** and add a new Silverlight project named `SilverlightBlobBrowser` with all the other settings left at their defaults as shown in the following screenshot:

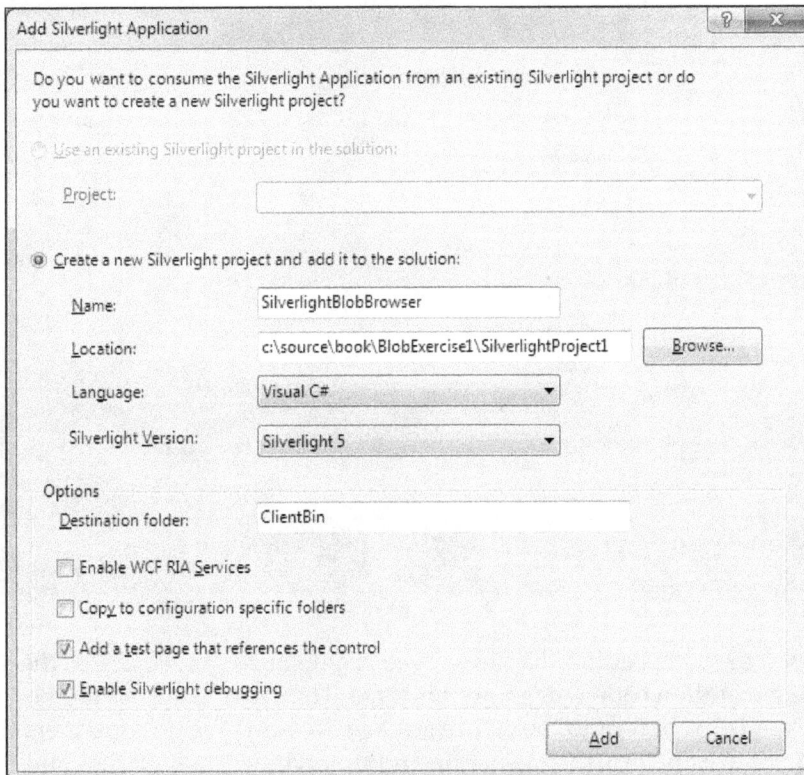

3. Right-click on the **BlobExerciseWebRole** ASP.Net project and add a new web form named `SilverlightHostPage.aspx`.

4. Immediately, right-click on `SilverlightHostPage.aspx`, and set it as the startup page.

5. Open the default test page `SilverlightBlobBrowserTestPage.html` that was generated by Visual Studio 2010.

6. Scroll down to the bottom, and copy everything within the `<form>`...`</form>` tags, including the form tags themselves.

7. Go back to `SilverlightHostPage.aspx` and replace the `<form>` tags with what was copied from the generated page. The resulting code should be similar to the following screenshot. Certain version numbers may look different, depending on your version of Silverlight:

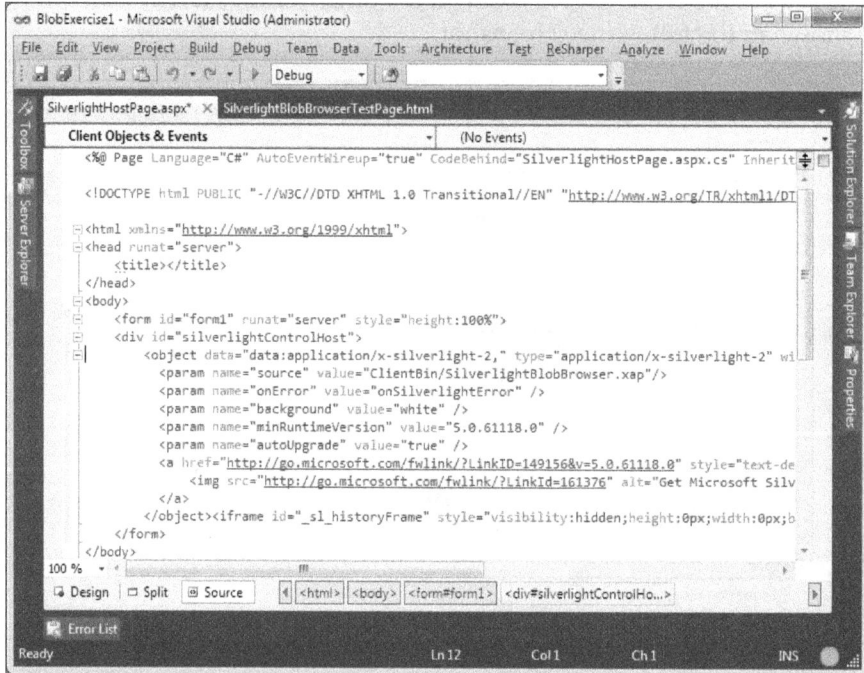

8. Open the code behind the file `SilverlightHostPage.aspx.cs`, the sample file generation code will go on this page. The `Page_Load(...)` method will be made to connect to the Azure storage account. Create containers that do not exist before, then generate and upload the test data files and the `clientAccessPolicy` file.

9. The first few lines of the `Page_Load` method should be familiar from *Chapter 4, Using Azure Queues with Silverlight*. The storage client library is used to retrieve the Azure storage account credentials from the configuration file, and then to get a handle to the Blob storage which is stored in the `blobStorage` variable. The code then calls the two helper methods that will be written in the following steps:

```
using System;
using System.Text;
using Microsoft.WindowsAzure;
using Microsoft.WindowsAzure.StorageClient;
namespace BlobExerciseWebRole
{
  public partial class SilverlightHostPage : System.Web.UI.Page
  {
    protected void Page_Load(object sender, EventArgs e)
    {
      // Retrieve a handle to the Azure storage account,
      // then create a proxy object to interact with Blob storage
      var account = CloudStorageAccount.FromConfigurationSetting
        ("AzureStorageConnectionString");
      var blobStorage = account.CreateCloudBlobClient();
      CreateCrossDomainPolicy(blobStorage);
      CreateTestFiles(blobStorage);
    }
  }
}
```

10. Once the credentials have been retrieved, the `Page_Load` method will then ensure that the Silverlight client is able to access the storage account, by placing a client access policy file inside the root of the domain. The following code will create a special container to hold the policy file, as it does not exist before. The permissions are then reset on the container and the client access policy file is created and uploaded, allowing all Silverlight clients to access the files:

```
private void CreateCrossDomainPolicy(CloudBlobClientblobStorage)
{
  const string rootContainer = "$root";
  // Create the container if it does not exist
  // Then reset the permissions on the container
  blobStorage.GetContainerReference
    (rootContainer).CreateIfNotExist();
  blobStorage.GetContainerReference
    (rootContainer).SetPermissions(
```

```
newBlobContainerPermissions
{
  PublicAccess = BlobContainerPublicAccessType.Blob
});
// The client access policy file is required so that Silverlight
// can make cross domain requests to this Azure storage account
var blob = blobStorage.GetBlobReference
  ("clientaccesspolicy.xml");
blob.Properties.ContentType = "text/xml";
blob.UploadText(
@"<?xml version=""1.0"" encoding=""utf-8""?>
<access-policy>
<cross-domain-access>
<policy>
<allow-from http-methods=""*"" http-request-headers=""*"">
<domain uri=""*"" />
<domain uri=""http://*"" />
</allow-from>
<grant-to>
<resource path=""/"" include-subpaths=""true"" />
</grant-to>
</policy>
</cross-domain-access>
</access-policy>");
}
```

11. The test data files will then be created by the web role. Similar to what happened in the preceding step, a host container will be created, and set to be accessed as public. Then, a simple loop is used to create five files named `file0.txt` to `file4.txt`. The storage client then uploads each new blob to the container:

```
private void CreateTestFiles(CloudBlobClientblobStorage)
{
  const string containerName = "blobexercise";
  // Create the container if it does not exist
  // Then reset the permissions on the container
  blobStorage.GetContainerReference
    (containerName).CreateIfNotExist()
  blobStorage.GetContainerReference
    (containerName).SetPermissions(newBlobContainerPermissions
  {
    PublicAccess = BlobContainerPublicAccessType.Blob
  });
```

```
for (inti = 0; i< 5; i++)
{
  // Format the filename, for example, blobexercise/file1.txt
  var fileName = string.Format(@"{0}/file{1}.txt", containerName,
    i);
  var blob = blobStorage.GetBlobReference(fileName);
  // Create a set of files with random data.
  // Simply print 'Hello World' with a line number based on the
    current loop.
  // This makes each file slightly different
  var stringBuilder = new StringBuilder();
  for(int j = 0; j <= i; j++)
  {
    stringBuilder.Append(j + " Hello World\n");
  }
  blob.UploadText(stringBuilder.ToString());
}
}
```

12. Press *F5* to run the program, and check if everything is working correctly. If all is working well, then you should be able to open a tool such as the Windows Azure storage explorer, and see the generated files in your container. The following screenshot shows the files inside the **blobexercise** container, with the special $root folder also having been created:

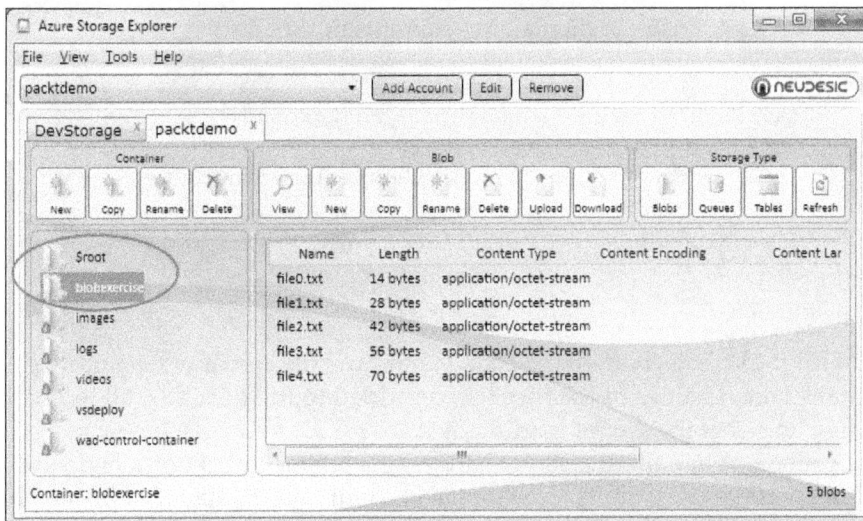

Retrieving and displaying the files from Azure Blob storage in Silverlight

At this stage of the chapter, the web role has been configured in a few ways to support the Silverlight client as follows:

- The client access policy file has been placed in the root of the storage account, allowing all Silverlight clients to read from the public containers

- A set of test files have been generated in a container, ready for the Silverlight client to retrieve and display them

To simplify the retrieval, we will simply hard-code the five files that the Silverlight client will display. Later in the chapter, we will learn how to list the contents of a container.

Start by adding the controls to the Silverlight application:

1. From the solution explorer, open `MainPage.xaml` which is inside the **SilverlightBlobBrowser** project.

2. Replace the grid with a stack panel, and then add three new controls within it:

    - `Listbox` to display the file names

    - `TextBox` to display the URL

    - `TextBlock` to display the contents of the file

```
<UserControl>
  <StackPanel x:Name="LayoutRoot" Background="White">
    <ListBox x:Name="blobListBox"
      SelectionChanged="BlobListBox_SelectionChanged" />
    <TextBox x:Name="urlTextBox" />
    <TextBlock x:Name="blobFileContents"/>
  </StackPanel>
</UserControl>
```

With the screen created, the code behind the file can now be modified. The hard-coded names of the files will be added to the `ListBox`, allowing the user to select the file for loading. A `SelectionChanged` event is placed on the `ListBox`. When the selection changes, the Silverlight client will download that text file from the Azure storage account and display it in the text block.

Modify the constructor of `MainPage.xaml.cs` so that the hard-coded file names are added to the `ListBox`:

```
using System;
using System.IO;
using System.Net;
using System.Windows.Controls;
namespace SilverlightBlobBrowser
{
  public partial class MainPage
  {
  publicMainPage()
  {
    InitializeComponent();
    // add each file to the ListBox
    for(int i = 0; i< 5; i++)
    {
      blobListBox.Items.Add(string.Format(@"file{0}.txt", i));
    }
  }
  }
}
```

3. To the `MainPage` class, add the event handler for the `SelectionChanged` event. The event handler will detect the filename selected in the `ListBox` and use it to construct the final URL of the file hosted on the Azure Blob storage. Be sure to change the account name to the account you used in your connection string. The final URL is placed into a textbox, allowing it to be copied at a later step. With the final URL, the Silverlight client is able to make a standard asynchronous HTTP request to retrieve the file. As this is an asynchronous call, a callback method is required. A **lambda** expression is used to set the text in the text block:

```
private void BlobListBox_SelectionChanged
  (object sender, SelectionChangedEventArgs e)
{
  // change the account name to the account used in the connection
    string
  const string accountName = "packtdemo";
  const string containerName = "blobexercise";
  // generate the URL based on the standard format and file name
  var filename = blobListBox.SelectedItem as string;
  var url =
    string.Format(@"http://{0}.blob.core.windows.net/{1}/{2}",
    accountName, containerName, filename);
  urlTextBox.Text = url; // place the URL into the TextBox to
    assist with debugging
```

```
    // use the URL to make a HTTP request for the file
    var client = new WebClient();
    client.DownloadStringCompleted += (sender2, e2) =>{
      blobFileContents.Text = e2.Result; };
    client.DownloadStringAsync(new Uri(url, UriKind.Absolute));
}
```

4. Press *F5* to compile the entire solution and run it. If everything works correctly, the Silverlight application should launch and display the ListBox with filenames. Click on a filename and the result should look similar to the following screenshot:

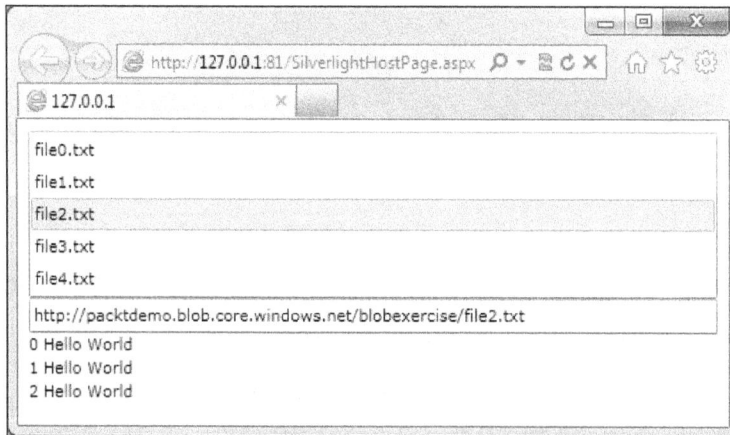

5. Try to copy the URL of the file from the TextBox and navigate to it using a web browser. Azure Blob storage exposes each file as a standard HTTP resource, which you can access using all the web technologies. The following screenshot shows Internet Explorer being used to navigate to the file:

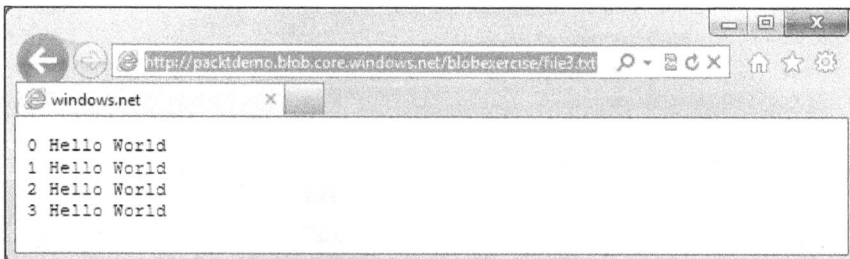

Using the shared access signatures to upload from Silverlight

This section is a little unique as Silverlight will be accessing the Azure storage account directly rather than allowing the web role to handle the interactions for us. This will require the use of **shared access signatures**.

Shared access signatures can temporarily grant permissions to work with an Azure container without disclosing the shared access key to end users.

In this section, we will generate and use shared access signatures to enable the Silverlight application to make calls to the Azure Storage REST API. With access to the REST API, the Silverlight client will be able to upload images to the container and also list the contents of the same. These two techniques will be used together to create a Silverlight application that allows the user to upload the images, and then have the images displayed back to them.

> This exercise shows how to use the shared access signature to upload the files, but the same technique can be used for retrieving the restricted files.

1. The `SilverlightHostPage.aspx.cs` file will be used to generate two shared access signatures. Modify the `Page_Load(...)` method and add a new single line, so that it calls a new `GeneratedSharedAccessSignature` method, which will be written in the next step:

```
using System;
using System.Text;
using Microsoft.WindowsAzure;
using Microsoft.WindowsAzure.StorageClient;
namespace BlobExerciseWebRole
{
  public partial class SilverlightHostPage : System.Web.UI.Page
  {
    protected void Page_Load(object sender, EventArgs e)
    {
    // Retrieve a handle to the Azure storage account,
    // then create a proxy object to interact with Blob storage
    var account =  CloudStorageAccount.FromConfigurationSetting
      ("AzureStorageConnectionString");
    var blobStorage = account.CreateCloudBlobClient();
    CreateCrossDomainPolicy(blobStorage);
```

```
        CreateTestFiles(blobStorage);
        GeneratedSharedAccessSignature(blobStorage);
      }
    }
}
```

2. Add the two new properties to hold the signatures, and then the code to generate them. The code creates a new container to hold the images, which is the standard code now. After the container has been generated, two shared access signatures are created. One is for writing to the container, and the second is for granting permission to list the contents of the container. Both these signatures are given a life span of 10 minutes to restrict malicious use:

```
public string ImageContainerListUrl { get; set; } // displayed on
  the ASPX page
public string ImageContainerWriteUrl { get; set; } // displayed on
  the ASPX page
private void GeneratedSharedAccessSignature
  (CloudBlobClientblobStorage)
{
  const string containerName = "imagecontainer";
  // Create the container if it does not exist
  // Then reset the permissions on the container
  var imageContainer =
  blobStorage.GetContainerReference(containerName);
  imageContainer.CreateIfNotExist();
  imageContainer.SetPermissions(
  newBlobContainerPermissions
  {
    PublicAccess = BlobContainerPublicAccessType.Blob
  });
  // create the write signature to allow upload
  var sas = imageContainer.GetSharedAccessSignature(new
  SharedAccessPolicy()
  {
    Permissions = SharedAccessPermissions.Write,
    SharedAccessExpiryTime = DateTime.UtcNow +
      TimeSpan.FromMinutes(10)
  });
  ImageContainerWriteUrl = new UriBuilder
    (imageContainer.Uri) { Query = sas.TrimStart('?')
    }.Uri.AbsoluteUri;
  // create List signature to allow listing blobs in the container
  sas = imageContainer.GetSharedAccessSignature(new
    SharedAccessPolicy()
```

```
{
    Permissions = SharedAccessPermissions.List,
    SharedAccessExpiryTime = DateTime.UtcNow +
        TimeSpan.FromMinutes(10)
});
ImageContainerListUrl = new UriBuilder
    (imageContainer.Uri) { Query = sas.TrimStart('?')
    }Uri.AbsoluteUri;
}
```

3. Modify the `SilverlightHostPage.aspx` page to include the two shared access signatures as initialization parameters that Silverlight can access. The final result should look like the following screenshot and the code snippet is as follows:

```
<param name="initParams" value="ImageContainerWriteUrl=<%=
    ImageContainerWriteUrl %>,ImageContainerListUrl=<%=
        ImageContainerListUrl %>" />
```

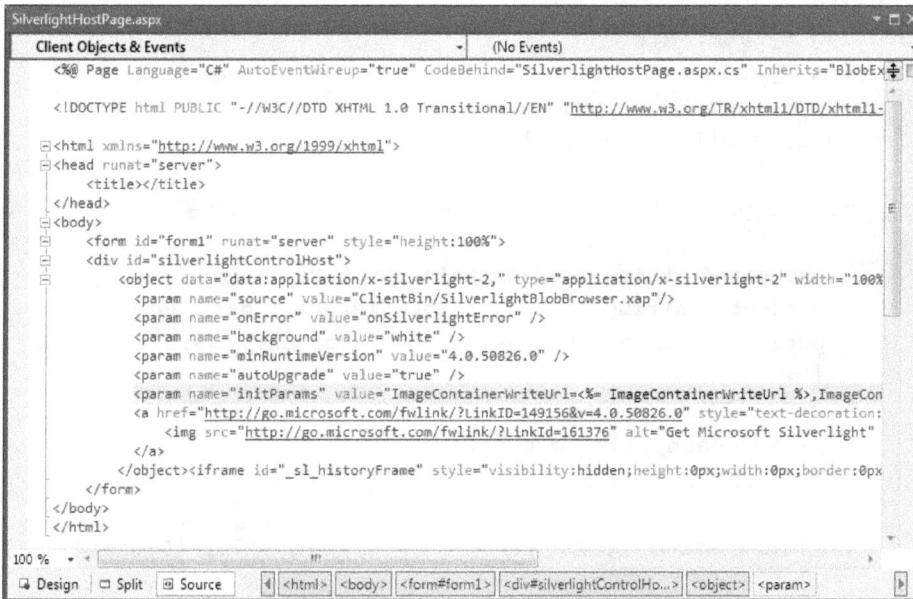

4. In the Silverlight project **SilverlightBlobBrowser**, open `App.xaml.cs`. Change the `Application_Startup` method, so that the `MainPageconstructor` has the initialization parameters from the hosting page passed onto it:

```
private void Application_Startup(object sender,
                                    StartupEventArgs e)
{
   this.RootVisual = new MainPage(e.InitParams);
}
```

5. Right-click on the Silverlight project and add a reference to **System.Xml.Linq**.

6. Open `MainPage.xaml.cs`. The constructor will be modified to take the initialization parameters, and extract the shared access signatures for using them later:

```
using System;
using System.Collections.Generic;
using System.IO;
using System.Linq;
using System.Net;
using System.Windows.Controls;
using System.Xml.Linq;
namespace SilverlightBlobBrowser
{
  public partial class MainPage
  {
    protected string ImageContainerWriteUrl { get; set; }
    protected string ImageContainerListUrl { get; set; }
    public MainPage(IDictionary<string, string>initParams)
    {
    InitializeComponent();
    // add each file to the ListBox
    for (int i = 0; i< 5; i++)
    {
      blobListBox.Items.Add(string.Format(@"file{0}.txt", i));
    }
    // Extract the shared access signatures from the
        initialization parameters
    string parameterName = "ImageContainerWriteUrl";
    if (initParams.ContainsKey(parameterName) &&
        !string.IsNullOrEmpty(initParams[parameterName]))
    ImageContainerWriteUrl = initParams[parameterName];
    parameterName = "ImageContainerListUrl";
    if (initParams.ContainsKey(parameterName) &&
        !string.IsNullOrEmpty(initParams[parameterName]))
```

```
ImageContainerListUrl = initParams[parameterName];
LoadImages();
}
}
}
```

7. Open `Page.xaml`. A new button will be added to allow the user to select an image to upload and a `StackPanel` will be used to display images. The final XAML file should look like the following screenshot:

```
<Button Content="Select file" Click="FileUploadButtonClick" />
<StackPanel x:Name="imageStackPanel" />
```

```
Design  ↑↓   XAML
<UserControl x:Class="SilverlightBlobBrowser.MainPage"
    xmlns="http://schemas.microsoft.com/winfx/2006/xaml/presentation"
    xmlns:x="http://schemas.microsoft.com/winfx/2006/xaml"
    xmlns:d="http://schemas.microsoft.com/expression/blend/2008"
    xmlns:mc="http://schemas.openxmlformats.org/markup-compatibility/2006"
    mc:Ignorable="d"
    d:DesignHeight="300" d:DesignWidth="400">

    <StackPanel x:Name="LayoutRoot" Background="White">
        <ListBox x:Name="blobListBox" SelectionChanged="BlobListBoxSelectionChanged" />
        <TextBox x:Name="urlTextBox" />
        <TextBlock x:Name="blobFileContents" />

        <Button Content="Select file" Click="FileUploadButtonClick" />
        <StackPanel x:Name="imageStackPanel" />
    </StackPanel>
</UserControl>

100 %  ▾
UserControl UserControl  ▸
```

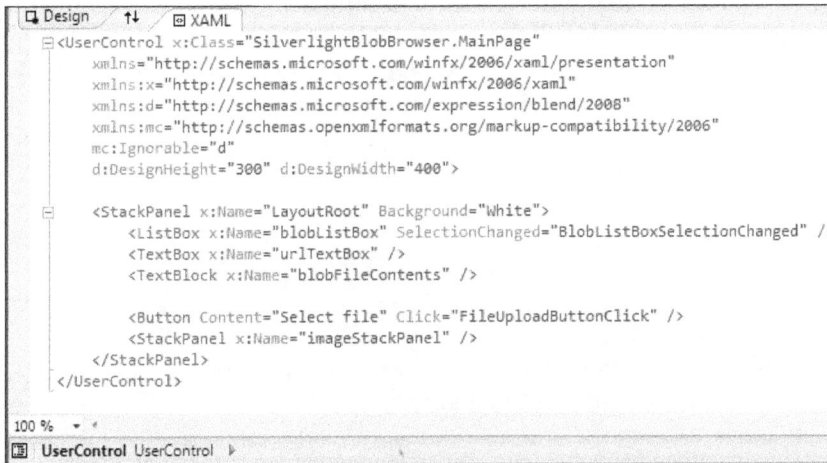

8. Open `MainPage.xaml.cs`. The code found in the container will be added to display the images. The shared access signature with the list permission is taken and the request of the list container contents is appended to the end of the URL. The URL is then used with `WebClient` to perform a standard HTTP GET command against the REST API. An event handler is added to `WebClient`, so that once the results have been returned the `ParseImageContainerContents` method is called to load the images. A small trick used in this method is such that Silverlight will cache the results for a URL, that is, it will always display the same container contents. By modifying the URL slightly with each request, it forces Silverlight to stop caching the results, that is, the contents of the new container will be listed after the image is uploaded:

```
public void LoadImages()
{
    // take the shared access signature, and append the REST command
    we want to invoke. in this case it is the "List the contents
```

```
   of the container" service
var url = ImageContainerListUrl +
  @"&restype=container&comp=list";
// This will slightly change the url with each call, preventing
  caching
url += "&ticks=" + DateTime.Now.Ticks;
// make a HTTP request for the contents of the container
var client = new WebClient();
client.OpenReadCompleted += (ParseImageContainerContents);
client.OpenReadAsync(new Uri(url, UriKind.Absolute));
}
```

9. The web request to the REST API will return an XML document listing the number of blobs inside the container. LINQ to XML is used to parse the results to find the URLs of each image. The LINQ to XML query looks for all <Blob> elements inside the returned document. A simple loop then goes through the results of the LINQ to XML query and manually adds new image controls to the stack panel by using the following code:

```
voidParseImageContainerContents(object sender,
  OpenReadCompletedEventArgs e)
{
  // read the results of the REST call to list the container
    contents
  var myReader = new StreamReader(e.Result);
  var xml = myReader.ReadToEnd();
  myReader.Close();
  // use LinqToXml to find the URLs of all blobs in this container
  var data = XElement.Parse(xml);
  var query = from blob in data.Descendants("Blob")
  selectblob.Element("Url").Value;
  imageStackPanel.Children.Clear();
  for each (var imageUrl in query)
  {
    // Silverlight has restrictions with https so ensure the
      images are http
    var httpImageUrl = imageUrl.Replace("https", "http");
    imageStackPanel.Children.Add(
    new Image
    {
      Height = 50,
      Source = new System.Windows.Media.Imaging.BitmapImage(new
        Uri(httpImageUrl))
    });
  }
}
```

10. If you were to run the Silverlight application at this point, it would load but would not display any images. If you use the Azure storage explorer tool to manually upload a few images and reload the application, each of the images would be loaded in StackPanel. The following steps will allow you to select a file to upload to the Blob storage from within the Silverlight application.

11. When the user clicks on the **select file** button, the event handler code will be added. The **event handler** opens a file selection dialog that will allow the users to browse their computer for an image to upload it. The filter property can be used to restrict those files which the user can select. Once a file has been selected, the UploadFile method is called to handle the file uploading:

```
private void FileUploadButtonClick(object sender,
   System.Windows.RoutedEventArgs e)
{
   var fileDialog = new OpenFileDialog();
   fileDialog.Multiselect = false;
   fileDialog.Filter = "All files (*.*)|*.*|PNG Images
      (*.png)|*.png|JPEG Images (*.jpg)|*.jpg";
   var fileSelected = fileDialog.ShowDialog();
   if(fileSelected == true)
   {
      UploadFile(fileDialog.File.Name, fileDialog.File.OpenRead());
   }
}
```

12. The UploadFile method will take the contents of the selected file, and upload it to Azure Blob storage. The shared access signature has stored the permissions to write to the Blob storage within itself, as well as the name of the container that should be used. A PUT command with the full path of the container, and the desired file name, is used to create a file inside the Blob storage. A combination of a binary writer and file stream are used to simultaneously read and upload the file:

```
private void UploadFile(string name, FileStreamopenRead)
{
   // take the Shared Access Signature with write permissions and
      the container information and add the filename
   var uriBuilder = new UriBuilder(ImageContainerWriteUrl);
   uriBuilder.Path += string.Format("/{0}", name);
   var uploadUrl = uriBuilder.Uri.AbsoluteUri;
   // a HTTP PUT request to upload a file
   var webRequest = (HttpWebRequest)
   System.Net.Browser.WebRequestCreator.ClientHttp.Create
      (new Uri(uploadUrl));
```

```
webRequest.Method = "PUT";
// upload the file to Azure Storage
webRequest.BeginGetRequestStream(ar =>
{
  // a BinaryWriter is used in conjunction with the webRequest
    to push data up using (var writer = new
    BinaryWriter(webRequest.EndGetRequestStream(ar)))
  {
    // The selected file is continuously read and written out to
      the BinaryWriter
    byte[] buffer = new byte[32768];
    int readBytes;
    while ((readBytes = openRead.Read
            (buffer, 0, buffer.Length)) > 0)
    {
      writer.Write(buffer, 0, readBytes);
    }
  }
  webRequest.BeginGetResponse(callback =>
  {
    // updating the UI needs to occur on the UI thread
    Dispatcher.BeginInvoke(LoadImages);
  }, null);
}, null);
}
```

13. Press *F5* to compile and run the application. Select a file to upload and then watch the images as they appear in the stack panel.

The Azure Content Delivery Network (CDN)

An advanced extension to Blob storage services is the **Windows Azure Content Delivery Network**. Usually, the files stored in the storage are hosted from a single geographical location. If the datacenter is in the US, but the user is living in Australia, there can be a large latency in getting the files to the user. A CDN can help to speed up the delivery of the files to end users by hosting files on "edge nodes" that are physically closer to the user than the original datacenter. The technology is currently employed by Microsoft as a way of distributing Windows updates, as well as the map tiles for Bing maps.

For systems that transfer large files, such as Windows updates, having the data physically closer increases the chance of it being delivered at higher data rates, due to the reduced number of links between the edge node and the Personal Computer (PC) of the user. A highly interactive application, such as Bing maps, can show a noticeable increase in the interactivity when the latency is decreased.

The following diagram shows how the edge nodes can be distributed in geographically remote locations, away from the original source:

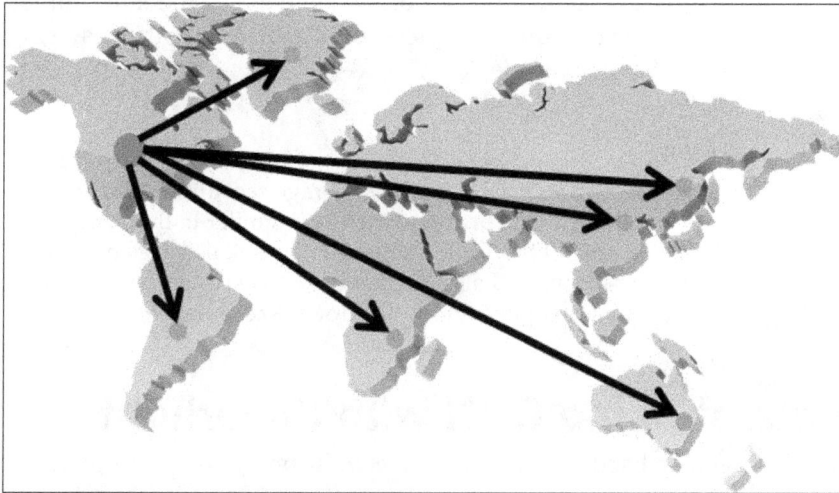

Once the CDN has been activated on an Azure storage account, it is as simple as changing the URL to take advantage of the technology. The domain of the website changes, but the path stays the same.

If the original URL of a Koala photo looked as follows:

```
http://<account name>.blob.core.windows.net/images/koala.jpg
```

Then once CDN has been enabled, the files are accessible by using the generated GUID-based URL as follows:

```
http://<guid>.vo.msecnd.net/images/
```

It is also possible to map CDN directly to your own website as a subdomain by using a CNAME record, for example, `http://<subdomain>.<your website>.com/images/`.

If a user in Sydney, Australia were to try accessing the photo of the Koala through the URL of CDN, the process would work like this. First, the PC of the user would be automatically redirected to use the physically closest edge node, which happens to be in Sydney, Australia. The file does not currently reside on this edge node, so there is a "cache miss". The edge node will reach out to the main datacenter that the file is hosted on, bringing it across the Internet, and caching it locally. It then serves it up to the requesting user. The file will then be cached for as long as the **TTL (Time To Live)** has been set up for, currently up to a maximum of 72 hours. This means that the first user requesting the file will not see any benefit as the file must still be sent internationally, but all the subsequent requests by that user, or other users, will use the cached version on that edge node.

> **Pricing**
>
> Enabling and using CDN on a Blob storage account will incur a cost for the usage. The pricing structure is similar to the charges associated with all the Table storage, with a small charge per 10,000 transactions and also the bandwidth costs. Ensure that you consult the pricing page on the Windows Azure website.

Benefits of using CDN with Silverlight

The Azure CDN can be used in two main ways to improve the performance of your Silverlight applications, either by caching the media elements displayed within the Silverlight application (images, audio, video, and so on), or by caching the Silverlight application itself within CDN.

In order to allow the Silverlight to utilize CDN to load the media elements, it simply requires a change in the URL. This is a very easy way to get improvements in the loading performance from a Silverlight application.

If the Silverlight application is large, it can be beneficial to host the Silverlight XAP file on CDN to decrease the loading time. Another technique is to split the Silverlight application into smaller "modules" using a framework, such as the Microsoft MEF or the Microsoft Prism. The core of the Silverlight application can be hosted within the Azure compute role, or can be stored in the Blob storage. Once the core of the Silverlight application has been loaded, the additional modules can then be loaded asynchronously from CDN to improve loading times.

In order to host a Silverlight XAP file within the Azure Blob storage, it requires some slight modifications to the project as follows:

1. In Visual Studio 2010, open the `properties` folder of the Silverlight application, and open `ApplicationManifest.xml`.

2. In the `<Deployment>` tag, add the attribute `ExternalCallersFromCrossDomain` which instructs the Silverlight application that it is allowed to be loaded from pages that are hosted on a different domain:

```
<Deployment
xmlns="http://schemas.microsoft.com/client/2007/deployment"
xmlns:x="http://schemas.microsoft.com/winfx/2006/xaml"
ExternalCallersFromCrossDomain="ScriptableOnly" >
```

3. Upload the XAP file to the Azure Blob storage. The file can be uploaded manually using a tool such as Windows Azure storage explorer. Ensure that you set the **ContentType** to **application/x-silverlight-app**, as shown in the following screenshot:

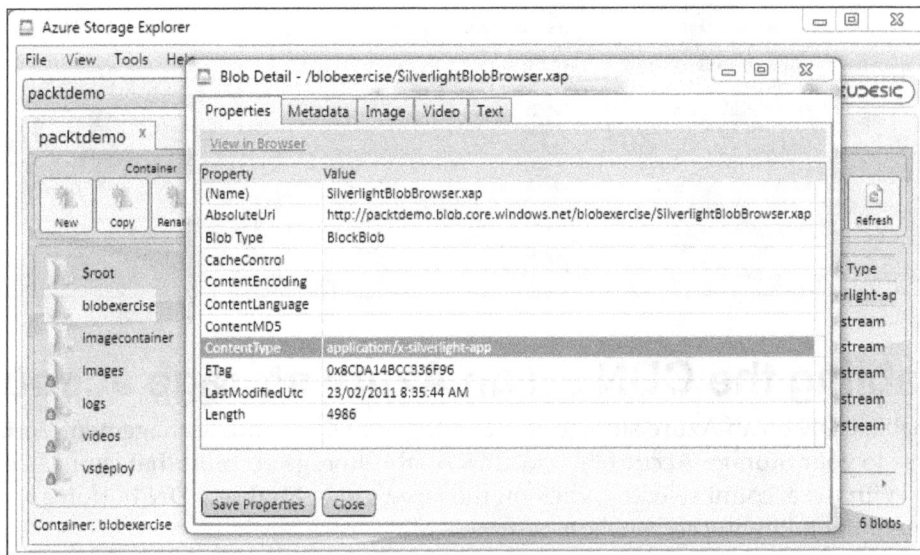

4. Copy the **AbsoluteUri** onto the clipboard.

5. Go back to Visual Studio 2010, and open **SilverlightHostPage.aspx**.

6. Change the source tag of the Silverlight application, so that the path is the URL of the Silverlight XAP file that is stored in the Azure Storage.

7. Add a new tag parameter which instructs the host page that it is OK to load a Silverlight control that is hosted elsewhere as follows:

```
<param name="enableHtmlAccess" value="true" />
```

8. The final **SilverlightHostPage.aspx** file should look similar to the following screenshot:

Enabling the CDN on an Azure storage account

To enable CDN on an Azure storage account, log in to the Azure Management Portal. Browse to your **Storage Accounts,** and click on the storage account that should be used. With the account selected, click on the large green **Enable CDN** button as shown in the following screenshot:

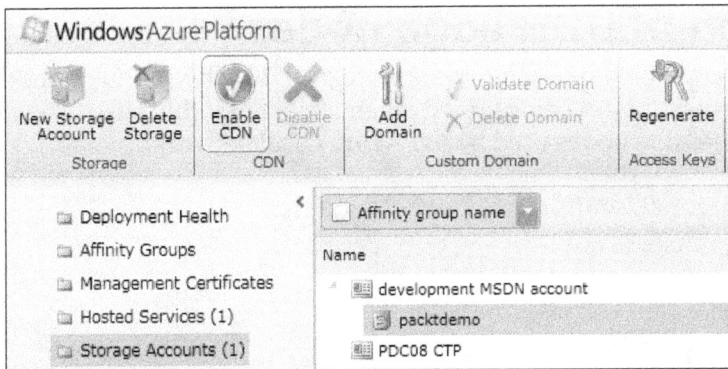

After the CDN has been enabled on that storage account, the properties window will update, and display the unique URL to access the CDN version of your files. The following screenshot shows an example of a storage account that has been CDN-enabled:

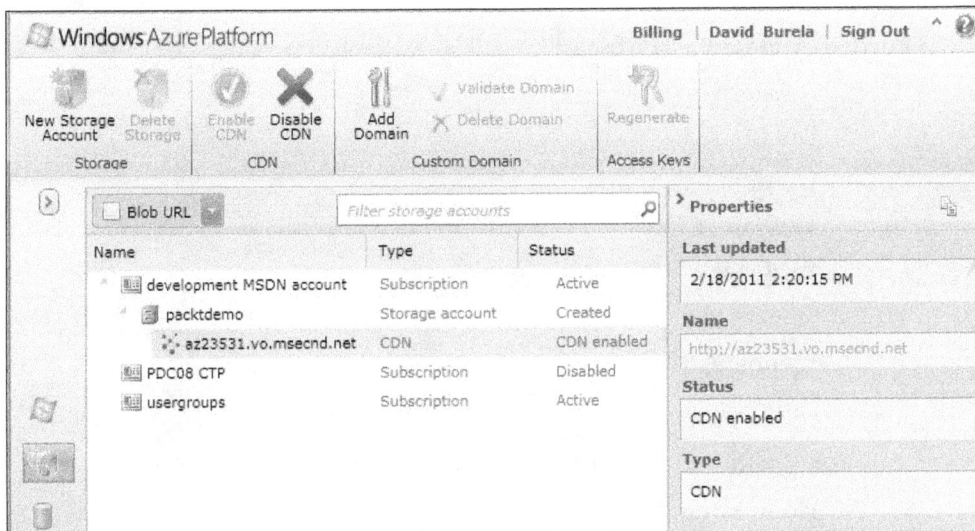

Location of CDN edge nodes

At the beginning of the year 2011, there were over 20 active CDN nodes distributed globally, with new nodes being added on an almost monthly basis. The following are some of the edge nodes used by the Azure CDN network:

- US
    - Ashburn, VA
    - Bay Area, CA
    - Chicago, IL
    - San Antonio, TX
    - Los Angeles, CA
    - Miami, FL
    - Newark, NJ
    - Seattle, WA

- Europe/Middle East/Africa
    - Amsterdam, NL
    - Dublin, IE
    - London, GB
    - Moscow, RU
    - Paris, FR
    - Stockholm, SE
    - Vienna, AT
    - Zurich, CH

- Asia-Pacific/Rest of World
    - Hong Kong, HK
    - São Paulo, BR
    - Seoul, KR
    - Singapore, SG
    - Sydney, AU
    - Taipei, TW
    - Tokyo, JP

Summary

In this chapter, Azure Blob storage was explored in depth, including the underlying mechanisms of how files are stored within the Blob service. We then created an Azure web role that generated files and stored each one of them in the Blob storage. A Silverlight application was then created to retrieve each of the generated text files from the Blob storage, and display them on the screen.

We then moved on to creating a Silverlight application that could access the REST API directly, enabling the Silverlight application to upload the images, and then list the images that are held in a Blob container.

The Silverlight restrictions around the cross-domain policies were explained. The concept of a client access policy XML file was introduced as a way to grant permissions to Silverlight applications to access services on different domains.

Finally, Content Delivery Network (CDN) was explained, as well as its use in improving the end-user performance of your applications.

The next chapter will introduce the Azure Table service, and the way it can be used to store non-relational data.

6
Storing Data in Azure Table Storage from Silverlight

The Windows Azure storage service is focused on the durable storage of persistent data. This chapter will be focusing on the Table feature of the storage service. The Table service allows the structured data to be persisted for a later usage.

In this chapter, we will discuss the following topics:

- Azure Table storage
- Azure Table storage versus SQL Azure
- Using Azure Table storage from Silverlight

Azure Table storage

Azure Tables are cheaper ways of storing large volumes of structured data. When used correctly, Azure Tables are extremely scalable and faster ways of storing and retrieving the data. The data stored in the Table storage does not have a fixed schema (like a table in a standard database). Instead, the entities are schema-less and flexible. Each of the columns can be better thought of as a name or a value pair. It is possible to store multiple entities in the same table that uses different properties.

Accessing Azure Table storage

Azure Table storage can be accessed in the same way as explained in *Chapter 4, Using Azure Queues in Silverlight*. The Table service is exposed through a REST API, and can be accessed directly or with the Windows Azure storage client library.

The URL to access Table storage can be broken down into the following components:

```
http://<StorageAccount>.table.core.windows.
net/<TableName>?$filter=<Query>
```

- **Storage account**: It is the name of the Azure storage account that was created in the Azure Management Portal
- **Table name**: It is a grouping of the related entities
- **Query**: It is the filter that affects the data that is returned (optional)

Under the covers, REST API is compatible with **OData**, a technology that will be introduced in later chapters.

Querying Azure Table storage

It is possible to use **LINQ** queries to retrieve data from the Azure Table storage. These queries allow you to specify the `where` clauses that filter the data that has to be sent back. However, it is important to realize that there are many things that are not supported in Azure Storage. It is not possible to sort the results at all by using an `OrderBy`, and you are not able to do a `count` query either. However, there are ways to work around these limitations.

Although it is not possible to specify an ordering of the results, the results are returned in a sorted order by the combination of the partition key and row key. By selecting what to put into the row key, it is possible to have Azure Storage to store the results in a sorted order which is then returned to you.

A second way to get around the ordering and count limitations is to do the operation locally in an Azure role. By using `AsEnumerable` in the LINQ query, it will force the outcome of the results locally. Other commands can be chained on top of it that will be done locally, rather than on the Azure storage service.

An example query would look similar to the following code snippet:

```
context.CreateQuery<MyEntity>("tablename").Where(p => p.Quantity >
100).AsEnumerable().OrderBy(p => p.Quantity);
```

The preceding query will allow the Azure Table service to filter the results by quantity on the server side. The `AsEnumerable` command will then execute the query, and bring the results locally. From there, the rest of the chained commands are executed locally, so that the `OrderBy` command would be done locally in memory.

In order to improve the performance, Azure Table storage will return only a maximum of 1,000 results at a time. If there are too many results, then the Table storage will return the first 1,000 results, and also a continuation header. The continuation header can be passed back to get the next 1,000 results. This can be repeated until there are no more results to return. This can be useful if you want to process the results in batches. However, this really can get rather tedious if you just want all the results to come back. The **data context class** has another method named `AsTableServiceQuery` that can be used to automatically handle the sending of the continuation tokens back to retrieve all results.

Under the covers

Each entity stored in the table requires three properties: a **partition key, row key,** and **timestamp**. The partition key is used to help Azure Storage to scale the table across multiple servers. The row key is the entity identifier with that partition. The partition key and the row key are used together as unique identifiers of the entity within that table. The tables are sorted by the combination of the partition key and the row key.

Each table can have two additional properties on top of the three mandatory ones for a total of 255 properties. These properties can be of type `binary`, `Bool`, `DateTime`, `double`, `GUID`, `int`, `int64`, or `string`. When thinking about **database tables**, 255 properties is a large number. However, it is important to remember that Table storage does not support relationships, so it may make sense to duplicate a lot of data and denormalize it into the table. Denormalizing the data may require a lot of additional properties to be used. Each entity is limited to a maximum of 1 MB each, while the partition key and row key can be up to 32 KB each.

The following diagram shows the structure of Azure Table storage. Table storage lives inside the Azure storage account. A table is created to group each logical set of related entities. The **entity definition** is not actually stored inside the Table storage, but is a class definition inside your code. This class definition instructs the Table storage about the properties that should be brought back to populate the object. Finally, properties are stored within the Azure Storage inside the table. These properties are simply the name or value pairs and can be defined whenever the developer sees them as fit.

As the following diagram shows, the tables are schema-less. It is possible for two separate entities to coexist within the same table. In this case, the class that brings back a `Person` entity would have two properties (`FirstName` and `LastName`), but an `Employee` entity would have four properties (`FirstName`, `LastName`, `JobPosition`, and `Salary`):

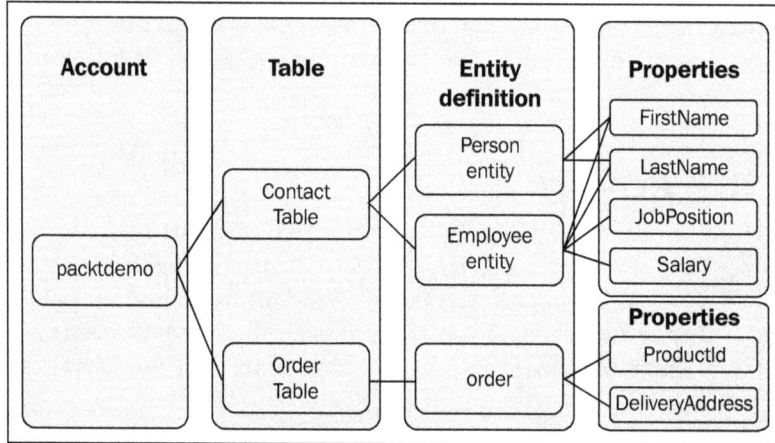

The tables need to be created initially in the code. This can be done by making a call to `CreateTablesFromModel`. The storage client library will automatically reflect over the code base and search for `IQueryable<T>` properties in the data context. The table name used within each `IQueryable<T>` is then used to create each of the tables in the Table storage account. It is only necessary to call this method once to create the table to hold the entities. The table schema is never explicitly defined, each entity holds their own properties; that is, there is no need to update the Table storage on the server if the entities change.

Partitions

In order to allow Azure Storage to scale with the increase in the volume of the data in your tables, the tables need to be partitioned to spread the load. The partition key in each entity instructs the system how the entities should be split up. Each partition is a logical grouping of entities that is likely to be queried together. If the table is for blog posts or news articles, it may make sense to group them by year. However, if the table is storing product orders, partitioning by year may not be fine-grained enough as there could be thousands of orders per year. A partition key based on the customer may allow the partitions to scale better.

The following diagram shows an example of how a table being partitioned by year would distribute the entities over a number of different servers. The partitions may be grouped together on the same machine if they are lightly queried partitions (2008 and 2009 in the diagram). If suddenly both 2008 and 2009 partitions were to be queried heavily, the storage service will automatically move the partitions onto different servers to distribute the load:

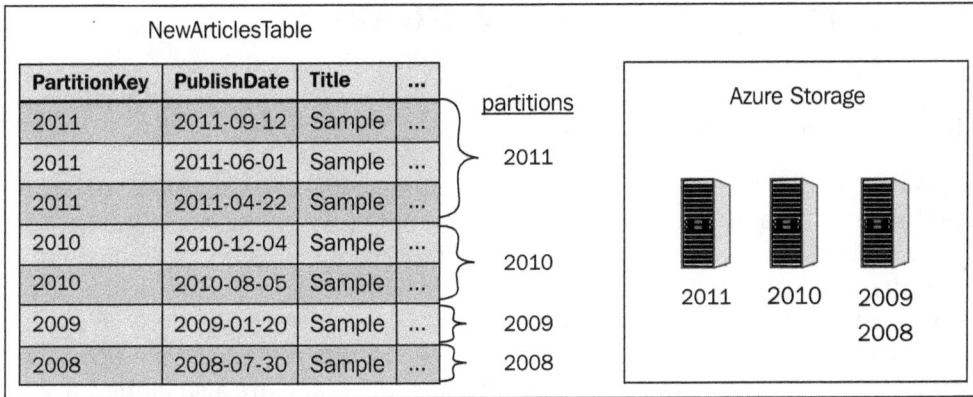

An appropriate partition key should be selected that will keep the relative size of each partition roughly equal to each other, so that you get a linear scale-out in performance. Scaling out your data, and keeping the partition size small not only lets you query within that partition very quickly, but also lets you query the partitions in parallel.

Flexible schema

The tables in Azure Storage do not have a fixed schema. Instead, each entity can be defined individually. Each entity can store any properties it likes. However, while retrieving values, the properties of the entity class will be populated with the matching columns from the table.

The flexible schema allows different entities to coexist within the same table. This can be useful if you want to store related entities together within the same partition keys. Storing a business entity and related audit information together in the same table can result in the data for both entities being retrieved with similar queries.

The flexible schema also means that you can modify the shape of an entity any time. If new properties are required, they can just be added to the entity class and the values will automatically be persisted.

If a property is no longer relevant, just remove it from the entity class and it will no longer be returned in your queries. However, the values of that property will still be stored in the Table storage. It is possible to write a code that goes through the entities and clears those values from the Table storage. However, storage is cheap, so it may be easier to just let the data remain there in case it is required later.

Concurrency and transactions

Table storage uses the timestamp on each row to handle **concurrency**. This service uses optimistic concurrency by default. The timestamps are automatically compared to determine whether there has been a concurrency conflict.

When save changes is called on a data service context, it will go and save each entity individually by default. Sometimes, you may want to save changes in a transaction, so that multiple entities are updated at once. Transactions can only be done on those entities that are in the same partition of the same table. As mentioned earlier, Azure Storage load balances partitions over a number of servers. A transaction can only work on a single partition at a time because all the entities need to be modified by that one server. Transactions have a limit of 100 entities, and are also limited to a payload, lesser than 4 MB.

In order to indicate the service that the changes should be saved in a batch, the `SaveChangesOptions` enumeration can be passed to the `SaveChanges` method as follows:

```
context.SaveChanges(SaveChangesOptions.Batch)
```

Azure Table storage versus SQL Azure

When someone is first introduced to the Windows Azure Platform, it is very common to hear the question asked, *Should I be using Azure Tables or SQL Azure?* The largest difference between the two offerings is in the way each of them stores the data:

- **Azure Table storage:** It is built on top of the Azure Storage platform. It comprises flexible or schema-less entities. There is no referential integrity between the tables, and no custom indexes. It can scale massive amounts of data due to the partition key.

- **SQL Azure:** It is an SQL Server that has been configured to be hosted on top of the Windows Azure in a high availability mode. It comprises standard SQL Tables with indexes and referential integrity. It may not scale as far as Azure Table storage.

A table within the Azure Table storage can be thought of as a single spreadsheet. In a spreadsheet, all the data is stored inside it, separate and distinct from any other data, as there is no referential integrity. Inside a spreadsheet, columns can be added and used any time. Azure Table storage acts very similar to this concept.

SQL Azure will look familiar to any .Net developer who has used **SQL Server 2008** previously. Tables have a fixed schema, have referential integrity, and can have custom indexes applied to them. Stored procedures, temp tables triggers are also specialized functions that are supported on top of the SQL Azure, which can help to port the existing applications. However, many features of the SQL Server are not available, and the service is not much scalable out of the box.

Scalability

Due to the architecture of Azure Table storage, it is currently more scalable than the SQL Azure. The current account limits on the Azure Storage accounts allow them to reach 100 TB in size. If the data is partitioned correctly across the multiple Azure Storage nodes, then the performance can be spectacular. In addition to it being partitioned across the multiple nodes, as Azure Storage data is always replicated over three instances, reads of Azure Table storage can also be automatically load balanced across the replicas to improve the performance.

SQL Azure by comparison is bounded to the single instance that the database is running on. If you are using a 50 GB database, then it will be a single SQL Azure instance that is executing your queries across the 50 GB worth of data. SQL Azure does not automatically scale-out the data it contains, but there are techniques that can be used such as **sharding** that can increase the scalability of SQL Azure, which will be discussed in Chapter 7, *Relational data with SQL Azure and Entity Framework*.

So which one should you choose

The general rule of thumb I use while trying to decide whether an enterprise should use Azure Tables or SQL Azure comes down to the expected scale of the application and the technologies that you need to support.

If you are porting an existing application that uses SQL Server, or you are planning to use technologies that rely on a relational database (LINQ to SQL, ADO.Net, and so on), then SQL Azure is the best choice.

Azure Table storage should be used in two primary scenarios, of which the first is for the specialized applications that are built from the ground up to take advantage of the scalability of the Azure Tables. If used correctly, Azure Tables can scale-out, and handle a tremendous amount of traffic.

The second scenario is whether the application will only be storing a very small amount of data, as it can be more cost-effective to use Azure Tables. The application will only be charged for the small amounts of storage that is being used, at Azure Storage rates. The examples of applications suitable for using the Azure Table storage would be storing blog comments, log or audit files, and so on. Azure Tables are also useful for worker roles to track the work they are doing.

Using Azure Table storage from Silverlight

In order to demonstrate the use of Azure Table storage from Silverlight, we will create a system that allows news articles to be published and also displayed to the user. The system will allow news articles to have a published date set for them, so that the articles can be created in the past, or scheduled for the future. When a user displays the latest news articles, it will only display the ones that have a published date preceding the current date or time. In this way, articles will be automatically published when the current date or time passes the published date, and is returned in the query.

Two entities will be created for this system: `NewsArticle` that contains full information about a news article, and `NewsArticleHeader` that only contains the title and the published date. As the content of a news article may be extremely long, returning a list of them may require a lot of data to be transmitted. `NewsArticleHeader` will allow us to return a list of available articles quickly, and lets the user decide the one that he/she wants to download.

Performing operations against the Azure Table storage requires the use of the shared access key. Due to this, the operations to interact with the Azure Table storage will be occurring in a web role, with the Silverlight application interacting with the web role through a WCF service.

Interacting with Table storage and creating a WCF service

To start building the system, the entities, a Table data service context, and a WCF service should be created. Start this process by creating a new Azure solution with a WCF service web role:

1. In Visual Studio 2010, create a new **Windows Azure Project** named **TableExercise1** as shown in the following screenshot:

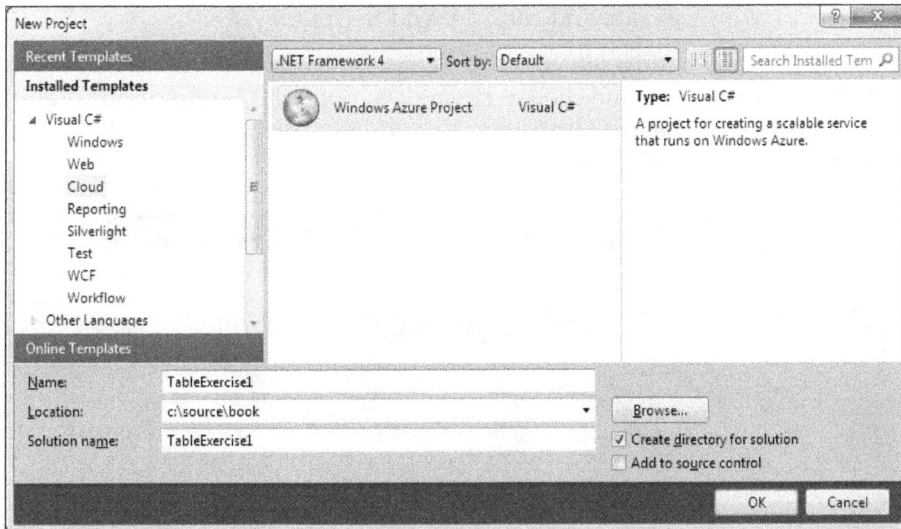

2. Add a WCF service web role into the project. Rename the WCF role to **WCFServiceWebRole** as shown in the following screenshot. Click on **OK** to create the application:

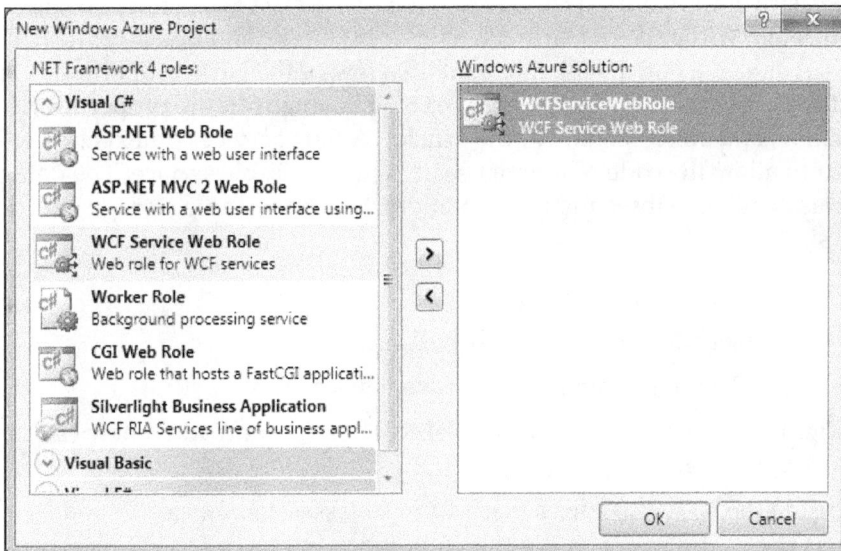

3. Once Visual Studio 2010 has finished creating the solution, expand the **TableExercise1** project, expand the `roles` folder, right-click on **WCFServiceWebRole**, and select **Properties**.

4. Select the **Settings** tab, and click on **Add Setting**.

5. Name the new setting as AzureStorageConnectionString, change it to a **Connection String**, and then click on **...** to open the configuration. Select **Use the Azure storage emulator**, and click on **OK**. The final result should look similar to the one shown in the following screenshot:

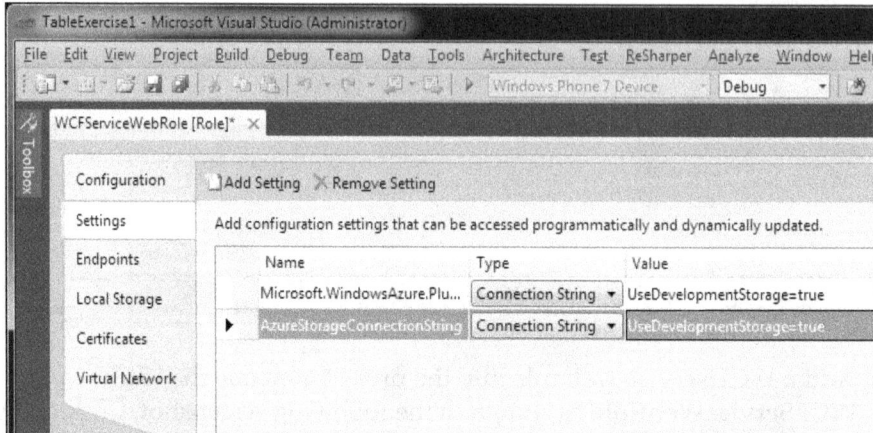

With the basics of the solution configured, the entity classes can now be added. The two entities that will be created are NewsArticleHeader and NewsArticle. The NewsArticleHeader entity will only contain a few of the basic properties of the news entity (Title, Date), but NewsArticle will contain all the properties (Title, Date, Author, and TextContent of the article). A data service context class will also be created to allow the code to interact easily with the Table service. The data service context class will have three methods to interact with the Table storage which are as follows:

   ° Create a news article
   ° Get a list of news article headers
   ° Get the full details of a single news article

1. Right-click on the **WCFServiceWebRole** project and add a new class named NewsArticle.

2. Inside the **NewsArticle.cs** file, add two classes: NewsArticle and NewsArticleHeader and implement them as shown in the following code snippet. Both classes have a subclass named TableServiceEntity, which simply provides three base properties (the partition key, row key, and timestamp). It is perfectly acceptable to subclass TableServiceEntity, and add the properties to the class yourself, allowing you to subclass another

class. The entities just need to be **POCOE** "CDN" (**Plain Old CLR Objects**), but for the ease of implementation, we will subclass:

```
using System;
using Microsoft.WindowsAzure.StorageClient;
namespace WCFServiceWebRole
{
  public class NewsArticle : TableServiceEntity
  {
    public string Title { get; set; }
    public string TextContent { get; set; }
    public string Author { get; set; }
    public DateTime PublishedDate { get; set; }
  }
  public class NewsArticleHeader : TableServiceEntity
  {
    public string Title { get; set; }
    public DateTime PublishedDate { get; set; }
  }
}
```

8. Click on **Add Reference** to add a reference to **System.Data.Services.Client**. This is required to communicate with the Table service through the storage client. The following screenshot shows the reference being added in the **Add Reference** window:

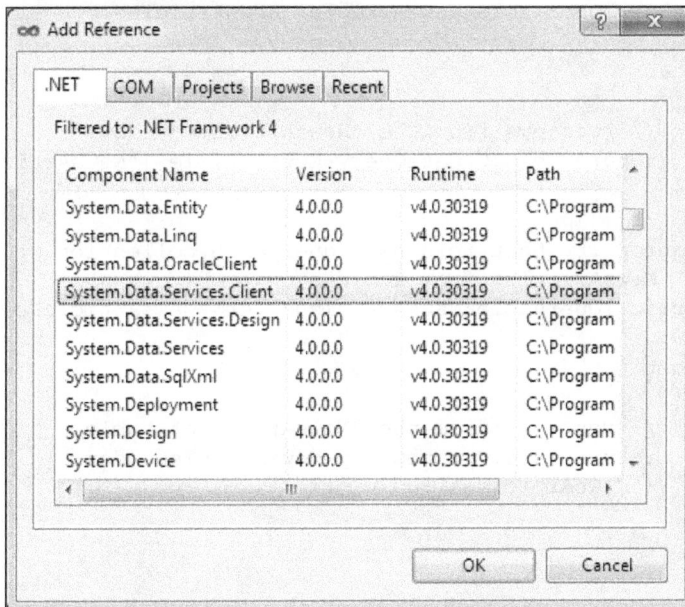

9. Right-click on the **WCFServiceWebRole** project, and add a new class named NewsArticleDataServiceContext.

10. Implement the NewsArticleDataServiceContext class as shown in the following code snippet. The class inherits from TableServiceContext, which provides all the basic functionalities to handle the authentication, communication with the Table service, serialization of the entities, and so on. The two properties are added to the class, each exposing the entities (NewsArticle and NewsArticleHeader) as IQueryable. This allows LINQ queries to be built with the where clauses specified. These entities have a different schema, but both have been defined to be retrieved from a single NewsArticles table. The data service context class automatically handles the deserialization of the data, and populates the properties of the entity:

```csharp
using System;
using System.Linq;
using Microsoft.WindowsAzure;
using Microsoft.WindowsAzure.StorageClient;
namespace WCFServiceWebRole
{
  public class NewsArticleDataServiceContext : TableServiceContext
  {
  public NewsArticleDataServiceContext(string baseAddress,
    StorageCredentials credentials)
   : base(baseAddress, credentials)
    {
    }
    public IQueryable<NewsArticle> NewsArticles
    {
      get
      {
        // retrieve from the "NewsArticles" table
        return this.CreateQuery<NewsArticle>("NewsArticles");
      }
    }
    // property that returns a queryable collection of
        NewsArticles from table storage
    public IQueryable<NewsArticleHeader> NewsArticleHeaders
    {
      get
      {
        // retrieve from the "NewsArticles" table
        return this.CreateQuery<NewsArticleHeader>
        ("NewsArticles");
      }
    }
  }
}
```

11. Into the `NewsArticleDataServiceContext` class, add a new method that will allow for the creation of a new `NewsArticle`. This method takes in four parameters: the title, the main content of the article, the author, and also the date to publish the article. The entities will be partitioned by month and year that the article will be published. This partition key makes sense for a blog, as it is a standard to see the archives grouped by month. As these are news articles, querying and retrieving back the most recent articles will need to have them sorted chronologically. This requires that we store the entities in a particular way, as it is not possible to define an `OrderBy` clause while querying the Table storage. The following method uses a trick to sort the entities. You should recall that the entities are sorted by the combination of a partition key and a row key. If we were to simply store the entities with the partition key as **YYYYMM** (201110 for October 2011), the articles would be stored in an ascending order, with the oldest article returned first. To overcome this, the partition key is generated by taking the year **9999** and **subtracting** the **current year**, and doing the same to the month portion. This reverses the order of the partitions and will return the entities in a descending chronological order instead, for example, October 2011 will become 798802. The same is done to the row key. Within each partition, the news articles for that month also need to be sorted in a descending chronological order. This is done by taking the maximum value of `Ticks`. `MaxValue` and subtracting the `Ticks` of the `DateTime` of the published date from it. However, two articles could be scheduled to be published at the same `DateTime`, so it is also important to add a GUID to this value to ensure **uniqueness**. Once all the values have been calculated, the entity is created, and added to the context. The context is triggered to save the changes back to the Table storage:

```
// Method to insert a new NewsArticle into the table
public void AddNewsArticle(string title, string textContent,
 string author, DateTime publishedDate)
{
    //Partition the data by the published year & month. Reverse the
      dates so that rows are stored in reverse chronological order
    var partitionKey = string.Format("{0:0000}{1:00}", (9999 -
      publishedDate.Year), (12 - publishedDate.Month));
    // Format the rowkey so that the rows will be stored in reverse
      chronological order.
    // Add a Guid to ensure uniqueness.
    var rowKey = string.Format("{0:10}_{1}",
     DateTime.MaxValue.Ticks - publishedDate.Ticks, Guid.NewGuid());
    // call methods on the base class
```

```
    this.AddObject("NewsArticles", new NewsArticle { PartitionKey =
      partitionKey, RowKey = rowKey, Title = title, TextContent =
        textContent, Author = author, PublishedDate =
          publishedDate });
    this.SaveChanges();
  }
```

12. Right-click on the **WCFServiceWebRole** project, select **Add new item** and add a **Global Application Class** named `Global.asax`.

13. Modify the `Application_Start` method inside `Global.asax`, so that it will construct the tables if they do not exist. This should only be called once in the application, as there is a performance penalty if you attempt to create a table that already exists. The following gets the account details from the configuration file. Once it has the account details, it creates all the required tables by looking at the table names used inside the `NewsArticleDataServiceContext` class. The `NewsArticleDataServiceContext` class inserts and retrieves all the entities within it from a single table named `NewsArticles`, so that a single table will be created:

```
using System;
using Microsoft.WindowsAzure;
using Microsoft.WindowsAzure.ServiceRuntime;
using Microsoft.WindowsAzure.StorageClient;
namespace WCFServiceWebRole
{
  public class Global : System.Web.HttpApplication
  {
    protected void Application_Start(object sender, EventArgs e)
    {
      var account = CloudStorageAccount.Parse
        (RoleEnvironment.GetConfigurationSettingValue
        ("AzureStorageConnectionString"));
      // create the tables by looking inside
        NewsArticleDataServiceContext and discovering the names
        of tables
      CloudTableClient.CreateTablesFromModel(
        typeof(NewsArticleDataServiceContext),
          account.TableEndpoint.AbsoluteUri, account.Credentials);
    }
  }
}
```

With the entities created as well as the data service context class to save and retrieve them, we can now focus on exposing the operations to the Silverlight client through a WCF service. The WCF service will expose three methods to the Silverlight application as follows:

○   Create a news article

○   Get a list of news article headers

○   Get the full details of a single news article

14. Open **IService1.svc** and modify the code to be the same as the following code snippet. The interfaced file will define the three methods that we wish our service to have comprising a create method that takes in the properties of the news article to be created, a list headers method that returns the 10 latest articles (as they are sorted chronologically in Table storage), and a method that will return a full news article:

```
using System;
using System.Collections.Generic;
using System.ServiceModel;
namespace WCFServiceWebRole
{
  [ServiceContract]
  public interface IService1
  {
    [OperationContract]
    void AddNewsArticle(string title, string textContent, string
      author, DateTime publishedDate);
    [OperationContract]
    List<NewsArticleHeader> GetLatestNewsArticleHeaders();
    [OperationContract]
    NewsArticle GetFullNewsArticle(string partitionKey, string
      rowKey);
  }
}
```

15. Open **Service1.svc** and modify the code to be the same as the following code. Firstly, the class constructor retrieves the account configuration and stores it in a private variable for the other methods to use. The AddNewsArticle method creates an instance of the NewsArticleDataServiceContext class using the credentials of the saved account in the private variable. The context is then invoked to create a new NewsArticle based on the parameters passed to it. The GetLatestNewsArticleHeaders uses the context to return the 10 latest news articles that were published before the current date. This schedules the news articles to be published at a later date.

The GetFullNewsArticle method uses the context to search for a single news article. Each entity is uniquely identified through the combination of a partition key and a row key, so that the table search will return a single result or nothing at all. As it is possible to identify a single entity uniquely through this combination, Azure Storage will throw an exception saying that it was not able to find the specific entity. The following code snippet will disable the exception from being thrown away, and will return a null value instead:

```
using System;
using System.Collections.Generic;
using System.Linq;
using Microsoft.WindowsAzure;
using Microsoft.WindowsAzure.ServiceRuntime;
namespace WCFServiceWebRole
{
  public class Service1 : IService1
  {
    private readonly CloudStorageAccount storageAccount;
    public Service1()
    {
      storageAccount = CloudStorageAccount.Parse
        (RoleEnvironment.GetConfigurationSettingValue
          ("AzureStorageConnectionString"));
    }
    public void AddNewsArticle(string title, string textContent,
      string author, DateTime publishedDate)
    {
      var context = new NewsArticleDataServiceContext
        (storageAccount.TableEndpoint.AbsoluteUri,
          storageAccount.Credentials);
      context.AddNewsArticle(title, textContent, author,
        publishedDate);
    }
    public List<NewsArticleHeader> GetLatestNewsArticleHeaders()
    {
      var context = new NewsArticleDataServiceContext
        (storageAccount.TableEndpoint.AbsoluteUri,
          storageAccount.Credentials);
      var results = context.NewsArticleHeaders.Where(p =>
        p.PublishedDate <= DateTime.Now).Take(10);
      return results.ToList();
    }
    public NewsArticle GetFullNewsArticle
    (string partitionKey, string rowKey)
    {
```

```
        var context = new NewsArticleDataServiceContext
          (storageAccount.TableEndpoint.AbsoluteUri,
             storageAccount.Credentials);
        context.IgnoreResourceNotFoundException = true; // prevents
          an exception being thrown if an entity is not found, and
          instead returns null
        var result = context.NewsArticles.Where
          (p => p.PartitionKey == partitionKey &&
             p.RowKey == rowKey);
        return result.FirstOrDefault();
      }
    }
  }
```

Creating the Silverlight application

The Silverlight application will be created to have two modes, that is, a viewing tab, and a tab to create new news articles. The Silverlight application will communicate with the WCF service to retrieve a list of many NewsArticleHeader. These will be displayed in a ListBox and will allow the user to select one to view. Once the user has made a selection, the WCF service will be queried to retrieve the full contents of that news article:

1. Add a new Silverlight project to the solution. Do this by right-clicking on **WCFServiceWebRole** and selecting **Properties**. Go to the **Silverlight Applications** tab, then click on **Add**. Name the Silverlight application as NewsArticleSilverlightProject.

2. Right-click on **NewsArticleSilverlightProjectTestPage.aspx** in the web role and select **Set as start page**.

3. Be sure to build the project to make sure that the WCF service is compiled.

4. Right-click on the Silverlight project and click on **Add Service Reference**.

5. Click on **Discover**. Select **Service1.svc** and rename the service reference to **NewsArticleServiceReference** as shown in the following screenshot:

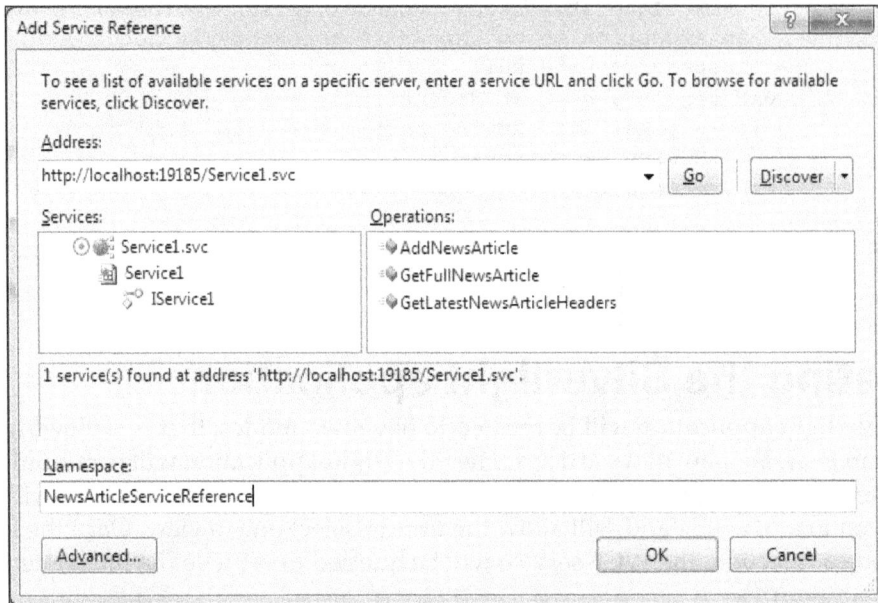

6. Open `MainPage.xaml`. The layout for the Silverlight application will now be created. Two tabs will be added to the screen of which one is to view the news articles and the other to create the news articles. A template is created in the resources that will be used later in `ListBox`. The template defines the way to display and format news articles when displayed in `ListBox`. From the `ToolBox`, drag a `TabControl` onto the design surface to allow Visual Studio 2010 to automatically add the correct assembly references. Then, modify the XAML as follows:

```
<UserControl x:Class="NewsArticleSilverlightProject.MainPage"
xmlns:sdk="http://schemas.microsoft.com/winfx/2006/xaml/
presentation/sdk">
  <UserControl.Resources>
    <!--Defines the template for displaying news articles in the
      ListBox-->
    DataTemplate x:Name="NewsArticleItemTemplate" >
    <StackPanel Orientation="Horizontal">
    <TextBlock Text="{Binding PublishedDate}" Width="150" />
```

```
    <TextBlock Text="{Binding Title}" />
    </StackPanel>
    </DataTemplate>
</UserControl.Resources>
<Grid x:Name="LayoutRoot" Background="White">
    <sdk:TabControl >
    <!--Defines the first tab to view news articles-->
    <sdk:TabItem Header="View">
    <!-- Tab contents added in later step -->
    </sdk:TabItem>
    <!--Defines the second tab to create news articles-->
    <sdk:TabItem Header="Create">
    <!-- Tab contents added in later step -->
    </sdk:TabItem>
    </sdk:TabControl>
    </Grid>
</UserControl>
```

7. Add the contents of the `View` tab. A number of controls are added: A query `Button` is added to invoke the WCF service, a `ListBox` to display the `NewsArticleHeaders`, and then two `TextBlocks` to display the author and the content of the selected news article. `ListBox` has a selection changing event on it, which will be used to trigger a call to the WCF service:

```
<sdk:TabItem Header="View">
    <Grid>
        <Grid.RowDefinitions>
        <RowDefinition Height="20" />
        <RowDefinition Height="0.5*" />
        <RowDefinition Height="20" />
        <RowDefinition Height="0.5*" />
        </Grid.RowDefinitions>
        <Button Content="Query table" Click="QueryButtonClick" />
        <ListBox x:Name="HeadersListBox" Grid.Row="1"
            SelectionChanged="HeadersListBoxSelectionChanged"
            ItemTemplate="{StaticResource NewsArticleItemTemplate}" />
        <TextBlock Grid.Row="2" x:Name="authorBlock" />
        <TextBlock Grid.Row="3" x:Name="contentBlock"
            TextWrapping="Wrap" />
    </Grid>
</sdk:TabItem>
```

8. Add the contents of the `Create` tab. It only has a single `Button` to invoke the WCF service, and then a number of `TextBlocks` and `TextBoxes` to take the user input:

```
<sdk:TabItem Header="Create">
  <StackPanel>
    <TextBlock Text="Title" />
    <TextBox x:Name="TitleTextBox" />
    <TextBlock Text="Author" />
    <TextBox x:Name="AuthorTextBox" />
    <TextBlock Text="Publish date" />
    <sdk:Calendar x:Name="publishedDateControl"
      HorizontalAlignment="Left" />
    <TextBlock Text="Article content" />
    <TextBox x:Name="ArticleContentTextBox" AcceptsReturn="True"
      Height="200" />
    <Button Content="Create" Click="CreateButtonClick" />
  </StackPanel>
</sdk:TabItem>
```

9. Open the code behind the file `MainPage.xaml.cs` and implement the **event handlers** of the controls. First, the event handler for the query button will be added. This event handler simply calls the WCF service and when the results are returned, they are set to be the `ItemsSource` of `ListBox`. The item template attached to `ListBox` will automatically handle the formatting. As the WCF service is used a number of times in the code behind the file, a `helper` method has also been created that will construct a proxy for us. It uses the same trick that we have seen a number of times to simplify the development:

```
private static NewsArticleServiceReference.Service1Client
  CreateServiceProxy()
{
  // This is the same code from chapter 3. To allow this code to
    work locally and in produciton.
  // Find the url for the current silverlight .xap file. Go up one
    level to get to the root of the site.
  var url = Application.Current.Host.Source.OriginalString;
  var urlBase = url.Substring(0, url.IndexOf("/ClientBin",
    StringComparison.InvariantCultureIgnoreCase));
  // Create a proxy object for the WCF service. Use the root path
    of the site and append the service name
  var proxy = new NewsArticleServiceReference.Service1Client();
  proxy.Endpoint.Address = new System.ServiceModel.
  EndpointAddress(urlBase + "/Service1.svc");
```

```
    return proxy;
}
private void QueryButtonClick(object sender, RoutedEventArgs e)
{
  var proxy = CreateServiceProxy();
  // use a lambda expression for the completed event as it is a
    single line.
  proxy.GetLatestNewsArticleHeadersCompleted +=
  (sender2, e2) =>
  {
    headersListBox.ItemsSource = e2.Result;
  };
  proxy.GetLatestNewsArticleHeadersAsync();
}
```

10. Next, implement the event handler for the `ListBox` selection changed event. The method first checks if there is a valid selection in the `ListBox`, it then creates a proxy, passes the row, and partitions the keys to the WCF service. Once a result is returned, the code then updates the screen to display the author and the text content of the article:

```
private void HeadersListBoxSelectionChanged(object sender,
  SelectionChangedEventArgs e)
{
  var item = HeadersListBox.SelectedItem as
    NewsArticleServiceReference.NewsArticleHeader;
  if (item != null)
  {
    var proxy = CreateServiceProxy();
    // use a lambda expression for the completed event as it is
      two lines
    proxy.GetFullNewsArticleCompleted +=
    (sender2, e2) =>
    {
      authorBlock.Text = String.Format("Author: {0}",
        e2.Result.Author);
      contentBlock.Text = e2.Result.TextContent;
    };
    proxy.GetFullNewsArticleAsync(item.PartitionKey, item.RowKey);
  }
}
```

11. Finally, add the event handler for the query button. This method just takes the values from the screen, and passes them to the WCF service. A single test is done to ensure that the user has selected a publish date. If they have not, then the date is by default today:

```
private void CreateButtonClick(object sender, RoutedEventArgs e)
{
  var proxy = CreateServiceProxy();
  var selectedDate = publishedDateControl.SelectedDate ??
    DateTime.Now;
  // default to today's date if none is selected
  proxy.AddNewsArticleAsync(TitleTextBox.Text,
    ArticleContentTextBox.Text, AuthorTextBox.Text, selectedDate);
}
```

12. Press *F5* to run the application.

13. Click on the **Create** tab, and create a number of articles on different days. Once created, go back to the **View** tab, and look at the articles. Your final application should look similar to the following screenshot:

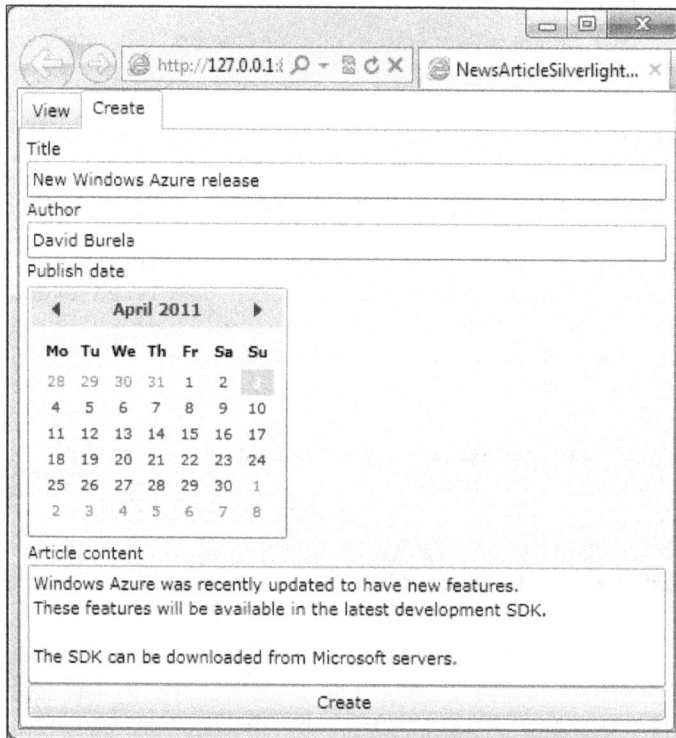

The other screenshot related to the preceding one is as follows:

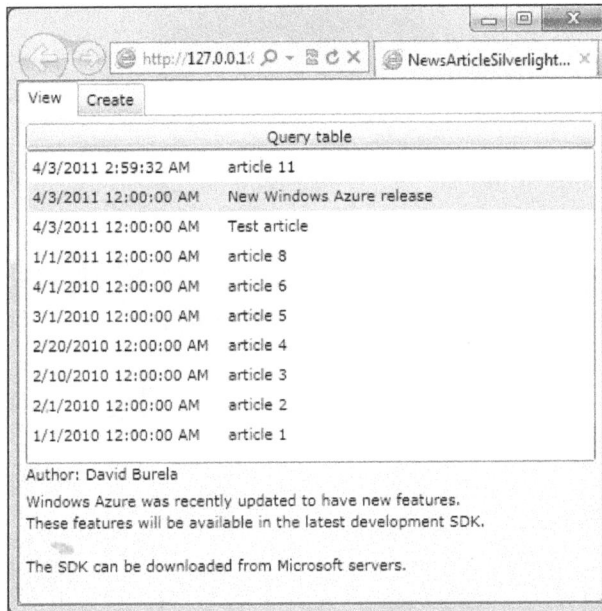

Summary

In this chapter, we looked at the considerations that should be used while deciding between Azure Table storage or SQL Azure. The type of software project you are working on dictates the choice of technology that is better for you. In general, most standard business applications may benefit from the speed of the implementation by using SQL Azure. Small niche implementations or systems on a massive scale may benefit from using Table storage.

Next, we explored how Table storage works under the covers, as well as how it uses partitions to scale the performance of the data retrieval.

Finally, a Silverlight application was created that demonstrated how to persist data back to Table storage, how the two entities of different shapes can be retrieved from the same table, as well as how to interact with it from a Silverlight client.

In the next chapter, we will look at how the relational data can be used in Silverlight with SQL Azure.

7
Relational Data with SQL Azure and Entity Framework

Many enterprise applications require a relational database to persist business data. Microsoft offers a cloud-scale, relational database named SQL Azure. SQL Azure allows developers to begin with the building of cloud solutions quickly. This chapter will use **Entity Framework** to simplify the data access.

In this chapter, we will discuss the following topics:

- SQL Azure
- What Entity Framework is
- Using SQL Azure in Silverlight

SQL Azure

SQL Azure offers a relational data store as part of the Windows Azure platform. It is highly available and requires less maintenance than a traditional on-premises SQL Server installation. SQL Azure is built on top of SQL Server technologies, which keeps the compatibility high with the existing technology stacks. This allows developers to jump quickly into a familiar environment and get started.

SQL Azure is a managed service. Microsoft handles all the basic maintenance and administration issues for you. You no longer need to physically administer faulty power supplies, broken hard disks, worry about disk space, and so on. Microsoft also handles the installation of security patches and updates of the operating system, the updation to the machines, unburdening you again.

At a superficial level, SQL Azure can be thought of as "SQL Server in the cloud", and you can use it as a local SQL Server instance. Most of the technologies used to access the SQL Server will continue to work with SQL Azure, for example, LINQ to SQL, Entity Framework, ADO.Net, and so on.

It is important to note that there are many SQL Server 2008 R2 features that are not supported within SQL Azure, such as the SQL Server Agents and jobs, FILESTREAM data, data compression, and so on. An up-to-date list of SQL Server feature limitations can be found on MSDN at the following URL:

`http://msdn.microsoft.com/en-us/library/windowsazure/ff394115.aspx`

SQL Azure versus Table storage

The differences between SQL Azure and Table storage were covered in the previous chapter, but we will quickly summarize it again:

- **Azure Table storage:** This is built on top of the Azure Storage platform and has flexible or schema-less entities. There is no referential integrity between the tables and no custom indexes and is highly scalable.
- **SQL Azure:** It is an SQL Server that has been ported to be hosted on top of Windows Azure. It supports standard SQL tables with indexes and referential integrity.

The type of the software project you are working on dictates the choice of technology better for you. In general, most standard business applications may benefit from the speed of the implementation by using SQL Azure. Small niche implementations or the systems on a massive scale may benefit from the use of Table storage.

Most traditional enterprise applications will most likely default to using SQL Azure, unless there is an identified need to build using Table storage.

Underlying architecture

As your database grows, it is essential to know what the underlying technology is, and the ways you can assist SQL Azure scale. Under the covers, Microsoft provides **redundancy** by saving each database across the multiple replicas of data (at least three). If the primary replica fails, SQL Azure will automatically fail over to one of the others as shown in the following diagram:

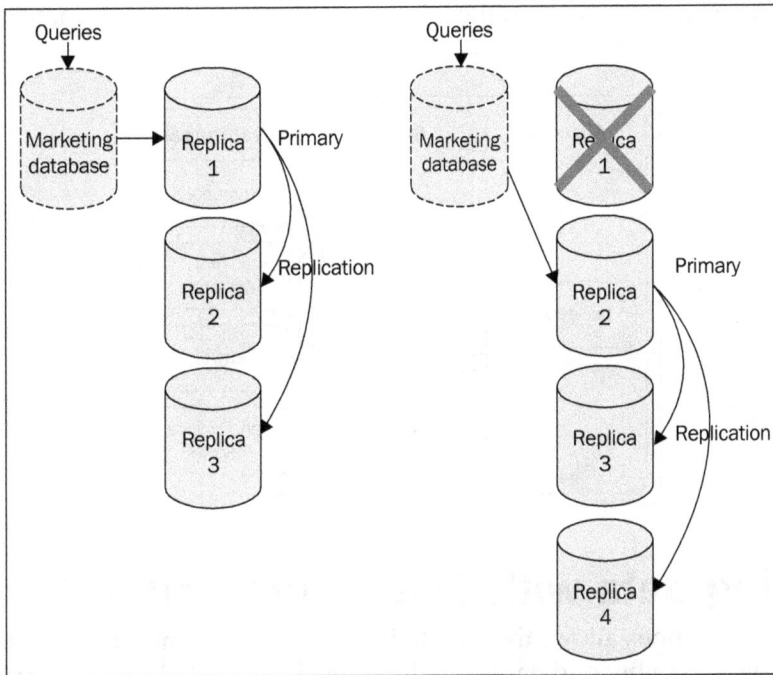

SQL Azure has three main logical layers when it comes to provisioning new databases:

- **Account**: This is the way that Microsoft bills you. Your standard Windows Azure account should give you the access.

- **Database server**: This is a logical database server and not a physical database server. The database server is placed in a single region, so that multiple database servers may be required if you are serving multiple regions. This is also the unit of billing, allowing you to group databases for marketing together on one server, and human resource databases on the other server, and also to track the billing charges.

- **Database**: It acts as a standard database, as you would expect from an SQL Server. It is a collection of tables, views, users, and so on. As the database server is only logical, each database can be placed on different physical machines by SQL Azure for performance reasons.

The following diagram visualizes the relationship between accounts, database servers, and databases:

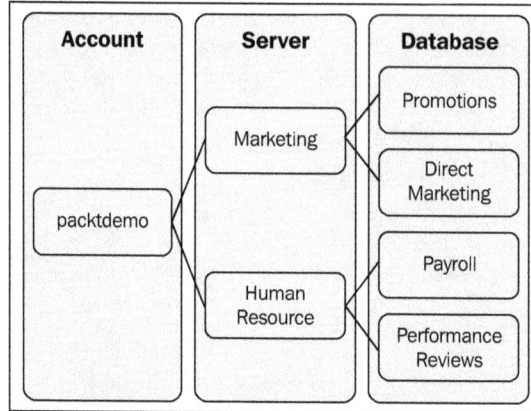

Sharding data with SQL Azure Federations

SQL Azure Federations allows the data to be sharded over a number of databases, improving the scalability of data. The federation allows SQL Azure to act similar to the SQL storage service tables with partition keys; however, federation rules are much more flexible than the partition keys. A rule could be defined that the customer data should be sharded based on the surname of the customer. The following diagram shows the data being segregated based on a rule with three conditions defined (A-K, L-R, and S-Z):

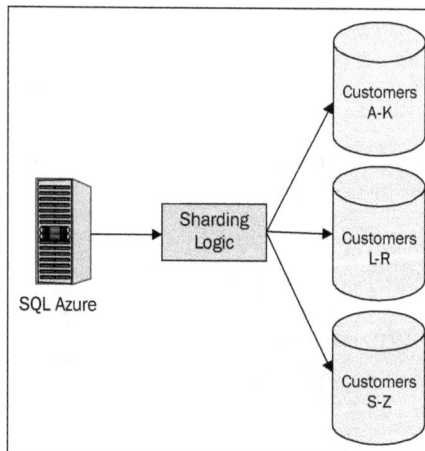

The federation rules are held in SQL Azure and requests are automatically forwarded to the correct database.

SQL Azure Federations is a technology that is still under active development by Microsoft. For further information, please refer to the MSDN documentation at the following URL:

```
http://msdn.microsoft.com/en-us/library/windowsazure/hh597452.aspx
```

What Entity Framework is

Traditionally, when creating applications that interact with a database, developers would be required to write a lot of underlying data access code. This is the code that is written for every project that retrieves the data, populates the data objects, accepts the updated commands, and so on.

The **Microsoft ADO.NET Entity Framework** (Entity Framework for short) is an **ORM (Object Relational Mapping)** Framework that saves developers from writing a lot of tedious boilerplate data access code. Entity Framework allows you to create data classes that represent your database tables, that is, the **Entity Data Model (EDM)**, and provides a simple way to query against your data store by using LINQ queries (Language Integrated Queries). These queries will automatically return the populated data objects which can be manipulated and persisted back to the database with a save command.

Under the covers, Entity Framework takes your LINQ queries, processes them through the EDM, and translates these commands into optimized SQL queries which it then executes through ADO.Net. Entity Framework does a good job of taking complex multi-table `join` and `where` statements defined in a LINQ query, and creating an optimized SQL which is then executed. The following diagram shows the relationship between your code, the Entity Framework, and the database:

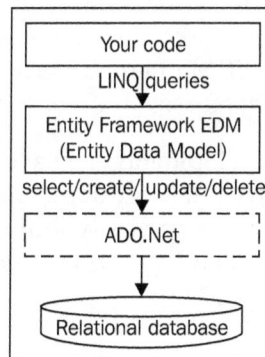

When the initial version of the Entity Framework was released in .Net 3.5 service pack 1, there was much bad press about it. Many people complained that it was hard to use, the requirement of deriving the data classes from a base class was limiting it, and also it was not "feature-complete" enough to be used as a first version. Later versions that were released with .Net 4.0 resolved most of these issues and it is now a good ORM Framework to use. If you had previously dismissed Entity Framework due to Version 1 issues, it is highly recommended that you look at it again.

Development options

Entity Framework provides three ways to create your EDM as follows:

- **Database first**: It allows the developer to take an existing database and reverse engineer it into an EDM. This EDM is then used to generate the code for the data classes. This method is useful for people who are more comfortable creating a database and relationships first in SQL Management Studio, or in other modeling tools. However, this technique can be rather limiting. Working in this way will keep you stuck in a **data-centric** frame of mind, where the database is the king.

- **Model-first**: This development allows you to use visual modeling tools within Visual Studio 2010 to create entities of your application. The EDM then generates the SQL script that will create the corresponding database for you, and also creates the data classes. This method is good for visual software developers. The new features in Entity Framework 4.1 mean that the code of the data classes generated by the EDM are **POCO (Plain Old CLR Object)** classes that are ready for you to extend as a partial class.

- **Code first**: This development was introduced in Entity Framework Version 4.1, and allows developers to write data classes as standard classes. Data classes do not require a base class, allowing for a lot of flexibility. DbContext is then subclassed to create the context of your database. All of this then automatically creates the EDM internally to query against. It can also automatically create the database.

The **model-first** and **code first** developments can have the advantage that the structure of entities is formed during the development and can be easily updated as the project develops. However, enterprises typically have a **database first** culture when it comes to data modeling. All the three methods are equally valid with Entity Framework.

Using SQL Azure in Silverlight

This exercise will demonstrate the use of SQL Azure, Entity Framework 4.0, WCF, and Silverlight. It is a simple application that allows you to track employees and also the department they are currently working in. The fundamentals learned here will allow you to easily create applications with a larger number of tables and entities.

This exercise will be built up in three stages. First, the SQL Azure database will be configured to prepare it for the development. Next, the Entity Framework model will be created which will automatically create the tables in SQL Azure for us. The WCF service will be created to interact with the EDM to **select** and **create** our entities. Finally, the Silverlight application will be created to display and create departments and employees. There is much XAML code required to display something complex, so much effort has been put into the stripping of the screen, down to the bare basics, to minimize the amount of code required to be typed. The following diagram shows the relationship between the components you will be creating:

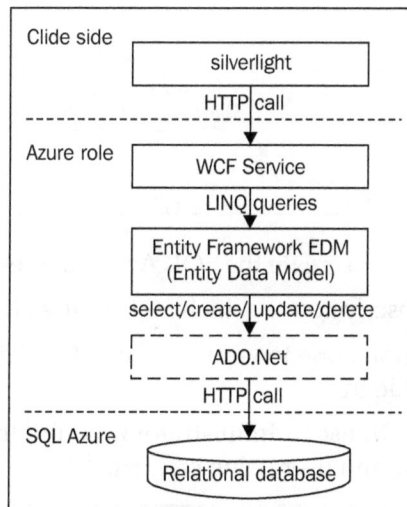

Configuring SQL Azure

First, you will start by configuring the SQL Azure database. You will be required to provision a new database, create an SQL user, configure the firewall to allow the Azure-hosted roles to access it, and also allow the access of your own IP address to develop against it as follows:

1. Log onto the Windows Azure Management Portal through the following URL:
   ```
   http://WindowsAzure.com
   ```

2. Once logged in, navigate to the **Database** section, then click on **Create a new SQL Azure Server** as shown in the following screenshot:

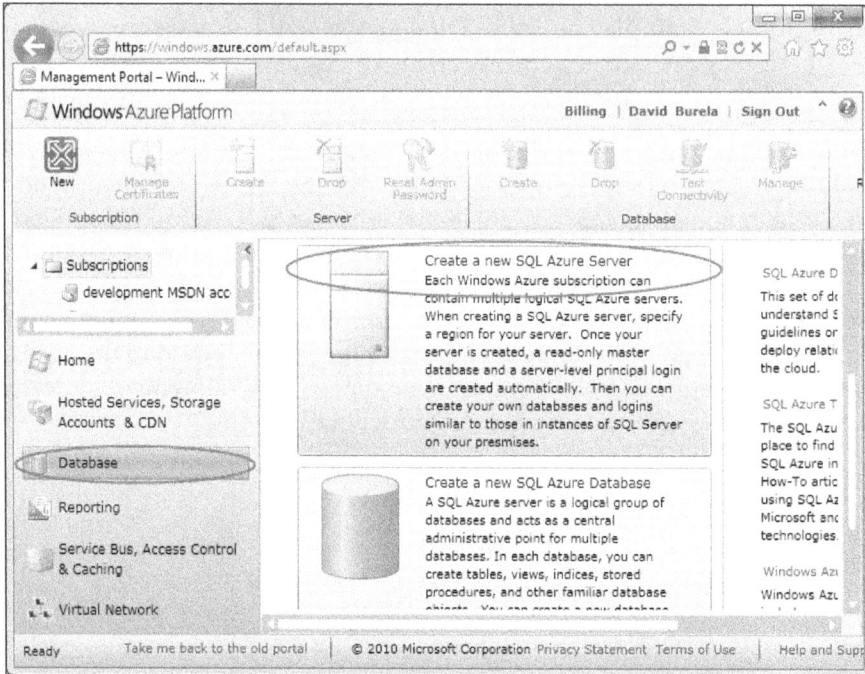

3. Complete the wizard to create the SQL Azure Server as follows:

   ° Select a subscription to which SQL Azure charges should be billed to

   ° Select a region close to your location at which the SQL Azure Server should reside in

   ° Create an SQL user administrator account; the following screenshot shows an admin user being created:

4. The final step of the wizard requires a firewall which protects the SQL Azure Server to be configured. Start by clicking on the checkbox that says **Allow other Windows Azure services to access this server**, as shown in the following screenshot. This will grant access to Windows Azure roles and other Azure services:

5. The next step is to grant your development machine access to the SQL Azure Server. Do this by clicking on the **Add** button. This will open a screen similar to the one shown in the following screenshot. Type your IP address, as shown, in **Your current IP address** into the **IP range start** and the **IP range end**. If you have a dynamic IP address, you will either need to update it each time, or enter the IP range that your Internet Service Provider (ISP) assigned:

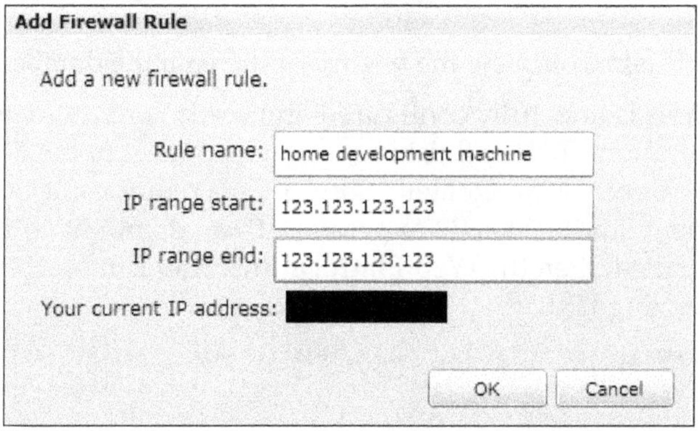

> **SQL Azure firewall rules**
>
> The firewall can be updated from the Azure Management Portal, as well as through the stored procedures. More information on updating the firewall rules using the stored procedures can be found on MSDN at the following URL:
>
> `http://msdn.microsoft.com/en-us/library/`
> `windowsazure/ee621783.aspx`

6. Click on **Finish** to complete the wizard and configure the SQL Azure Server.

7. Go back to the Windows Azure Management Portal, click on **Create a new SQL Azure database**. Complete the wizard by selecting your subscription and the SQL Azure Server that was created in the preceding step. Then, give the database an appropriate name as shown in the following screenshot:

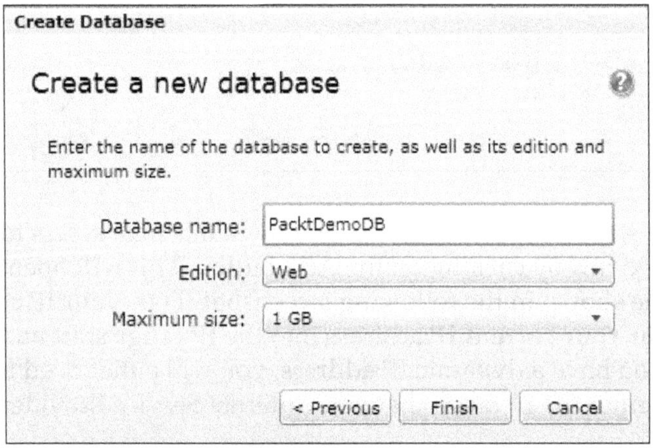

8. Click on **Finish**. Complete the wizard and create the database.

9. The database is now fully configured and ready for you to use in your applications. Before finishing, we will connect to the database using **SQL Server Management Studio**. This requires the SQL Server Management Studio 2008 R2 or greater. If you do not have a management studio installed, then the **Web Platform Installer** can be used to obtain it at the following URL:

`http://www.microsoft.com/web/downloads/`

10. When the SQL Azure Server is created, a random name is generated for you. You can obtain the server name by viewing it in the Windows Azure Management Portal. The following screenshot shows an example of a server name that was given, in this case, it is **xmpmeaywch**:

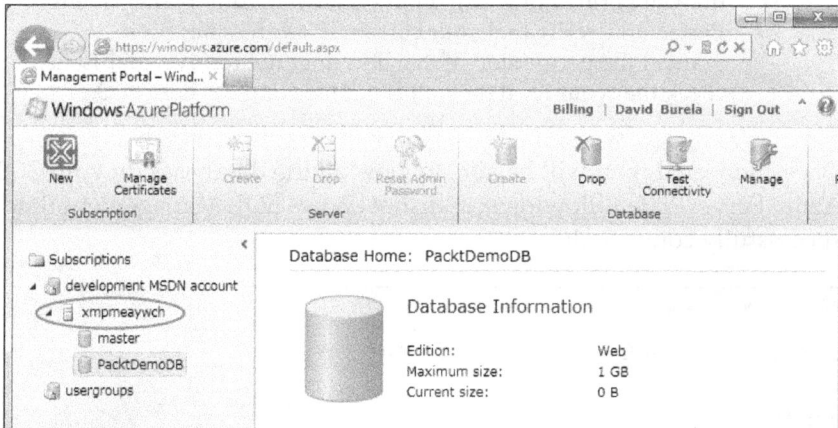

11. Open SQL Management Studio.

12. When prompted to connect to a server, enter the following details and your entries will appear as shown in the following screenshot:

    ○ **Server name**: `<generated server name>.database.windows.net`

    ○ **Login**: `<admin username>@<generated server name>`

    ○ **Password**: your password

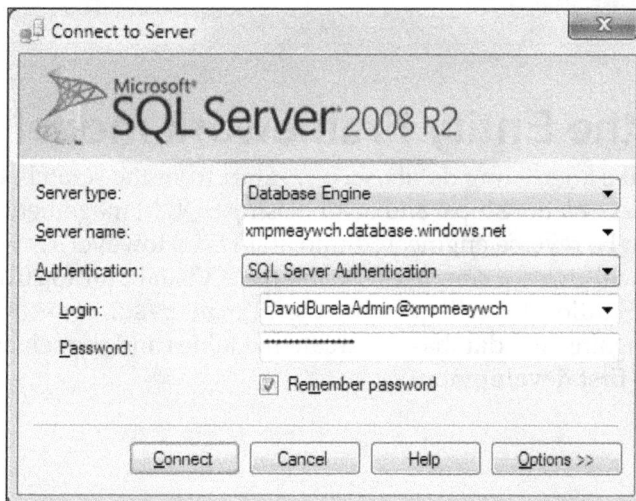

> **Unable to connect to the SQL Azure Server**
>
> If an error message indicates that you are unable to communicate with the server, there may be an issue with the firewall permissions. Log on to Windows Azure Management Portal, and verify that your current IP address has been granted the permission. If that also does not resolve your issue, check that your local firewall is not blocking the **port 1433**.

13. Once connected, you will be able to view all the databases on your SQL Azure Server. The following screenshot shows SQL Management Studio successfully connected:

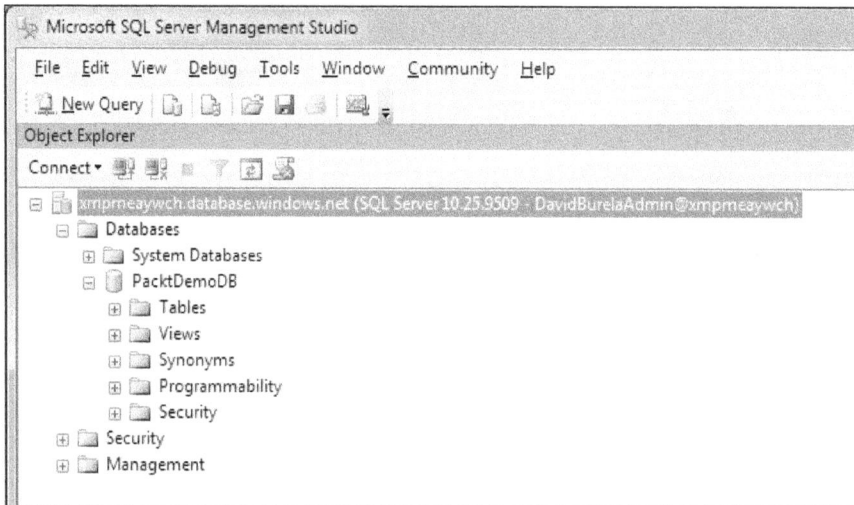

Creating the Entity Framework model

It is possible to take an existing database, or to start from the scratch, by creating all the database tables, relationships, and so on. Using SQL Management Studio, the database can then be reverse engineered into an EDM. However, as we are starting a new project, we will create a simple EDM and have Visual Studio 2010 generate the database. Visual Studio 2010 will generate the `Transact-SQL (T-SQL)` scripts which can be executed against the database to create the tables and the relationships. This is known as **model-first development**.

First, the Visual Studio 2010 solution needs to be created with the appropriate projects. We do this as follows:

1. In Visual Studio 2010, create a new **Windows Azure Project** named **SqlAzureExercise1** as shown in the following screenshot:

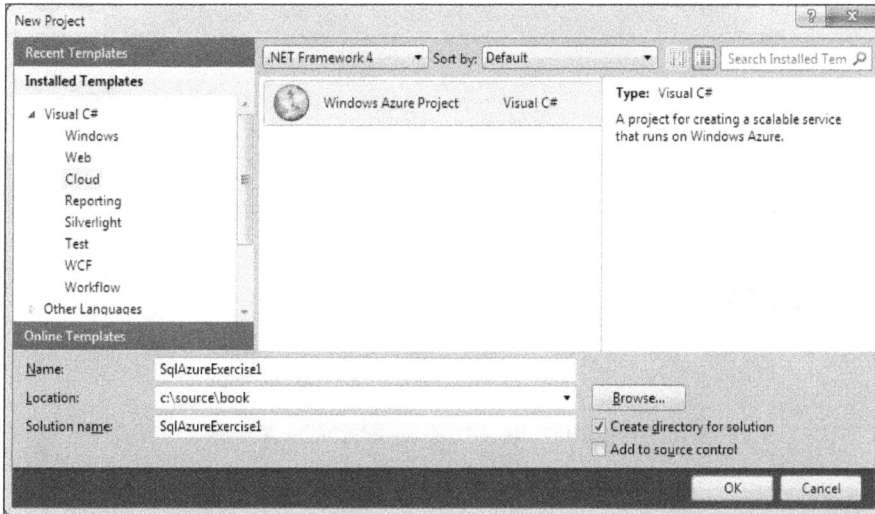

2. Add a **WCF Service Web Role** to the project. Rename the WCF role to **WcfServiceWebRole** as it has been done in the following screenshot. Click on **OK** to create the application:

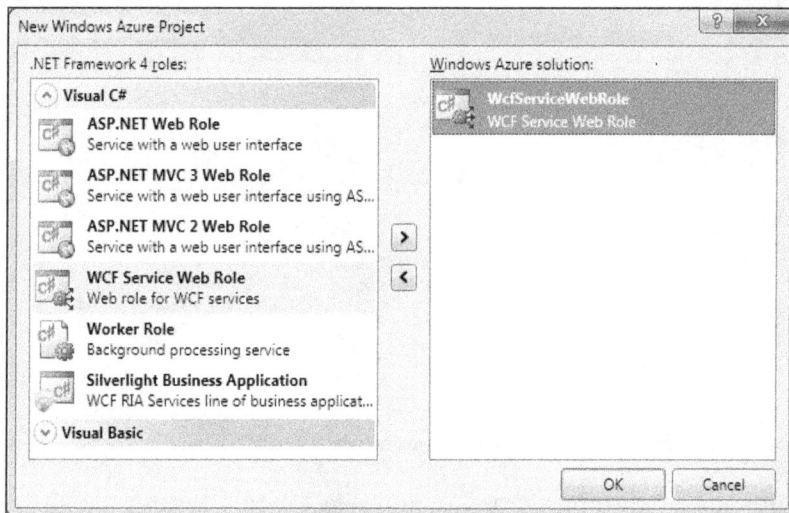

3. Right-click on the **WcfServiceWebRole** project and click on **Add | New Item**.

4. In the search box, search for **entity**. Create a new **ADO.Net Entity Data Model** and call it **WorkplaceModel.edmx** as shown in the following screenshot:

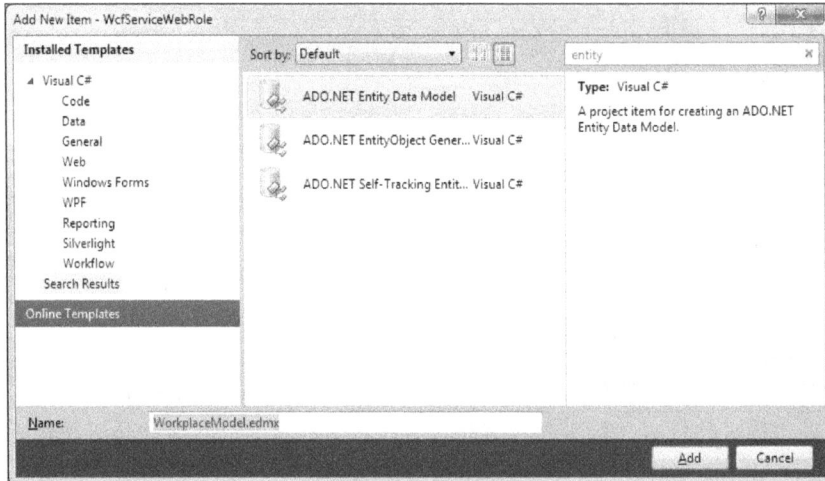

5. A wizard will pop up, allowing you to generate a model from an existing database (database first), or to start from an empty model (model-first). Select **Empty model** and click on **Finish** as shown in the following screenshot:

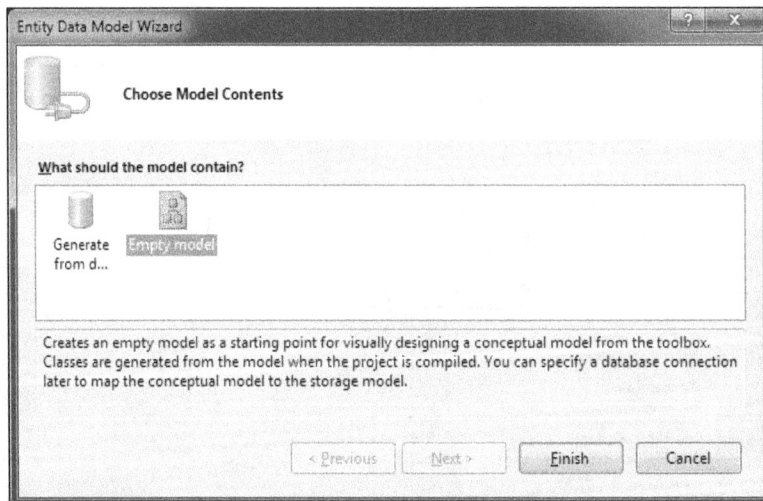

6. Right-click on the empty canvas, and select **Add | Entity...** as shown in the following screenshot:

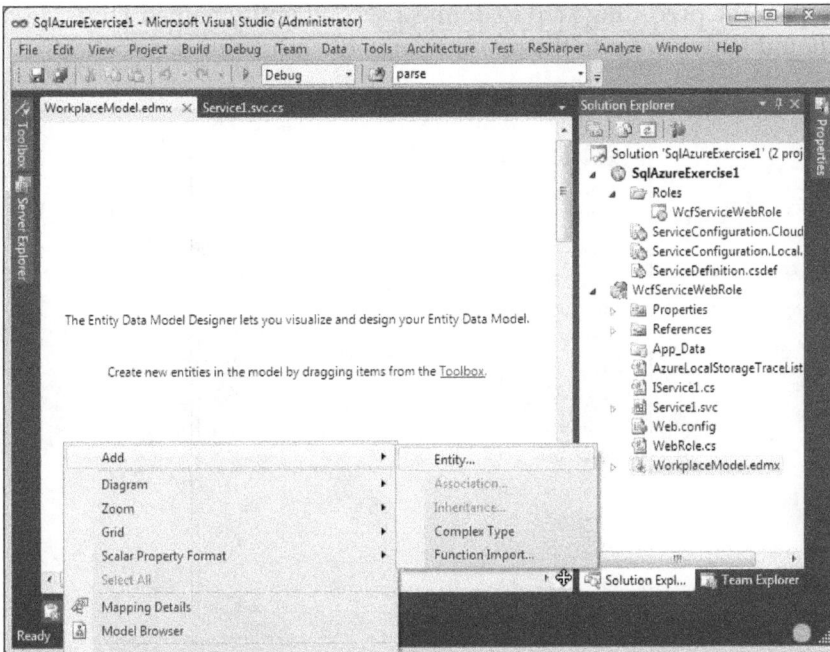

7. Define a new entity named **Employee**. The default values should be left as shown in the following screenshot. These will automatically create a primary key on the entity:

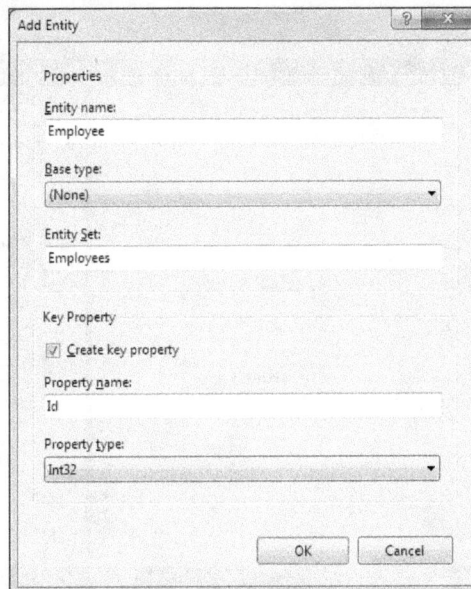

8. Repeat the preceding step to define a second entity named **Division**. It should look similar to the one shown in the following screenshot:

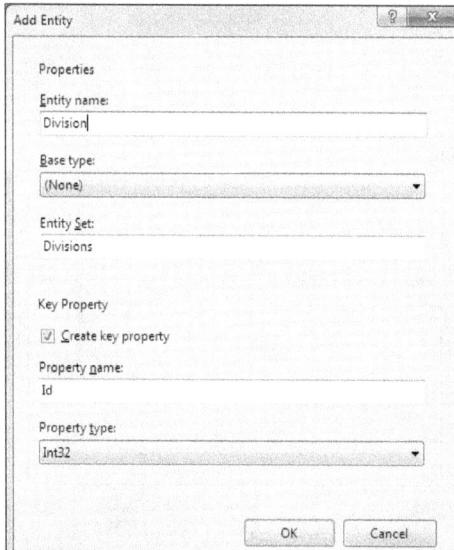

9. After the two entities have been created, the EDM canvas should look similar to the following screenshot:

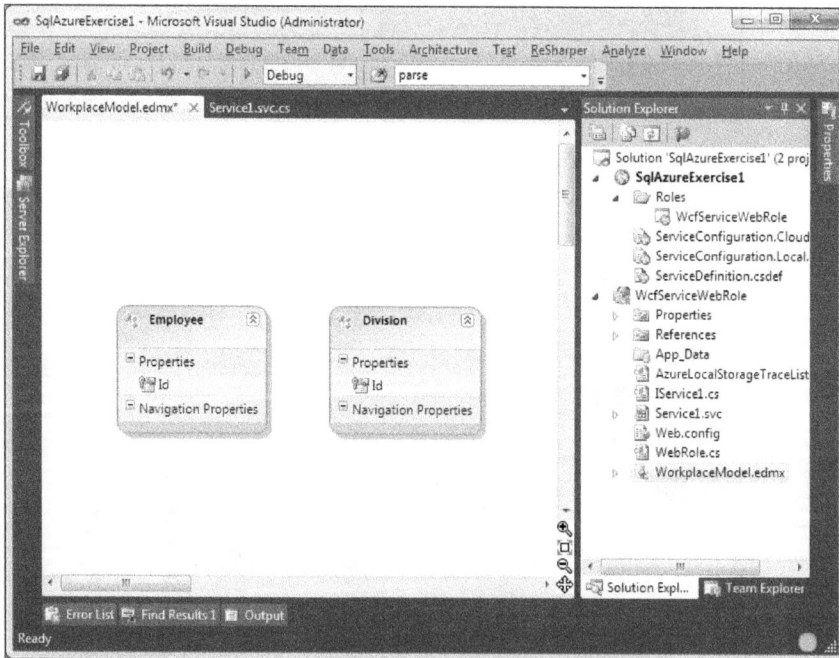

10. It is now time to add additional properties to each of the entities. To the `Employee` entity, right-click on the **Employee** entity, and add three new scalar properties: `Name`, `Position`, and `DateOfBirth`. Right-click on the `DateOfBirth` property, and select **properties**. Then, in the properties window, change the data type from **String** to **DateTime**. Leave the other two properties to their default type as **String**.

11. Add two new scalar properties to the **Division** entity: `Name` and `Description`. Leave them as the default **String** type.

12. There needs to be an association between `Employee` and `Division`. In SQL, this would require a foreign key and an association that enforces a referential integrity. This can be modeled easily in the EDM. Right-click on the **Division** entity and click on **Add Association**. The default settings should be correct. Set the **Multiplicity** of the **Employee** entity to * **(Many)**, so that it displays **Division can have * (Many) instances of Employee. Use Division. Employees to access the Employee instance** and set the **Multiplicity** of the **Division** entity to **1 (One)**, so that it displays **Employee can have 1 (One) instance of Division. Use Employee.Division to access the Division instance** at the bottom, as shown in the following screenshot. The checkbox **Add foreign key properties to the 'Employee' Entity** will automatically add a new foreign key property to be used in the referential integrity:

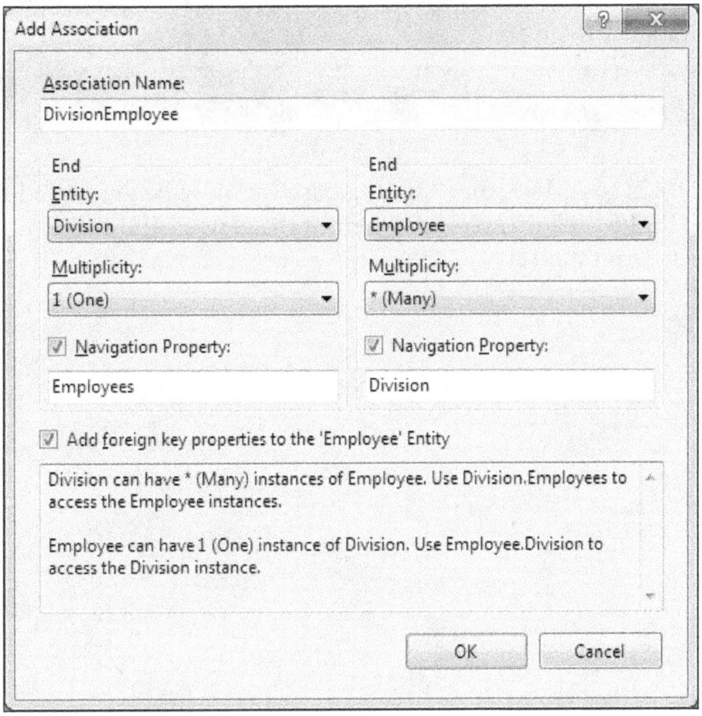

13. The final EDM should look similar to the following screenshot with two entities, that is, an association and a foreign key on the `Employee` entity. The **Navigation Properties** make it easy to access the **Division** child object from **Employee**, and also to access the **Employee** parent object from the **Division**:

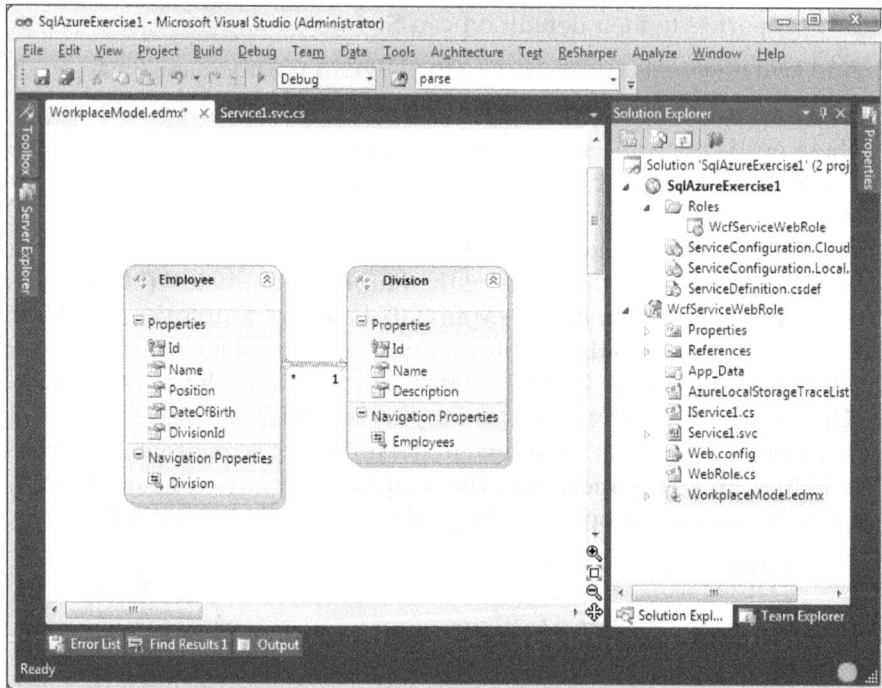

14. The EDM is complete, the SQL database can now be generated from this model. Right-click on an empty part of the canvas and select **Generate database from model**.

15. A pop up will be displayed, asking for the connection details of your SQL server. Enter the same details that were used to connect from within the SQL Management Studio. The result should look similar to the following screenshot:

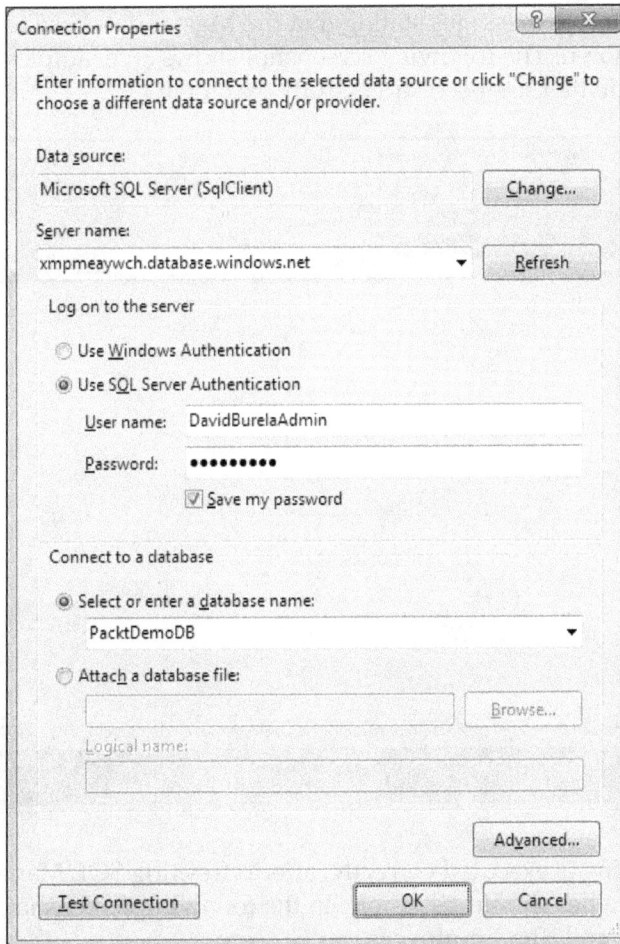

16. Click on the options to save everything within the web.config file and click on **Finish**. The T-SQL script will be generated, ready to be executed against your SQL Azure database.

17. From the Visual Studio 2010 designer, click on the **Execute SQL** button to run the script and create the appropriate tables, indexes, and referential integrity constraints. If a pop up dialog asks for the SQL connection details again, enter the same SQL Azure connection details. Be sure to change the database drop-down in Visual Studio 2010 to your database, that is, **PacktDemoDB**, otherwise error messages stating that the **Master database cannot be edited** may be shown. The following screenshot shows an example of the resulting T-SQL code that has been successfully executed:

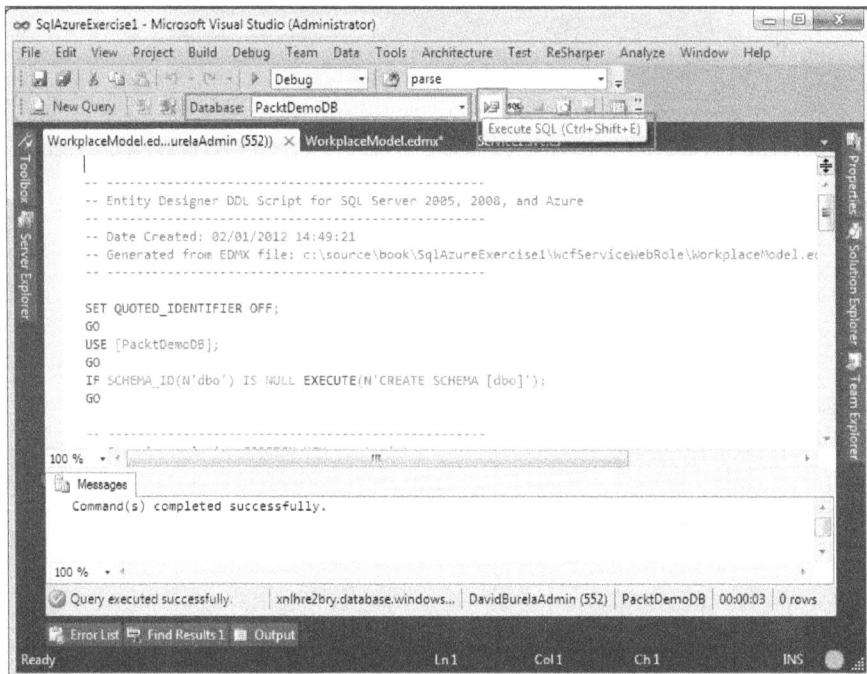

18. If everything is executed correctly, after refreshing SQL Management Studio, two new tables should be visible. In the following screenshot, the tables **dbo. Divisions** and **dbo.Employees** can be seen:

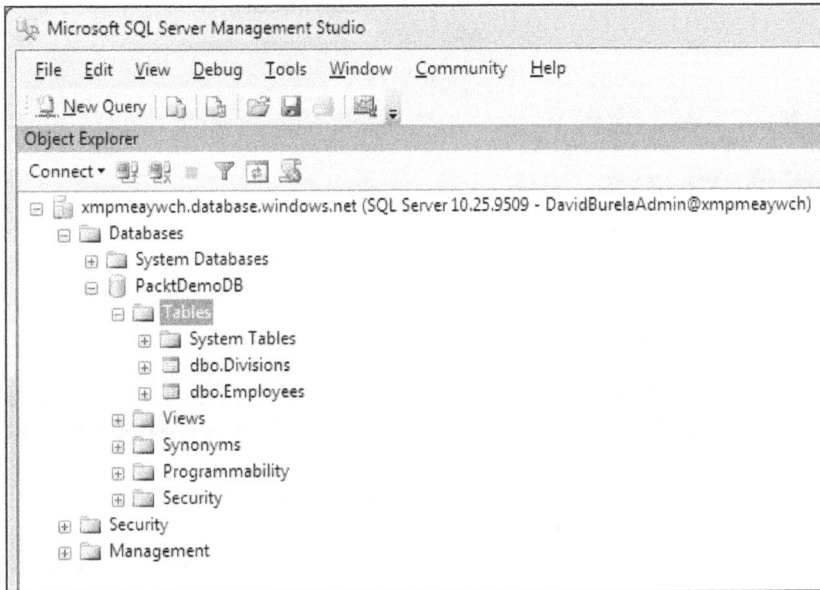

Database first development

If you have an existing database, you can select **Generate from database** and a new wizard will start. This will allow you to select which tables, views, and stored procedures should be imported into the EDM.

Creating the WCF service

The EDM and the supporting database objects in SQL Azure have been created and are ready to be used. A WCF service will now be defined to allow a Silverlight client to retrieve and create the entities. Four methods that will be defined in the service are `SelectEmployees`, `CreateEmployee`, `SelectDivisions`, and `CreateDivision`:

1. Open `IService1.svc`. Modify the code, so that it is similar to the following code snippet. Here, four methods are defined to select or create both employees and divisions:

```
using System.Collections.Generic;
using System.ServiceModel;
namespace WcfServiceWebRole
{
    [ServiceContract]
    public interface IService1
```

```
  {
    [OperationContract]
    List<Employee> GetEmployees();
    [OperationContract]
    List<Division> GetDivisions();
    [OperationContract]
    void CreateEmployee(Employee employee);
    [OperationContract]
    void CreateDivision(Division division);
  }
}
```

2. Open `Service1.svc`. Modify the class, so that the select methods are
   defined. In both the methods, first `entityContext` is created from the
   `WorkplaceModelContainer` class. This automatically reads the connection
   string from the `config` file, connects to the SQL Azure Server, thus making it
   ready for you to submit the commands. A LINQ query is then used to access
   the `Employees` table through the `entityContext`. Finally, the results are
   converted into a list that is returned back to the calling client:

```
using System.Collections.Generic;
using System.Linq;
namespace WcfServiceWebRole
{
  public class Service1 : IService1
  {
    public List<Employee> GetEmployees()
    {
      var entityContext = new WorkplaceModelContainer();
      var results = from e in entityContext.Employees
      select e;
      return results.ToList();
    }
    public List<Division> GetDivisions()
    {
      var entityContext = new WorkplaceModelContainer();
      var results = from d in entityContext.Divisions
      select d;
      return results.ToList();
    }
  }
}
```

3. Continue editing `Service1.svc` and add the two methods that allow the user to create new entities. Here, `entityContext` is created again. This time the `Employees` table is referenced, but instead of querying it, we attach a new object to the table. The object attached to the table is the new employee object that is passed from the client. When `SaveChanges` is called, Entity Framework will detect that a new object has been attached, and should be created in the database:

```
public void CreateEmployee(Employee employee)
{
  using (var entityContext = new WorkplaceModelContainer())
  {
    entityContext.Employees.AddObject(employee);
    entityContext.SaveChanges();
  }
}
public void CreateDivision(Division division)
{
  using (var entityContext = new WorkplaceModelContainer())
  {
    entityContext.Divisions.AddObject(division);
    entityContext.SaveChanges();
  }
}
```

Something that you may notice is the use of the `using` statements in the create methods, which were missing in the select methods. The `WorkplaceModelContainer` implements `IDisposable`, which means we can use the `using` statement to clean up things immediately when we realize that we are no longer going to use the database connection. This is fine when creating new objects, as we know definitely, when we are finished with the connection. The select methods behave differently. Although we have created `ToList` to hold the objects in a list, when WCF serializes the objects, it will automatically retrieve the child objects transpose, so reads from even the database. This causes the Entity Framework to try to access the database again which will result in an exception being thrown, as it has already been disposed off.

The garbage collector will automatically clean up the `WorkplaceModelContainer` when it is no longer used. Therefore, there is no requirement to use the `using` statement, but it can be cleaner to use it when you know there will be no side effects.

Creating the Silverlight application

A Silverlight application will now be created to consume WCF services. The first few steps should start to look familiar from the preceding exercises:

1. Add a new Silverlight project to the solution. Do this by right-clicking on the **WcfServiceWebRole** project and selecting **Properties**. Go to the **Silverlight Applications** tab, and then click on **Add**. Name the Silverlight application as **WorkplaceSilverlightProject**.

2. Right-click on **WorkplaceSilverlightProjectTestPage.aspx** in the web role, and select **Set as start page**.

3. Be sure to build the project to ensure that the WCF service has been compiled.

4. Right-click on the Silverlight project and click on **Add Service Reference**.

5. Click on **Discover**. Select **Service1.svc** and rename the service reference to **WorkplaceServiceReference** as shown in the following screenshot:

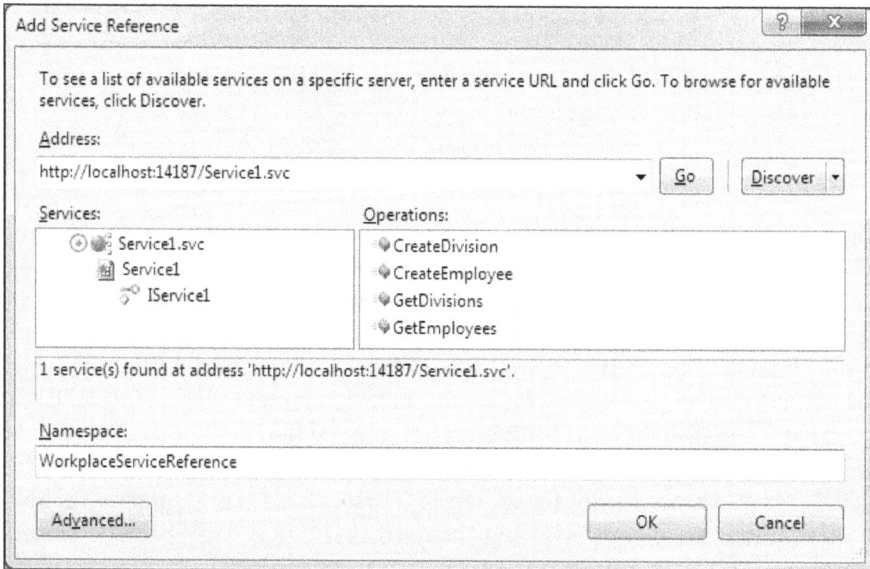

6. `TabControl` will be used in this exercise. This requires an additional reference. Right-click on **WorkplaceSilverlightProject**, and select **Add Reference**. Add a reference to `System.Windows.Controls`.

7. Open `MainPage.xaml`. The layout for the Silverlight application will be created now. The two tabs will be added to the screen: one to create `Employees`, and a second to create `Divisions` that the employee works in. Four templates will also be added, making them ready to be used later in different `ListBoxes`. There is much XAML code here, due to all the data needed to be visually formatted, which results in a lot of template code. After this step, the amount of code that needs to be written is much less:

```xml
<UserControl x:Class="SilverlightProject.MainPage"
xmlns:sdk="http://schemas.microsoft.com/winfx/2006/xaml/
presentation/
  sdk">
  <UserControl.Resources>
  <!--Mini division template to select which division an employee
    works in-->
    <DataTemplate x:Name="MiniDivisionItemTemplate" >
      <StackPanel Orientation="Horizontal">
        <TextBlock Text="{Binding Name}" FontWeight="Bold" />
        <TextBlock Text="{Binding Description}"
          Margin="10,0,0,0" />
      </StackPanel>
    </DataTemplate>
    <!--The full template used to display all Employees on
      the main screen-->
      <DataTemplate x:Name="EmployeeItemTemplate" >
        <StackPanel Orientation="Horizontal">
          <TextBlock Text="{Binding Name}" FontWeight="Bold" />
          <TextBlock Text="{Binding DateOfBirth,
          StringFormat='yyyy/mm/dd'}" Margin="10,0,10,0" />
          <TextBlock Text="{Binding Division.Name}"  />
        </StackPanel>
      </DataTemplate>
      <!--used as a sub template within the Division template, to
        show all employees that in that division-->
      <DataTemplate x:Name="MiniEmployeeItemTemplate" >
        <StackPanel Orientation="Horizontal">
          <TextBlock Text="{Binding Name}" FontWeight="Bold" />
          <TextBlock Text="{Binding Position}"
            Margin="10,0,10,0" />
        </StackPanel>
      </DataTemplate>
      <!--The full template used on the main page-->
      <DataTemplate x:Name="DivisionItemTemplate" >
        <StackPanel Orientation="Horizontal">
        <StackPanel Orientation="Horizontal">
```

```
            <TextBlock Text="{Binding Name}" FontWeight="Bold" />
            <TextBlock Text="{Binding Description}"
                Margin="10,0,10,0" />
          </StackPanel>
          <ListBox ItemsSource="{Binding Employees}"
          ItemTemplate="{StaticResource MiniEmployeeItemTemplate}" />
        </StackPanel>
      </DataTemplate>
   </UserControl.Resources>
   <!--The MainPage visual elements begin here here-->
   <Grid x:Name="LayoutRoot" Background="White" >
     <sdk:TabControl >
     <sdk:TabItem Header="Employees">
     <!-- employee code goes here -->
     </sdk:TabItem>
     <sdk:TabItem Header="Divisions">
     <!-- division code goes here -->
     </sdk:TabItem>
     </sdk:TabControl>
   </Grid>
</UserControl>
```

8. Add the employee tab by replacing the `<!-- employee code goes here -->` section with the following code. The employee tab is defined as the one having two columns and two rows, resulting in four quadrants. The upper-left corner is dedicated to the details entered to create a new employee. There are textboxes to accept input for `employeeName` and `employeePosition`. A `Calendar` control is also placed to select the date of birth. The last control in this corner is the create button. It will invoke the event handler which will result in the creation of an employee. The upper-right corner has a simple `ListBox` that allows the user to select the division that the new employee being created is associated with. The lower half of the screen has a `ListBox` that displays all the existing employees. It has `ItemTemplate` applied to it that defines how to display the data of the employee:

```
<Grid >
  <Grid.ColumnDefinitions>
    <ColumnDefinition Width="*" />
    <ColumnDefinition Width="*" />
  </Grid.ColumnDefinitions>
  <Grid.RowDefinitions>
    <RowDefinition Height="auto" />
    <RowDefinition Height="*" />
  </Grid.RowDefinitions>
```

```xml
<!--Section to create a new Employee-->
<StackPanel Grid.Row="0" Grid.Column="0">
  <TextBlock Text="Name" />
  <TextBox x:Name="employeeName" />
  <TextBlock Text="Position" />
  <TextBox x:Name="employeePosition" />
  <TextBlock Text="Date of birth" />
  <sdk:Calendar x:Name="employeeDob" />
  <Button Content="Create Employee"
    Click="CreateEmployeeButtonClick" />
</StackPanel>
<!--Selection box to select the divison the employee currently
  works in-->
<StackPanel Grid.Row="0" Grid.Column="1" >
  <TextBlock Text="Divisions" />
  <ListBox x:Name="divisionSelect" ItemsSource="{Binding
    Divisions}" ItemTemplate="{StaticResource
      MiniDivisionItemTemplate}" />
</StackPanel>
<!--Listbox to display all the employees-->
<ListBox Grid.Row="1" Grid.ColumnSpan="2" BorderBrush="Black"
  BorderThickness="4" ItemsSource="{Binding Employees}"
    ItemTemplate="{StaticResource EmployeeItemTemplate}" />
</Grid>
```

9. Add the division tab by replacing the `<!-- division code goes here -->` section with the following code. The division tab is defined as the one having two rows. The top half of the screen is dedicated to the creation of a new division and has two textboxes that accept `divisionName` and `divisionDescription`. The bottom half of the screen has a `ListBox` that displays all of the current divisions:

```xml
<Grid>
  <Grid.RowDefinitions>
    <RowDefinition Height="auto" />
    <RowDefinition Height="*" />
  </Grid.RowDefinitions>
  <!--Section to create a new Division-->
  <StackPanel>
    <TextBlock Text="Name" />
    <TextBox x:Name="divisionName" />
    <TextBlock Text="Description" />
    <TextBox x:Name="divisionDescription" />
    <Button Content="Create Division"
      Click="CreateDivisionButtonClick" />
```

```
    </StackPanel>
    <!--Listbox to display all the divisions. The ItemTemplate also
      formats the display so that employees working in each Division
      are shown-->
    <ListBox Grid.Row="1" ItemsSource="{Binding Divisions}"
      ItemTemplate="{StaticResource DivisionItemTemplate}" />
  </Grid>
```

10. Open the `MainPage.xaml.cs` code behind the file. Modify it, so that the class has two public properties: one to hold the employees and the other to hold the divisions that are available for use. The same helper method that has been used in the preceding few chapters is again used here. This helps to construct the WCF proxy that works both locally and when deployed onto an Azure server. The constructor should be changed, so that it sets `DataContext` of the page to be itself, allowing the data binding of the page to public properties. The constructor then initializes public properties and calls the two methods that load all employees and divisions:

```csharp
using System;
using System.Collections.ObjectModel;
using System.Linq;
using System.Windows;
using System.Windows.Controls;
using WorkplaceSilverlightProject.WorkplaceServiceReference;
namespace WorkplaceSilverlightProject
{
  public partial class MainPage : UserControl
  {
    public ObservableCollection<Employee> Employees { get; set; }
    public ObservableCollection<Division> Divisions { get; set; }
    private static Service1Client CreateServiceProxy()
    {
     // This is the same code from chapter 3. To allow this code
        to work locally and in production.
     // Find the url for the current silverlight .xap file. Go up
        one level to get to the root of the site.
      var url = Application.Current.Host.Source.OriginalString;
      var urlBase = url.Substring(0, url.IndexOf("/ClientBin",
        StringComparison.InvariantCultureIgnoreCase));
      // Create a proxy object for the WCF service. Use the root
          path of the site and append the service name
      var proxy = new Service1Client();
      proxy.Endpoint.Address = new
        System.ServiceModel.EndpointAddress(urlBase +
          "/Service1.svc");
```

```
          return proxy;
      }
      public MainPage()
      {
          InitializeComponent();
          this.DataContext = this;
          Employees = new ObservableCollection<Employee>();
          Divisions = new ObservableCollection<Division>();
          LoadDivisions();
          LoadEmployees();
      }
  }
}
```

11. Implement `LoadDivisions` and `LoadEmployees` methods. Both these methods follow the same pattern. First, the public property is cleared of all the existing data within it. Then, the WCF proxy is initialized through the helper method. When the WCF service returns the data, the callback will loop through each of the items and add it to the main page public property lists. Finally, the WCF method is invoked asynchronously:

```
private void LoadDivisions()
{
  Divisions.Clear();
  var proxy = CreateServiceProxy();
  proxy.GetDivisionsCompleted += (sender, e) =>
  {
    e.Result.ToList().ForEach(p => Divisions.Add(p));
  };
  proxy.GetDivisionsAsync();
}
private void LoadEmployees()
{
  Employees.Clear();
  var proxy = CreateServiceProxy();
  proxy.GetEmployeesCompleted += (sender, e) =>
  {
    e.Result.ToList().ForEach(p => Employees.Add(p));
  };
  proxy.GetEmployeesAsync();
}
```

12. Add the event handler for the `Createdivision` button. This method creates a new division object and sets the properties of the same using the values in the textboxes. Once the object has been created, it is submitted to the WCF service asynchronously. A callback method is added to the completed event to reload the divisions. This will refresh the data on the screen:

```
private void CreateDivisionButtonClick
    (object sender, RoutedEventArgse)
{
  var department = new Division();
  department.Name = divisionName.Text;
  department.Description = divisionDescription.Text;
  var proxy = CreateServiceProxy();
  proxy.CreateDivisionCompleted += (sender2, e2) =>
  {
    LoadDivisions();
  };
  proxy.CreateDivisionAsync(department);
}
```

13. Add the event handler for the `CreateEmployee` button. This method creates a new employee object and sets the properties of the same using the values in the textboxes. The calendar control is checked to ensure that a valid selection has been made, and defaults the value to the current date. Once the object has been created, it is submitted to the WCF service asynchronously. A callback method is added to the completed event to reload the employee data and also the divisions. The divisions are reloaded as there might be a new employee registered against it recently:

```
private void CreateEmployeeButtonClick
    (object sender, RoutedEventArgse)
{
  var employee = new Employee();
  employee.Name = employeeName.Text;
  employee.Position = employeePosition.Text;
  employee.DateOfBirth = employeeDob.SelectedDate ?? DateTime.Now;
  // default to today's date if none is selected
  // Check that a valid Department has been selected
  var selectedDepartment = divisionSelect.SelectedItem as
    Division;
  if (selectedDepartment != null)
  employee.DivisionId = selectedDepartment.Id;
  var proxy = CreateServiceProxy();
  proxy.CreateEmployeeCompleted += (sender2, e2) =>
  {
```

```
    // Reload all the data, as there may be new relationships
    LoadEmployees();
    LoadDivisions();
  };
  proxy.CreateEmployeeAsync(employee);
}
```

14. Press *F5* to compile and run the application.

15. Navigate to the **Division** tab and create a few divisions.

16. Navigate to the **Employee** tab, enter the employee details, select a division, and then click on the **Create Employee** button.

17. After creating a few divisions and employees, the **Employees** tab should look similar to the one shown in the following screenshot:

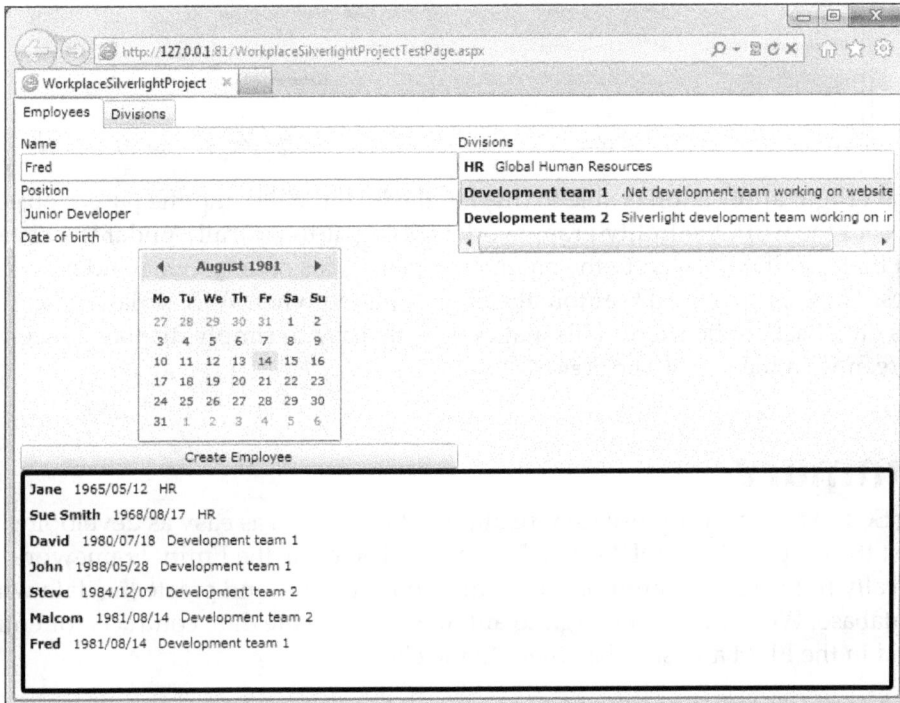

18. The **Divisions** tab should look similar to the one shown in the following screenshot:

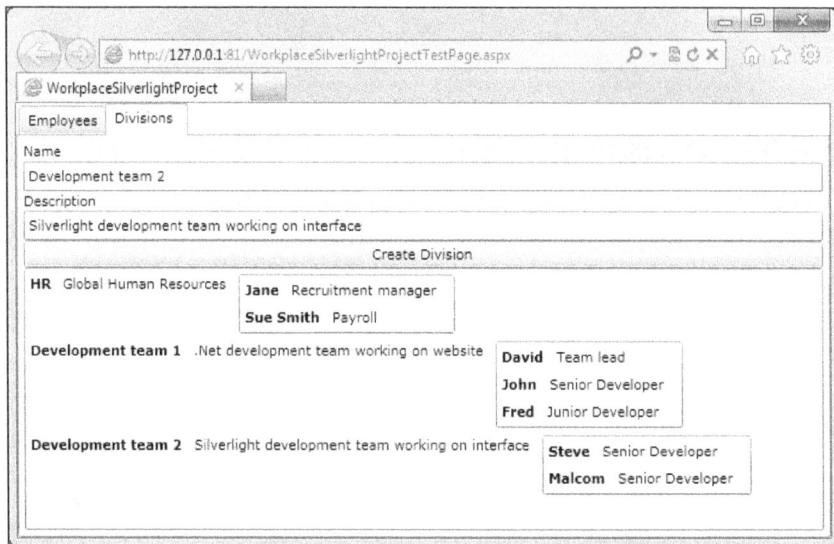

The Silverlight application is able to display the linked child and the parent objects because of the work the Entity Framework is doing automatically under the covers. Recall that the EDM placed to the navigation properties on `Employee` and `Division` entities. These properties are automatically populated when WCF serializes and passes data back to the client. This makes it really easy to simply display data on the screen with the use of `ItemTemplates`.

Summary

Using SQL Azure as a cloud-based, relational data store is as easy as developing against the on-premises SQL Server. Using a tool, such as the Entity Framework, can drastically reduce the amount of code required to retrieve and create the data within the database. WCF is smart enough to automatically create data contracts for entities defined in the EDM and serialize them to the client.

These basics of interacting with SQL Azure can be taken further in your own applications with multi-relational tables.

The Entity Framework model that was created here can be used to expose the data to clients through **RIA Services** or **OData**. These topics will be covered in *Chapter 8, RIA Services and SQL Azure* and *Chapter 9, Exposing OData to Silverlight Applications*.

The next chapter will continue to use SQL Azure and Entity Framework, but this time it will use RIA Services to share data rather than a standard WCF Service.

8
RIA Services and SQL Azure

The previous chapter on using SQL Azure with WCF services involved a lot of code being handwritten. Methods to expose each data type (Employee and Division) needed to be created, as well as the individual methods to allow the client to create new entities. The WCF methods also did not make it easy to query a subset of data.

RIA Services helps developers to be more productive by simplifying data access between the server and client. This chapter will explore the following topics:

- RIA Services
- Using Silverlight with RIA Services, SQL Azure, and Entity Framework

RIA Services

RIA Services is a framework that simplifies the process of building enterprise applications on the Silverlight platform. It makes it easy for a Silverlight client to query data on a server (from a database or other data store) and for the client to create, edit, and delete the data. RIA Services also provides additional features such as allowing validation rules to be defined that are run at both server side and client side.

RIA Services is composed of a few components:

- **Entities** that are to be shared between server and client (in this chapter, these will be generated automatically by Entity Framework)
- **Entity metadata** allows additional validation rules to be attached to entities and also specifies which data should be serialized
- **Domain service** exposes methods that the client can invoke to query data or to submit changes to entities (create, edit, or delete)

This chapter will use SQL Azure as the source of data as it is the typical scenario seen in enterprise software. Other backing stores can be used such as Azure Table storage.

More details on RIA Services is available at the following URL:

`http://www.silverlight.net/getstarted/riaservices/`

Architecture

Under the covers, RIA Services is simply a WCF service with additional compile-time features. These compile-time features simplify the consumption of the service by generating client-side code for the client application to use. This client-side code allows the Silverlight application to work with the domain service as a local class with `invokable` methods.

Whenever the server code is updated (for example, with changes to the structure of the entities, the entity validation, or to the domain service methods), the generated Silverlight code is automatically updated. This has a significant impact on the developer's productivity. Developing against a traditional WCF method can lead to mismatches between the server-side method and the generated proxy classes if a developer forgets to update the service reference.

The following diagram shows how RIA Services compares to traditional "3-tier" architecture. The traditional architecture diagram has many defined components on both the server side and client side. Notice how some of the components are duplicated between the server and client code (model definitions, validation code, and so on). The RIA Services diagram shows that there is a lot of code reuse between the server and client side.

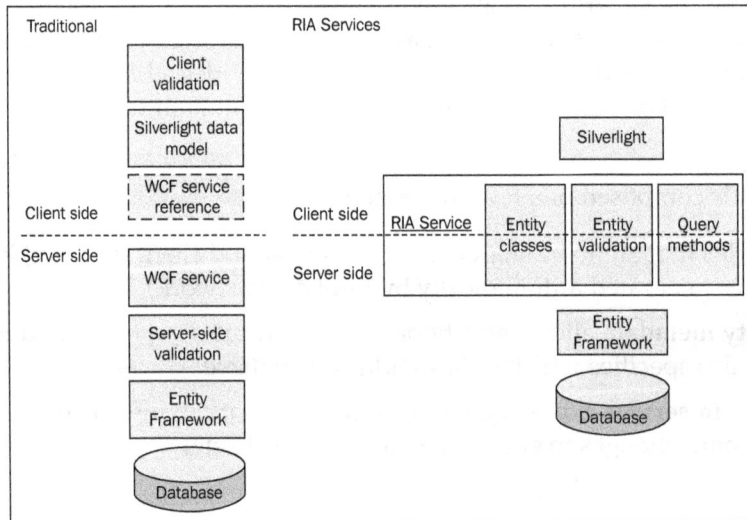

As RIA Services is still WCF under the covers, the services can also be consumed by other applications. For example, there are additional RIA Services components that can further expose the RIA Service endpoint as a SOAP or JSON friendly endpoint.

Querying a domain service

The server-side operations appear as invokable client-side operations. These operations are exposed as IQueryable results; this is what provides RIA Services with its flexibility.

In the previous chapter on SQL Azure and WCF Services, the query that defined what data should be returned to the client was hard coded in the WCF method. There were only a certain number of predefined data sets that could be returned. If the client wanted to perform any advanced operations, such as ordering the data, providing additional query filters, or page over large datasets, then it would involve a lot of additional code. Another solution is to send many redundant data over the wire to the Silverlight client and have the client perform the filtering and paging in memory. Sending redundant data to the client is inefficient and also a potential security risk.

A sample scenario involves a Silverlight screen that has a DataGrid. The DataGrid is used to display the results from an RIA Service method that returns 800 rows of employee data. The Silverlight client wants to filter the results, so that only employees with the surname "Smith" are returned. The DataGrid should also only show 20 results at a time, so as not to overwhelm the user. Naively, the server could simply transmit all 800 results, then have the client filter it down to 60 rows that contain the surname "Smith", and then let the grid page over the 60 results in memory.

RIA Services overcomes this problem of querying data through an exposed IQueryable method. The Silverlight client can define additional query conditions that are executed at the server side. The conditions `WHERE surname == "smith"` and `bring 20 rows of results for the first page of data` can be sent to the domain service. The domain service appends these additional conditions to the LINQ query defined in the domain service query. As LINQ has a deferred execution model, all of the conditions are combined and LINQ submits a single optimized SQL query to the database that includes all of the client and server-side conditions.

Tracking changes

The domain context class keeps track of entities when they are sent to the client. Whenever an entity is modified, deleted, or added to the collection, the domain context keeps track of this. When the client has finished modifying the entity collection, a single call to `.SubmitChanges()` will push the change set back to the server.

There is no need to manually call an `update` or an `insert` method as was required in the SQL Azure and WCF service chapter. Instead, the `update` and `insert` methods are automatically called.

RIA Services toolkit

The RIA Services toolkit provides additional classes and tools that help to create RIA Services applications. The core RIA Services framework is considered stable and has a slow release cycle. The toolkit is refreshed more frequently and has additional experimental features that may not be completely set in stone yet.

Examples of additional features in the toolkit are as follows:

- Improved MVVM support through the use of the `CollectionView` class
- T4 template code generation support
- ASP.Net `DomainDataSource`
- Ability to expose a SOAP or a JSON endpoint
- Azure Table storage support
- A jQuery client

It is very useful to keep yourself informed of what new features become available in each refresh of the toolkit.

Using Silverlight with RIA Services, SQL Azure, and Entity Framework

This exercise will demonstrate how simple it can be to build enterprise Silverlight applications that are built on top of RIA Services. The data will come from an SQL Azure database that was created in the previous chapter. Different features of RIA Services will be demonstrated in this exercise, such as the ease of sending data to the Silverlight client, filtering, paging, and data validation.

Configuring SQL Azure

This chapter assumes that your SQL Azure instance has been set up already from the previous chapter. The SQL Azure server, database, and firewall rules should all be configured already. It also assumes that `PacktDemoDB` has been created, and contains two tables: `Division` and `Employee`.

If this has not been done, please follow the instructions in *Chapter 7, Relational Data with SQL Azure and Entity Framework*. Follow the steps to configure the SQL Azure Server, create the Entity Framework model, generate the SQL script to create the database tables, and run the script against your SQL Azure database. Once that has been completed, close the Visual Studio solution and continue with the rest of this exercise.

Entities

In the previous chapter, we created the EDM (Entity Data Model) with a **model-first** approach. In this chapter, there is no need to recreate the model from scratch. Instead, the tables in the existing database will be reverse engineered to explore **database first** development. We do this as follows:

1. In Visual Studio 2010, create a new **Windows Azure Project** named **RiaServiceExercise1**, as shown in the following screenshot:

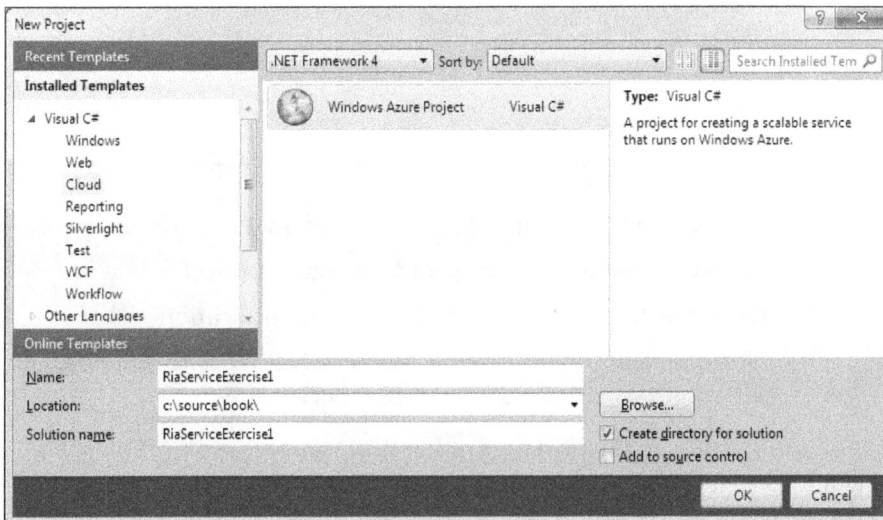

2. Instead of adding web or worker roles, a different project type will be added. Add a **Silverlight Business Application** into the project. Rename the role to **WorkplaceApplication**, as shown in the following screenshot, and click on **OK** to create the application:

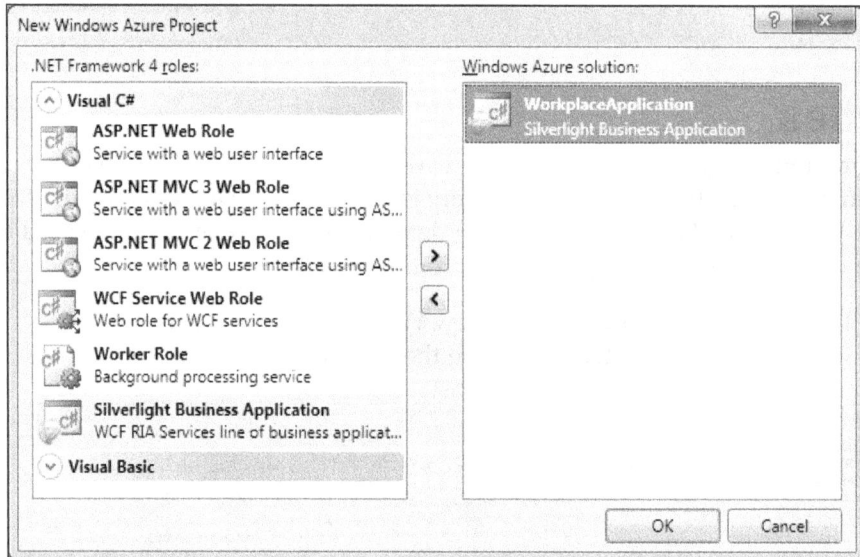

3. Once Visual Studio has created the solution, you will see three projects:

   ○ **RiaServiceExercise1**: The standard Azure project

   ○ **WorkplaceApplication**: The Silverlight application

   ○ **WorkplaceApplication.Web**: An ASP.Net website that hosts the Silverlight .xap file, as well as RIA Services

4. Inside the ASP.Net **WorkplaceApplication.Web** project, right-click on the **Models** folder, and click on **Add | New Item**.

5. In the search box, search for **entity**. Create a new **ADO.Net Entity Data Model** and name it **WorkplaceModel.edmx**, as shown in the following screenshot:

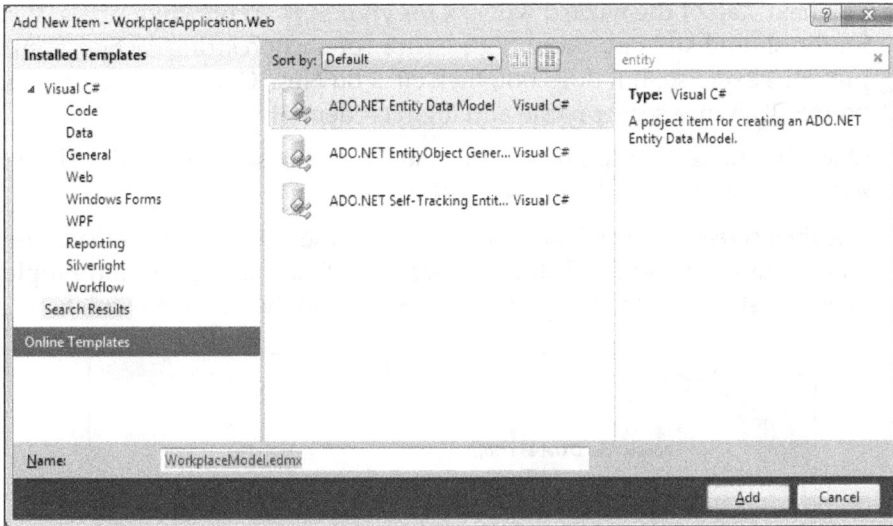

6. A wizard will open, allowing you to reverse engineer an existing database (database first), or to start from an empty model (model-first). This time, select **Generate from database**, and click on **Next** as shown in the following screenshot:

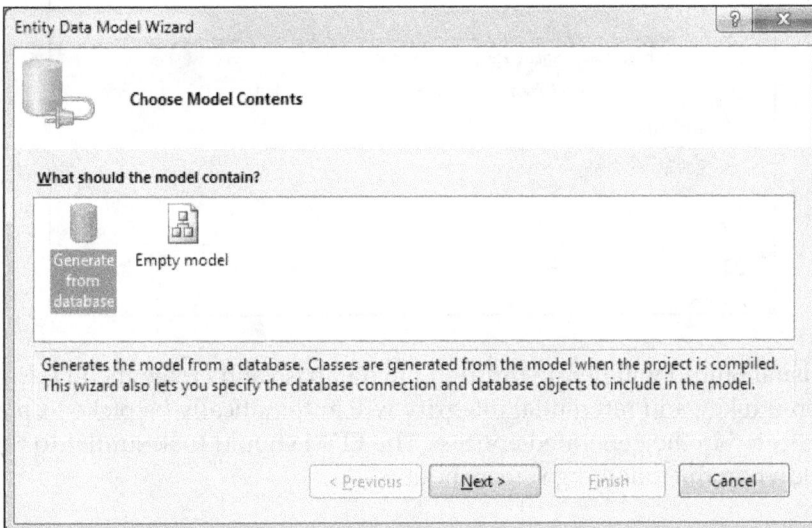

7. The next step of the wizard will ask for your SQL Azure credentials. Visual Studio should still have your SQL Azure connection string cached from the previous exercise. If it does not, then click on **New Connection** and enter your SQL Azure server name and login credentials.

8. Once the connection has been confirmed, select to save all the details in the Web.config file, and then click on **Next**.

9. The final screen of the wizard will connect to the SQL Azure database and scan for tables, views, and stored procedures. Select **Divisions** and **Employees** tables, as shown in the following screenshot, and then click on **Finish**:

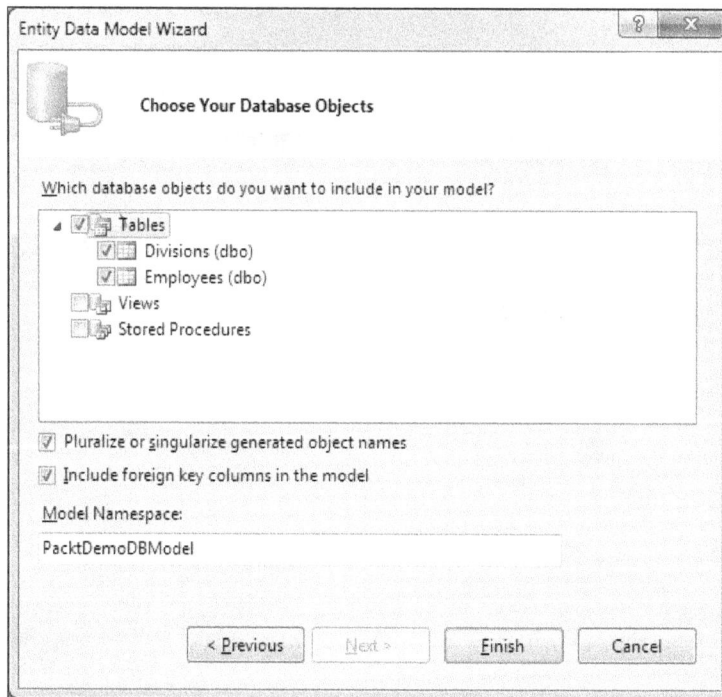

10. Visual Studio will iterate through the database and create the EDM. The foreign key and referential integrity will automatically be picked up and reflected in the generated entities. The EDM should look similar to the one shown in the following screenshot:

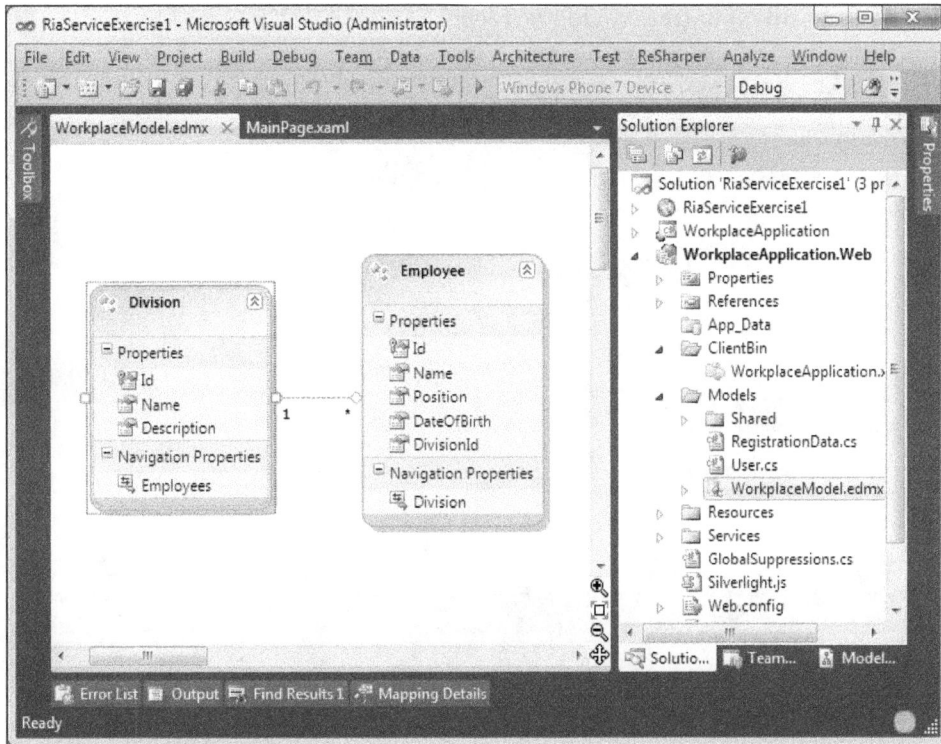

Domain service

With the entity model created, they can now be exposed to the Silverlight client through a **domain service**. In this example, we will autogenerate a basic domain service based on the EDM. We do this as follows:

1. Build the project to ensure that the EDM has been compiled.

2. Inside the **WorkplaceApplication.Web** project, right-click on the **Services** folder, and click on **Add | New Item**.

3. In the **Add New Item** dialog box, click in the search box and type
    domain. Select **Domain Service Class**, and name the new item
    WorkplaceDomainService.cs, as shown in the following screenshot:

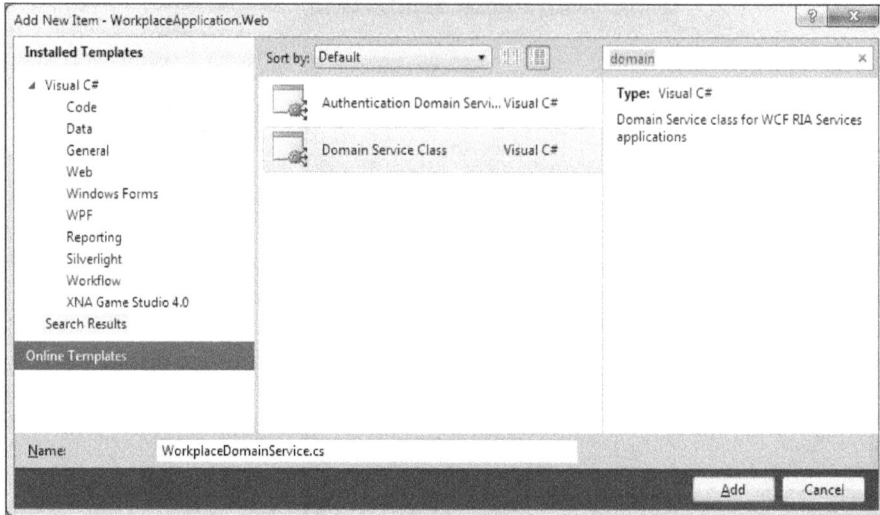

4. In the drop-down menu, select your entity model.

> **Why aren't my entities appearing in the drop down?**
>
> If your entity model is not appearing in the drop down of
> available DataContext classes, then you may not have built
> your project recently. After adding a new entity model, you
> need to build the project, so that the entities are generated.

5. Click on the checkboxes next to **Division** and **Employee**. This indicates to
    the domain service code generator that it should expose this entity to the
    Silverlight client. The Silverlight client will be able to query, filter, and select
    these entities. Click on the checkboxes that say **Enable editing**. This instructs
    the code generator to generate the methods that will allow the Silverlight
    client to create, update, and delete the entities. The final selections should
    look similar to the one shown in the following screenshot. When it does,
    click on **OK**:

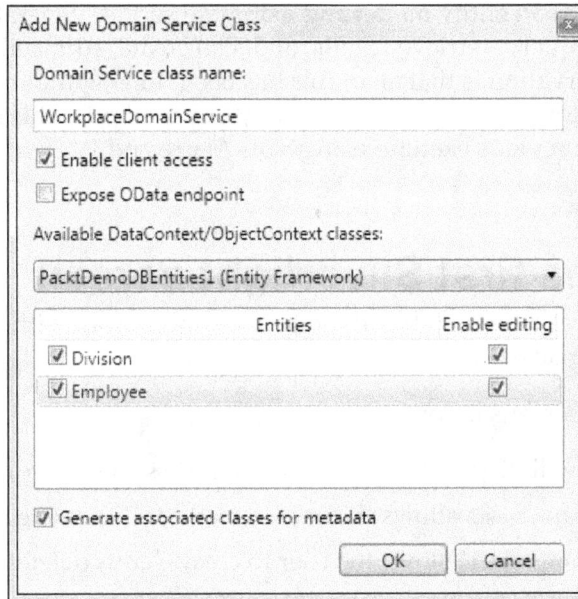

6. The code generator will create a basic `WorkplaceDomainService` class. It will have a number of methods defined that allow the Silverlight client to interact with the entities in meaningful ways. There will be `Get`, `Insert`, `Update`, and `Delete` methods for `Employee` and `Division`. The `GetDivisions` and `GetEmployees` methods will simply return all rows in those tables. It is possible to create other `get` methods that return a specific subset of data.

7. In the `WorkplaceDomainService.cs` file, add the following method. The method will return all divisions where there are more than two employees. It uses a LINQ query to select a subset of the `Divisions` table and returns the results. It is important to notice that the method is returning the results as `IQueryable` and not `IEnumerable`. This allows the Silverlight client to apply its own additional criteria (such as the name of the division) and have the server pass those criteria to the SQL Azure Server when it does the selection:

```
public IQueryable<Division> GetDivisionsWithMultipleEmployees()
{
  var results = from d in ObjectContext.Divisions
  where d.Employees.Count>= 2
  select d;
  return results;
}
```

The solution now has an entity model and a domain service generated, ready for the Silverlight client to query, retrieve results, and also create, edit, and delete entities. An interesting observation is that all of this has been done without writing a line of code so far (except for the additional GetDivisions method). This is a lot quicker to bootstrap than the previous exercise using SQL Azure and WCF methods to expose the data.

Creating the first Silverlight screen

With the RIA service created and ready to be consumed from within Silverlight, the first screen can be created.

There will be three screens in total:

- Home.xaml will display Divisions with the associated Employees
- DivisionPage.xaml allows the user to create/edit/delete Divisions
- EmployeePage.xaml allows the user to create/edit/delete Employees

The first screen that will be created is DivisionPage.xaml, so that there is a way to create the initial data. This screen will access data through the RIA Service by manually creating a context and querying it for data. Subsequent screens in this exercise will use more automated ways of accessing data:

1. Right-click on the **WorkplaceApplication** project and click on **Add reference**. Add a reference to System.Windows.Controls.Data. This will be required later for DataGrid.

2. Inside the **WorkplaceApplication** project, open MainPage.xaml. The controls to navigate around the application will be added to the menu bar of the Silverlight application.

3. Inside the Border element named LinksBorder, you will find HyperlinkButton that is in the menu bar. Underneath the Link1 hyperlink, enter the following code. The code will add two new links to the pages that will be created later:

```
<HyperlinkButton Style="{StaticResourceLinkStyle}"
  NavigateUri="/DivisionPage" Content="Division"
  TargetName="ContentFrame" />

<HyperlinkButton Style="{StaticResourceLinkStyle}"
  NavigateUri="/EmployeePage" Content="Employee"
  TargetName="ContentFrame" />
```

4. Inside the **WorkplaceApplication** project, right-click on the **Views** folder and click on **Add | New Item**. Add a new Silverlight page named `DivisionPage.xaml`.

5. Edit `DivisionPage.xaml`, so that it has a `DataGrid`, `DataForm`, and a `submit Button`. The `DataGrid` binds to the `DomainContext` object and displays the `Divisions` collection (the `DomainContext` will be created in the next step). The `DataForm` binds to the `Division` collection and uses a binding to the `DataGrid's` selected item to displays the current selection. `DataForm` allows the user to create/edit/delete Division objects. Finally, the `submit changes button` will have `DomainContext` to submit the changes back to the database:

```
<navigation:Page …
xmlns:controls="clr-namespace:System.Windows.
Controls;assembly=System.Windows.Controls.Data"
xmlns:toolkit="clr-namespace:System.Windows.
Controls;assembly=System.Windows.Controls.Data.DataForm.Toolkit">

  <ScrollViewer x:Name="LayoutRoot">
    <StackPanel>
      <controls:DataGrid x:Name="divisionGrid"
        ItemsSource="{Binding DomainContext.Divisions}"
        Height="200" />
      <toolkit:DataForm x:Name="divisionDataForm"
        ItemsSource="{Binding Path=DomainContext.Divisions}"
        CurrentItem="{Binding Path=SelectedItem,
        ElementName=divisionGrid, Mode=TwoWay}" />
      <Button Content="Submit changes" Click="SubmitButtonClick"/>
    </StackPanel>
  </ScrollViewer>
</navigation:Page>
```

6. Open the code behind the file `DivisionPage.xaml.cs` and modify the code as shown in the following code snippet. First, there is a `public` property `DomainContext` that exposes `WorkplaceDomainContext` to the XAML bindings. This object is what allows the code to query the data, and also tracks changes done to the entity collection (creation, edits, and deletes) and submits the change set back to the RIA service. Next, the constructor initializes the `DomainContext` property and sets the binding of the screen to be itself. The `OnNavigatedTo` method populates the `WorkplaceDomainContext` collections with the data returned from a query. First, the query is defined by selecting the appropriate query object from `DomainContext` (the `GetDivisionsWithMultipleEmployeesQuery` could have been selected as an alternative). With a handle to the query, additional conditions can be added by LINQ commands, such as `where` and `OrderBy`.

Finally, the SubmitButtonClick method ends any edits that may still be pending, and then gets DomainContext to submit all changes that have been made (create/edit/delete):

```
using System.Windows;
using System.Windows.Controls;
using System.Windows.Navigation;
using WorkplaceApplication.Web.Services;

namespace WorkplaceApplication.Views
{
  public partial class DivisionPage : Page
  {
    public WorkplaceDomainContextDomainContext { get; set; }

    public DivisionPage()
    {
      InitializeComponent();
      DomainContext = new WorkplaceDomainContext();

      // set the DataContext of DivisionPage.xaml to be itself
      this.DataContext = this;
    }

    // Executes when the user navigates to this page.
    protected override void OnNavigatedTo(NavigationEventArgs e)
    {
      var query = DomainContext.GetDivisionsQuery();
      DomainContext.Load(query);
    }

    private void SubmitButtonClick(object sender,
      RoutedEventArgs e)
    {
      // exit out of edit mode.
      divisionDataForm.CommitEdit();
      DomainContext.SubmitChanges();
    }

  }
}
```

7. Press *F5* to compile and run the application. Navigate to the **Division** page. If you are using the same database from the last exercise, you may see the data being displayed now. Click on the **+** button in the data form to create new Division entities. After creating a few, press the **Submit** button to submit all the changes back to the RIA Service which will add them to the SQL Azure database. After adding a few, the screen should look similar to the one shown in the following screenshot:

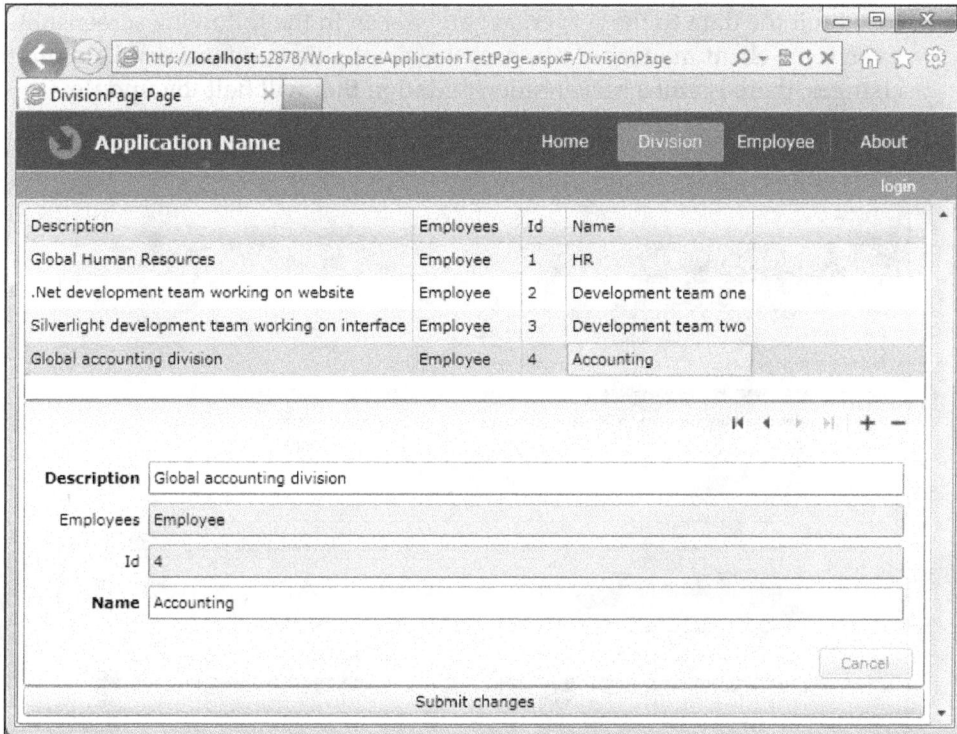

8. The grid and the data form both generate their columns and fields automatically based on the entity that is being displayed. In the previous screenshot, you can see that the ID field is grayed out, as you are not able to edit the primary key. The data form is also smart enough to automatically add a client-side validation to the UI. The Entity Framework model defined the Division entity as having `Name` and `Description` properties that are both non-nullable. If you attempt to leave either of those fields blank, there will be client-side validation errors that must be corrected before you are allowed to submit the data to the server, as can be seen in the following screenshot. Even if the client manages to bypass the client-side validation and submit the changes, there is still a server-side validation that will halt the update:

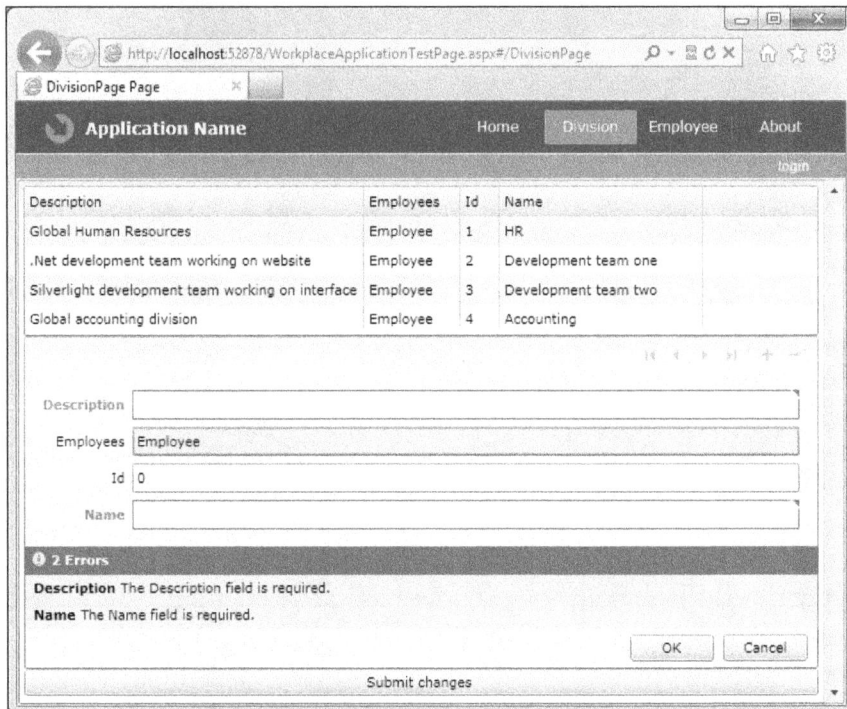

Using a Domain Data Source to access data

The `DivisionPage` interacted with the RIA service by creating a `DomainContext` and manually querying it and submitting changes back to the server. The `EmployeePage` will be created to work with `DomainDataSource`. We do this as follows:

1. Right-click on the Silverlight project **WorkplaceApplication** and click on **Add Reference**.

2. Add a reference to `System.Windows.Controls.DomainServices`. This library has the `DomainDataSource` control that will be used in this screen.

3. Right-click on **Views** and click on **Add | New Item**.

4. Add a new Silverlight page and name it `EmployeePage.xaml`.

5. Modify `EmployeePage.xaml`, so that it is similar to the following code. A `DomainDataSource` control named `dds` is added to the screen. The control then has its `DomainContext` element set with an instance of the `WorkplaceDomainContext`. This allows the screen to query the `WorkplaceDomainContext` through the `dds`. The `dds` will be populated with data from the `GetEmployees` query. `DataGrid` and `DataForm` are then data bounded to the `dds` this time instead of the `DomainContext` as was seen in the last screen:

```
<navigation:Page …
xmlns:domain="clr-namespace:WorkplaceApplication.Web.Services"
xmlns:controls="clr-namespace:System.Windows.
Controls;assembly=System.Windows.Controls.Data"
xmlns:toolkit="clr-namespace:System.Windows.
Controls;assembly=System.Windows.Controls.Data.DataForm.Toolkit"
xmlns:riaControls="clr-namespace:System.Windows.
Controls;assembly=System.Windows.Controls.DomainServices">

    <ScrollViewer x:Name="LayoutRoot">
      <StackPanel>
      <!--Non visual controls-->
        <riaControls:DomainDataSource Name="dds" AutoLoad="True"
          QueryName="GetEmployees" >
          <riaControls:DomainDataSource.DomainContext>
            <domain:WorkplaceDomainContext />
          </riaControls:DomainDataSource.DomainContext>
        </riaControls:DomainDataSource>

      <!--Visual controls-->
      <controls:DataGrid x:Name="employeeGrid"
        ItemsSource="{Binding Data, ElementName=dds}"
                    Height="200" />
      <toolkit:DataForm x:Name="employeeDataForm"
          ItemsSource="{Binding Path=Data, ElementName=dds}"
          CurrentItem="{Binding Path=SelectedItem,
                    ElementName=divisionGrid}" />
      <Button Content="Submit changes" Click="SubmitButtonClick"/>
      </StackPanel>
    </ScrollViewer>
</navigation:Page>
```

6. Modify the `EmployeePage.xaml.cs` code behind the file. This time, only a single method is required, as everything else is done in XAML. Add the event handler for the `submit changes button`, so that it triggers the `DomainDataSource` (`dds`) to submit all the changes:

```
private void SubmitButtonClick(object sender, RoutedEventArgs e)
{
  dds.SubmitChanges();
}
```

7. Press *F5* to compile and run the application.

8. Navigate to the **Employee** page.

9. Click on the **+** to create a new Employee. You will notice that an Employee requires the foreign key ID of the Division that it belongs to, as can be seen in the following screenshot. This is not very user friendly and requires the user to know ahead of time what the Division ID is:

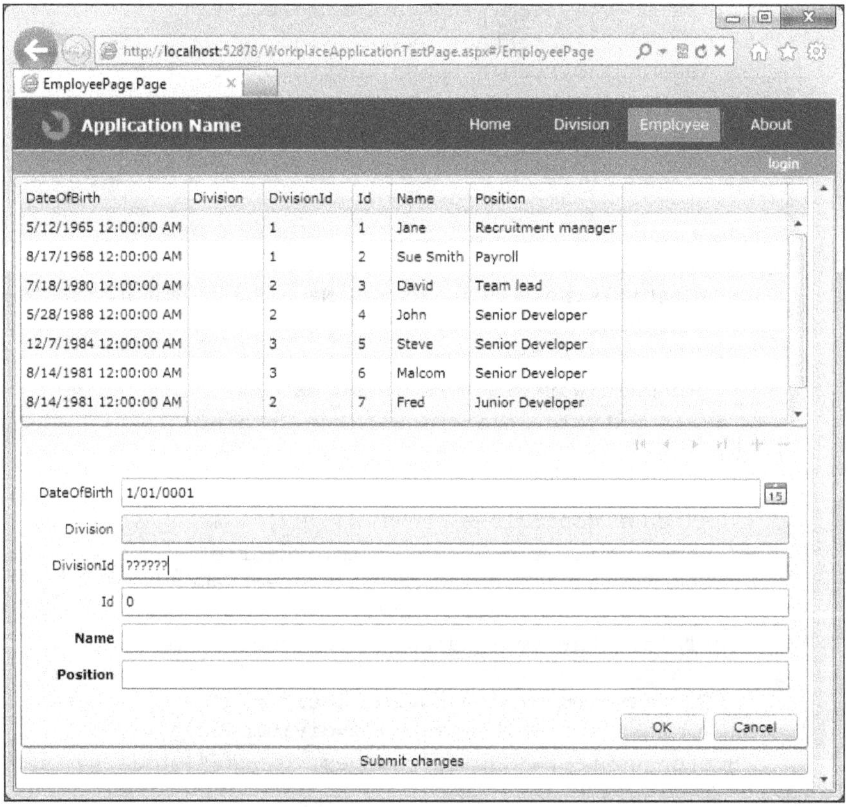

10. To make it easier for the user to select the Division to which the Employee belongs, a drop down will be used instead. When the `DataForm` automatically generates the fields based on the entity, it raises an event when it starts to create each field. You have the chance to intercept this and create a specific field in a customized way.

11. Open the code behind the file `Employee.xaml.cs`. When the `employeeDataForm` is generating the `Division` field for the `Employee`, it will be intercepted and a `ComboBox` is created instead. The drop-down box will display all of the available Divisions. Start by instructing `DomainDataSource` to run the `GetDivisionsQuery`, so that it pre-populates the Division collection in the `dds`. Next, add an event handler on the data form on the `AutoGeneratingField` event. The event handler checks whether it is the `Division` field that is being created. If it is, it creates a new `ComboBox` and sets the bindings to that. The data comes from `dds`, and the selection will be the `Division` property on the `Employee` that is currently being edited:

```
using System.Windows;
using System.Windows.Controls;
using System.Windows.Controls.Primitives;
using System.Windows.Data;
using System.Windows.Navigation;

namespace WorkplaceApplication.Views
{
  public partial class EmployeePage : Page
  {
    public EmployeePage()
    {
      InitializeComponent();

      // pre-populate the DomainDataSource with the Division data
      var context = (Web.Services.WorkplaceDomainContext)
        this.dds.DomainContext;
      var query = context.GetDivisionsQuery();
      context.Load(query);

      employeeDataForm.AutoGeneratingField +=
        employeeDataForm_AutoGeneratingField;
    }

    voidemployeeDataForm_AutoGeneratingField
      (object sender, DataFormAutoGeneratingFieldEventArgs e)
    {
      if (e.PropertyName == "Division")
      {
```

```
var divisionComboBox = new ComboBox { DisplayMemberPath =
  "Name" };
var itemsSource = new Binding("Divisions") { Source =
  this.dds.DomainContext };
var selectedItem = new Binding("Division") { Mode =
  BindingMode.TwoWay };
divisionComboBox.SetBinding
  (ItemsControl.ItemsSourceProperty, itemsSource);
divisionComboBox.SetBinding
  (Selector.SelectedItemProperty, selectedItem);

var divisionField = new DataField
{
  Content = divisionComboBox,
  Label = e.Field.Label
};

e.Field = divisionField;
  }
}
```

12. Press *F5* to compile and run the project.

13. Navigate to the **Employee** page. When selecting different Employees, the drop-down box should automatically select the correct **Division**, as shown in the following screenshot:

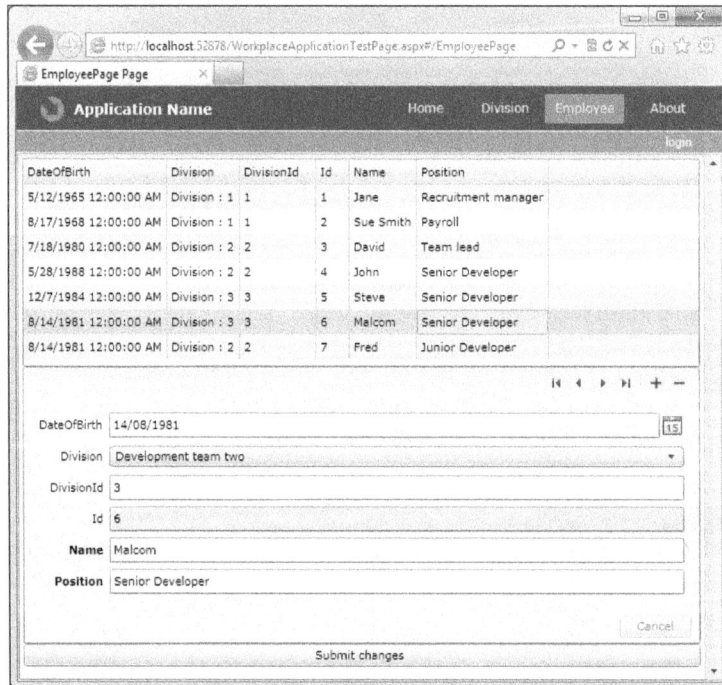

Paging, sorting, filtering, and child objects

For the final screen (Home.xaml), DomainDataSource will be used again, but Visual Studio 2010 will be used to automatically generate the controls. The screen will display all of the divisions. When a division is selected, a child table will display all the employees who are assigned to that division. Other features that will be implemented on this screen are paging, sorting, and filtering. We do this as follows:

1. Open Home.xaml.

2. Remove TextBlock named HeaderText.

3. From the menu bar in Visual Studio, click on **Data** | **Show Data Sources**. Visual Studio will show all the entities that have been exposed by the RIA Service and have a default select query, for example, GetDivisions().

4. Drag the **Division** entity from the **Data Sources** window and drag it into the StackPanel, as shown in the following screenshot. Visual Studio will automatically create a DataGrid and define the columns based on the **Division** entity. Feel free to change the order of the columns in XAML:

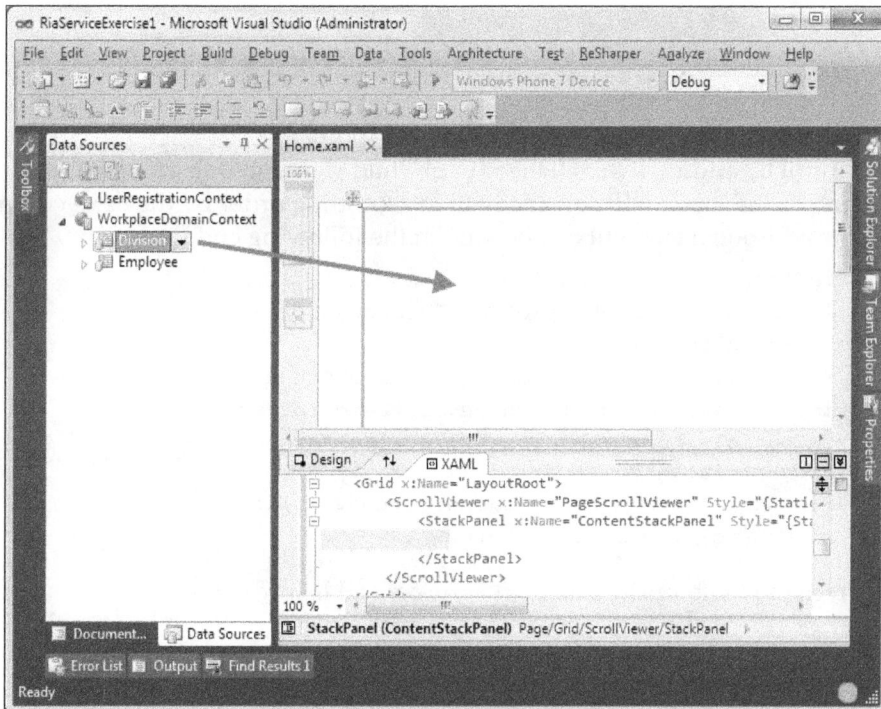

5. Remove the width attribute on the `DataGrid` control, so that it fills the `StackPanel` horizontally.

6. Press *F5* to compile and run the application. The Silverlight application should start, and the grid should automatically be populated with data as shown in the following screenshot:

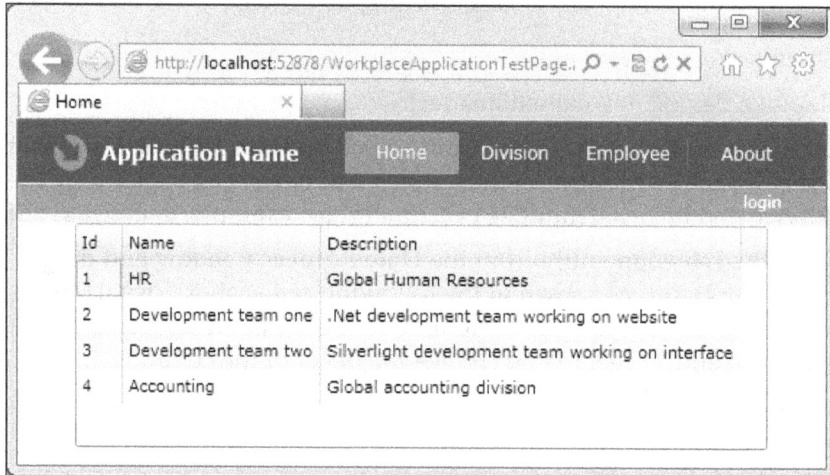

7. Sorting and paging will be added next. Modify the `DomainDataSource` control by adding a `SortDescriptor` child element to it. The `SortDescriptor` will sort the data in ascending order by the `Name` column. The additional element can be seen in the following code snippet:

```
<riaControls:DomainDataSource …>
<riaControls:DomainDataSource.DomainContext>
<my1:WorkplaceDomainContext />
</riaControls:DomainDataSource.DomainContext>
<riaControls:DomainDataSource.SortDescriptors>
<riaControls:SortDescriptor Direction="Ascending"
  PropertyPath="Name" />
</riaControls:DomainDataSource.SortDescriptors>
</riaControls:DomainDataSource>
```

8. From the toolbox, drag a `DataPager` control below `DataGrid`.

9. From the **Data Sources** window, drag the **Division** entity onto the `DataPager` as shown in the following screenshot. This will bind `DataPager` up to the same **Divisions** collection on the `DomainDataSource` created inside the page:

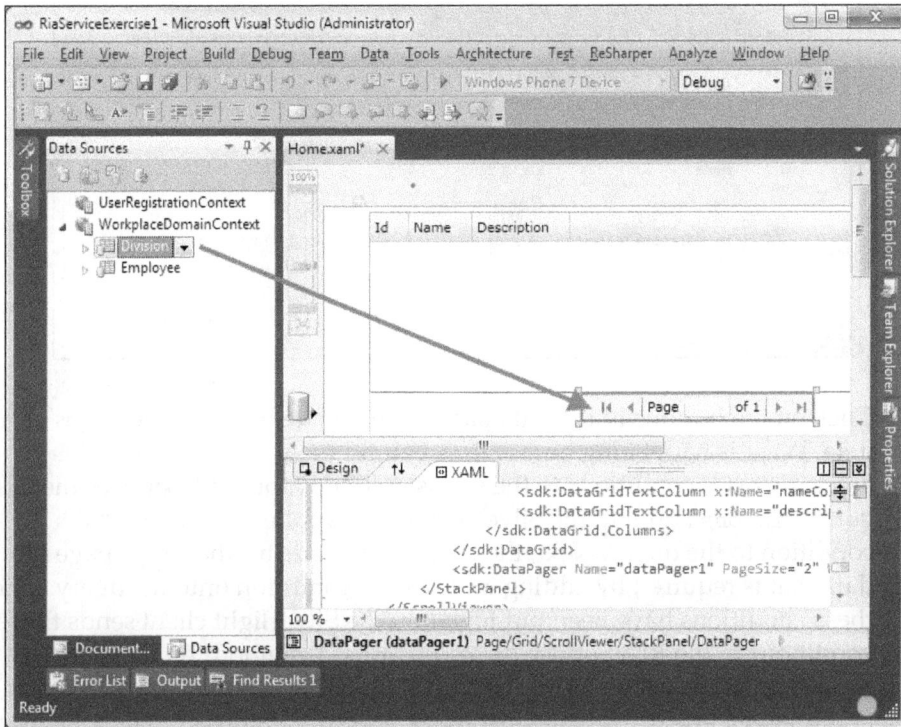

10. Clean up the `DataPager` by setting `PageSize` to 2, and removing the `Height` and `Width` attributes. A larger page size can be used, but setting it to 2 saves you from needing to create a lot of test data.

11. Press *F5* to compile and run the application. The screen should look similar to the one shown in the following screenshot:

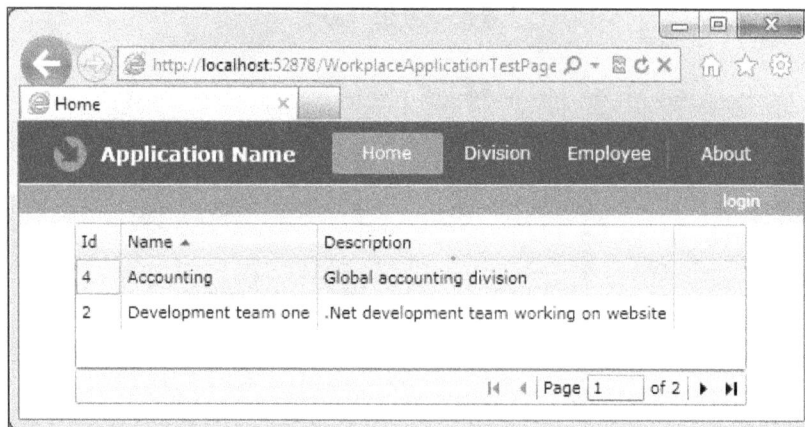

12. Click on the buttons in the data pager to navigate between the pages of data. What is happening here is that, behind the scenes, Silverlight is applying extra conditions to the exposed IQueryable RIA Services method GetDivisions(). First, the Silverlight client applies the .OrderBy() condition to the query. Next, the client only loads up the single page of data that is required by adding a .Take(2) condition onto the query. Once these conditions have been put together, the Silverlight client sends those conditions to the RIA Service GetDivisions() method. As the method returns an IQueryable, those conditions (OrderBy and Skip) will execute at the server side directly against the SQL Azure database. When the user clicks on **Next** to navigate to the second page of data, the client will add a .Skip(2).Take(2) condition instead. This will skip the first two items of data, and return the next two items. This is an efficient way of allowing the Silverlight client to define exactly what data it needs, in what order, but have it all be executed as a single efficient SQL query.

13. Next, the child grid will be added. Inside the **Data Sources** window, expand the **Division** entity, so that the child property **Employees** is visible. The **DivisionId** does not need to be shown as the **Division** has been selected in the parent grid. Click on the **DivisionId** property and change the control it will use to **None**.

14. Drag the **Employee** entity onto the `StackPanel` underneath `DataPager` as shown in the following screenshot:

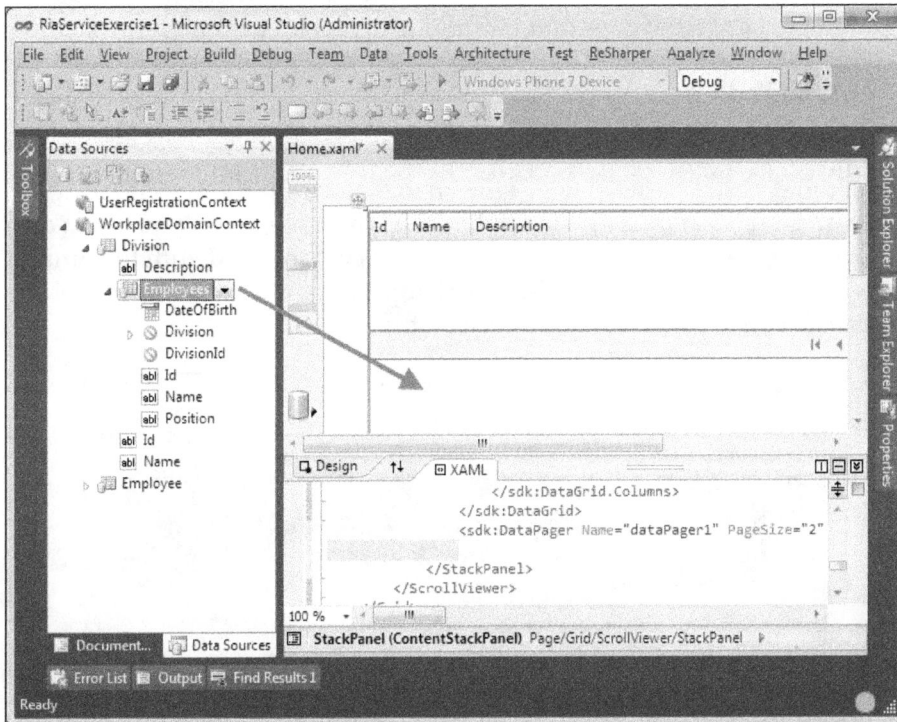

15. Press *F5* to compile and run the application. You will find that the child grid does not work as you would expect. Selecting a **Division** in the parent grid does not display any **Employees**. This is because RIA Services needs to be instructed to send extra data to the client.

16. By default, Entity Framework works in a lazy loading manner. Open the `WorkplaceDomainService.cs` class and modify the `GetDivisions()` method, so that the Employees child table is included in the results:

```
public IQueryable<Division> GetDivisions()
{
  return this.ObjectContext.Divisions.Include("Employees");
}
```

17. Next, by default, RIA Services is conservative with the amount of data that is sent across the wire. Even if the Entity Framework populates the Employees property, it will not be serialized to the client. The Division metadata class needs to be modified, so that it is told to also send the Employees. Open the `WorkplaceDomainService.metadata.cs` file. Find the `DivisionMetadata` class and add the `[Include]` attribute to the `Employees` property, as follows:

```
[Include]
publicEntityCollection<Employee> Employees { get; set; }
```

18. Now press *F5* and rerun the application. This time, when you select a Division, the `employeesDataGrid` should be populated with the Employees who work in that Division. The final application should look similar to the one shown in the following screenshot:

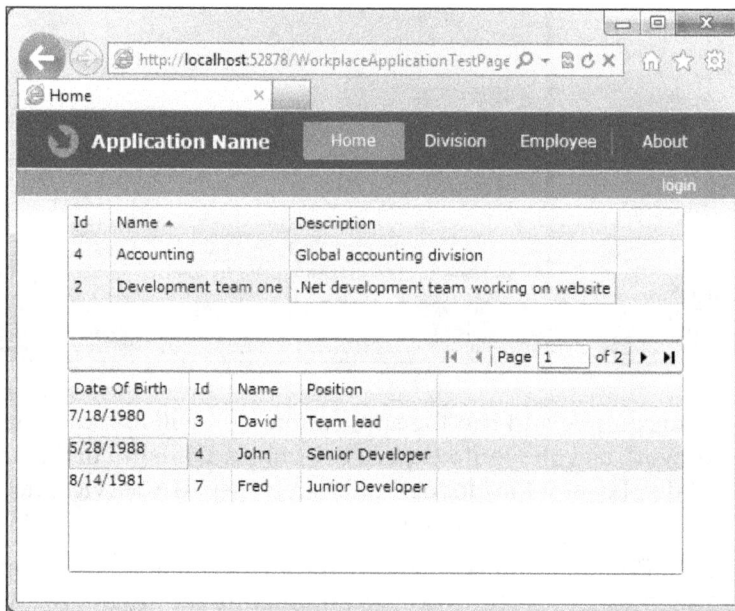

Under the covers of RIA services

At compile time, Visual Studio 2010 looks at the exposed entities and methods in the domain services. It uses the server-side code to generate the client-side code that can automatically interact with the server. To see this generated code, follow these steps:

1. In Visual Studio 2010, expand the **WorkplaceApplication** project in the **Solution Explorer**.

2. Click on **Show All Files**. This will show all of the hidden files that are used by Visual Studio. Expand the **Generated_Code** folder. Inside, there should be a file named **WorkplaceApplication.Web.g.cs**, as shown in the following screenshot:

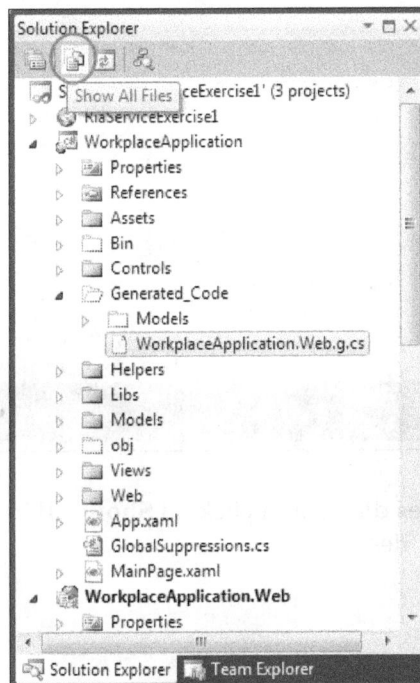

3. Open `WorkplaceApplication.Web.g.cs`. This file is generated automatically by the link to the RIA Service. Inside, there are definitions of `Division` and `Employee` classes. There is also a lot of code dedicated to the automatic connecting to the RIA Service, tracking changes to the entities, and so on.

4. Right-click on the **WorkplaceApplication** project and select **Properties**. The link to the RIA Service can be seen in the following screenshot. This is how Visual Studio automatically generates the proxy class to the RIA Service. All of this allows Silverlight to query the service as if it were just a local data source:

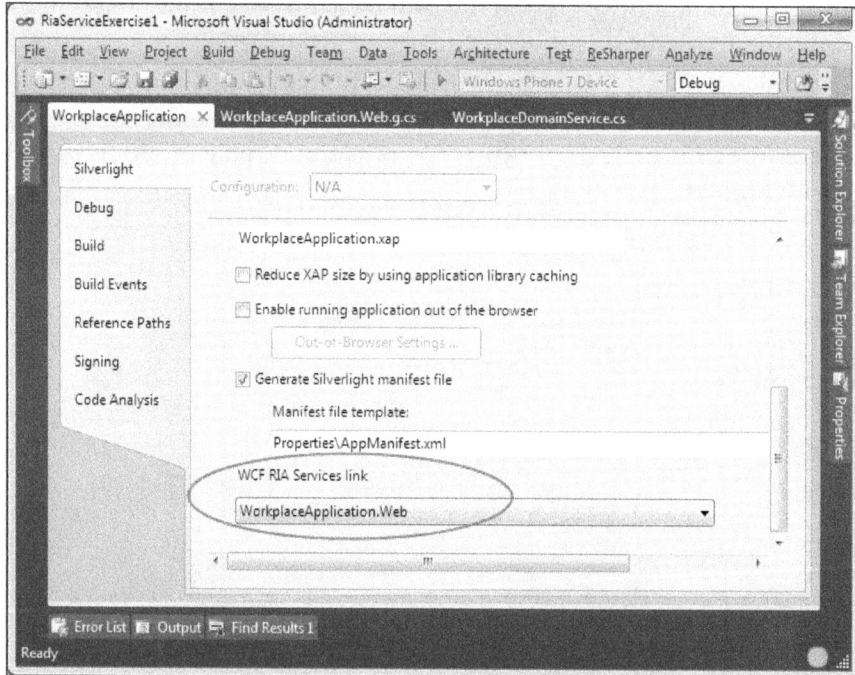

5. Close the properties dialog and click on **Show All Files** again to hide the system-generated files.

Summary

This chapter looked at how RIA Services can greatly simplify the development of an enterprise line of business applications. RIA Services makes it very simple for a Silverlight client to consume a domain service as if it were a local data repository.

A Silverlight application was created that showed a number of the productivity enhancements that RIA Services provides:

- Shared client-side and server-side validation of entities
- Client-side domain context that tracks changes to entity collections
- IQueryable methods in the domain service that allow the client to specify query conditions
- Easy paging, filtering, sorting of data

The next chapter will introduce OData which is a way to expose data directly to a client through HTTP. This allows a client to query data through the use of a URL.

9
Exposing OData to Silverlight Applications

Enterprises typically have multiple silos of data held in systems across their entire network. Work has been done to get the service interoperability through **SOA (Service Oriented Architecture)**. However, until recently, there has not been much work put into the data interoperability across applications. **OData** is an open standard that can be used to share data in an interoperable way.

This chapter will explore what OData is, and how it can be consumed and exposed in your applications. The following topics will be covered:

- OData
- Consuming OData services
- Sharing data by using OData

OData

The **Open Data Protocol (OData)** is a web protocol that enables the querying and updating of the data in a framework-agnostic manner. OData has been built by combining a number of existing web technologies together (HTTP, AtomPub and JSON), which allows any technology framework to consume or to produce OData services. As it is built on top of the existing web standards, it allows for a greater level of interoperability with existing frameworks.

Microsoft created Odata as a way to allow greater sharing of data between applications and systems. As a result, there are a number of implementations of it online (eBay, Netflix, and Twitpic), in server applications (SharePoint, SSRS, WCF services), and client application frameworks (iPhone apps, Windows Phone 7, and Silverlight applications).

More information about OData can be found at the main website:

```
http://www.odata.org
```

Value for the enterprise

OData can simplify the creation and sharing of data between the applications within an enterprise. There are two important ways that it can help:

- Having a standard way for all your applications to access the data can greatly simplify the development of applications throughout your enterprise, for example, iPhone, Silverlight, and so on
- Having a standard way of exposing and consuming the data also leads to a second benefit of being able to chain the data through the services

A piece of data may be sitting within a **SharePoint** list which is exposed as an OData feed. A service could consume data, transform it, and expose the results as another OData service, which could then be consumed by another service, and so on.

Accessing data

When starting out, it cannot be helpful to think of OData as a new framework that needs to be learned, but to instead think of it as an agreed pattern of data access (similar to a REST service). OData can be more easily thought of as a defined way of exposing the data that allows for easy discoverability and consumption.

Everything in OData is done through the use of the **Unique Resource Identifiers (URIs)**. OData is built on the idea that each entity, or an item or a resource should be uniquely identifiable by this URI. If your data set has a number of product categories, for example, you could retrieve the whole collection of them by going to the following URL:

```
http://odata.MyServer.com/ProductCategories
```

This would return a collection of product category entities in an AtomPub format. It is also possible to retrieve a single entity through the URI it contains, for example, the information of the product category with an ID of five can be accessed through the following URI:

```
http://odata.MyServer.com/ProductCategories(5)
```

All OData operations are invoked through the manipulation of the URI path. Without using special frameworks, it is possible to specify sets of data that should be queried, the filters that should be applied, and so on, all of them with a carefully crafted URI.

While it is possible to retrieve information about a single entity and a set of entities, it is also possible to navigate through entities. If the OData service is exposing the relational entities, the child or the parent objects can be retrieved through the URI. For example, to access all products contained under the fifth product category, they could be accessed as follows:

```
http://odata.MyServer.com/ProductCategories(5)/Products
```

HTTP Get requests are used to retrieve the data. The other HTTP verbs can be used to create and edit the data. To create a new entity, it requires an HTTP Post operation along with the entity data inside the request packet. Editing of entities can be done through a Put operation directed at the URI of the entity that should be updated.

It is perfectly fine to work with an OData service directly through the manual manipulation of HTTP requests (by either using the address bar in a browser, or making direct calls to the web client). However, there are a number of **Software Development Kits (SDKs)** available for different platforms that can help to simplify the consumption of these services. For example, the OData SDK built into Silverlight allows developers to interact with the service through LINQ queries. The SDK will take the query, and convert it into a URI that can then be used with the service.

URI construction

The URI of an OData request can be broken down into the following three components:

- **Service root URI**: It is the service endpoint of the OData service
- **Resource path**: It indicates the entity or the set of data that should be worked with
- **Query options**: They allow filters and conditions to be applied to the data set

The format of the URI can be seen as follows:

```
http://<Service root URI>/<Resource path>?<Query options>
```

We have an example of the preceding format as follows:

```
http://odata.MyServer.com/Customers?$filter=startswith(Name,'john')&
$orderby=age
```

In the preceding example, the OData service is exposed at the subdomain:

```
http://odata.Myserver.com/
```

The resource path (/Customers) indicates that the list of customers should be queried. Finally, the query options indicate that only customers whose names are starting with 'John' should be returned, and that the results should be ordered by the age property.

The following example is a bit more complex:

```
http://MyServer.com/InventoryService.svc/ProductCategories(5)/
Products?$top=10&$filter=substringof(Name,'pen') and price gt 1.24
```

This time, the OData service is being exposed directly through the following path:

```
http://MyServer.com/InventoryService/
```

The following portion of the URI, that is, the ProductCategories(5) or Products indicates that the data set you work with should be the list of the products, which are associated with ProductCategory with ID as 5. The filter query has a few components within it. First, the $top=10 component indicates that only the first 10 results should be returned. The next component of the query options defines filter parameters, that is, $filter=substringof(Name,'pen') and price gt 1.24. The URI may look strange with spaces within the URI, but it is all correct. The filter specifies that only products that contain the word pen, and have a price greater than (gt) 1.24 should be returned.

With a little more experience, it becomes easy to navigate through relationships of an OData service, and to filter the results using the URI.

OData versus RIA Services

A common question that is asked is, *In what situations should I use RIA Services and when should I use OData?*

The rule of thumb that I use when creating applications is as follows:

- **Controlling the frontend plus the backend (Silverlight)**: If you are creating the service and you are only creating a Silverlight client, RIA Services is your best choice due to the productivity improvements.

- **Controlling the frontend plus the backend (non-Silverlight)**: If you are controlling the service, but are exposing it to the non-Silverlight clients (such as iPhone, Android, Excel, and so on), OData is the sensible choice because of its interoperability benefits.

- **Controlling only the client**: If you are building a client and consuming a service from someone else, then OData would be a good choice if they will expose it.

RIA Services is the best choice if you are building the service and Silverlight application yourself due to its ability to quickly develop an application. In the other situations, OData may make more sense.

One useful feature in the RIA Services toolkit is the ability for a domain service to expose itself as an OData endpoint. This ability enables you to build an RIA Service for high productivity with your Silverlight application, yet expose the data to other clients. This approach is the best from both the worlds, and allows other clients to consume and query the OData service freely.

Consuming OData services

There are lists of applications and frameworks that can consume OData services on the OData website. An example of these existing applications can be found at the following URL:

`http://odata.org/consumers`

Developers who wish to download SDKs that will allow them to consume OData natively from within their applications can find the links on the following page:

`http://odata.org/developers/odata-sdk`

The following is a short list of platforms and applications that support the consumption of OData services:

- Web browsers
- Ajax or JavaScript or jQuery
- Silverlight
- Windows Phone 7
- iPhone
- Android
- Excel
- LINQPad
- PHP
- Java
- Any platform that allows the creation of an HTTP request

Using Internet Explorer

The easiest way to get started with OData is to query an existing service manually with a web browser. There are a number of existing OData services listed at `http://odata.org/producers` that can be browsed. The OData service for `http://Netflix.com` will be used in this exercise to demonstrate how to navigate and query a service as follows:

1. Open Internet Explorer.

2. Open **Internet Options** by clicking on the cog in the upper-right corner of the screen. Navigate to the **Content** tab. Click on the **Settings** button for the feeds as shown in the following screenshot:

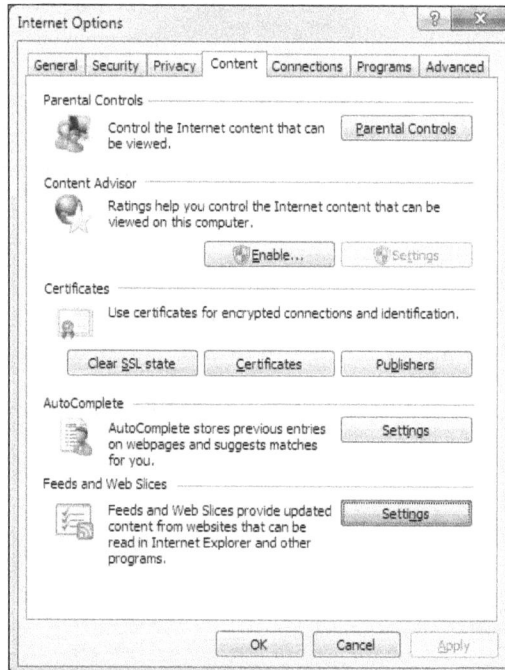

3. Turn off the feed reading view by unchecking it as shown in the following screenshot. This will stop Internet Explorer from rendering the XML as a feed, and will instead display the raw XML data:

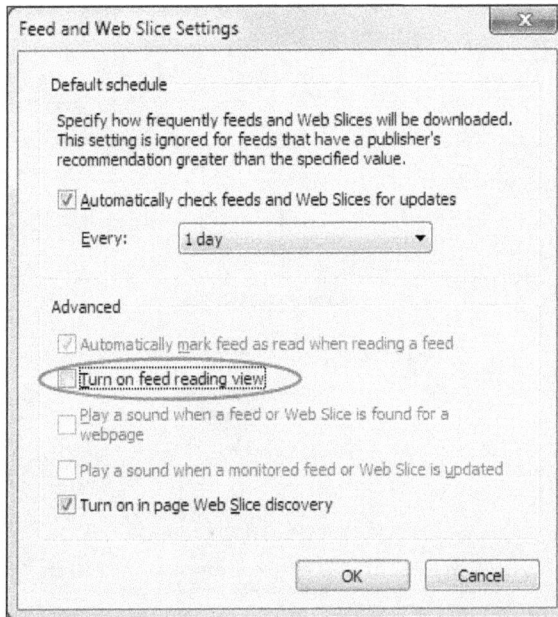

4. Navigate to the Netflix OData endpoint at the following URL:

   `http://odata.netflix.com`

5. This will automatically redirect you to the latest version of the OData service, which at the time of writing was v2, at the following URL:

   `http://odata.netflix.com/v2/Catalog/`

> **Case sensitivity**
>
> Be careful while navigating an OData service, as the URI is case sensitive. Attempting to navigate to /genres may result in a 404 error being returned, whereas /Genres will work fine.

6. The catalog endpoint shows all of the root entity sets that can be queried. The entity sets **Genres, Titles, TitleAudioFormats, TitleAwards, People, TitleScreenFormats**, and **Languages** can be seen in the following screenshot:

7. Each of the entity sets can be navigated by changing the URI. Navigate to the genres set by adding /Genres to the end of the URI as follows:

```
http://odata.netflix.com/v2/Catalog/Genres
```

Warning!

This may take a long time to load as there are hundreds of genres in the Netflix system.

8. As there are too many genres to look at, try filtering the data to show only romantic genres with the following URI:

```
http://odata.netflix.com/v2/Catalog/Genres?$filter=startswith
(Name,'romantic')
```

The following screenshot shows the two genres that fit that criterion: **Romantic Comedies** and **Romantic Dramas**.

The unique URI of the Romantic Comedies genres can be seen highlighted in the following screenshot as the `id` attribute:

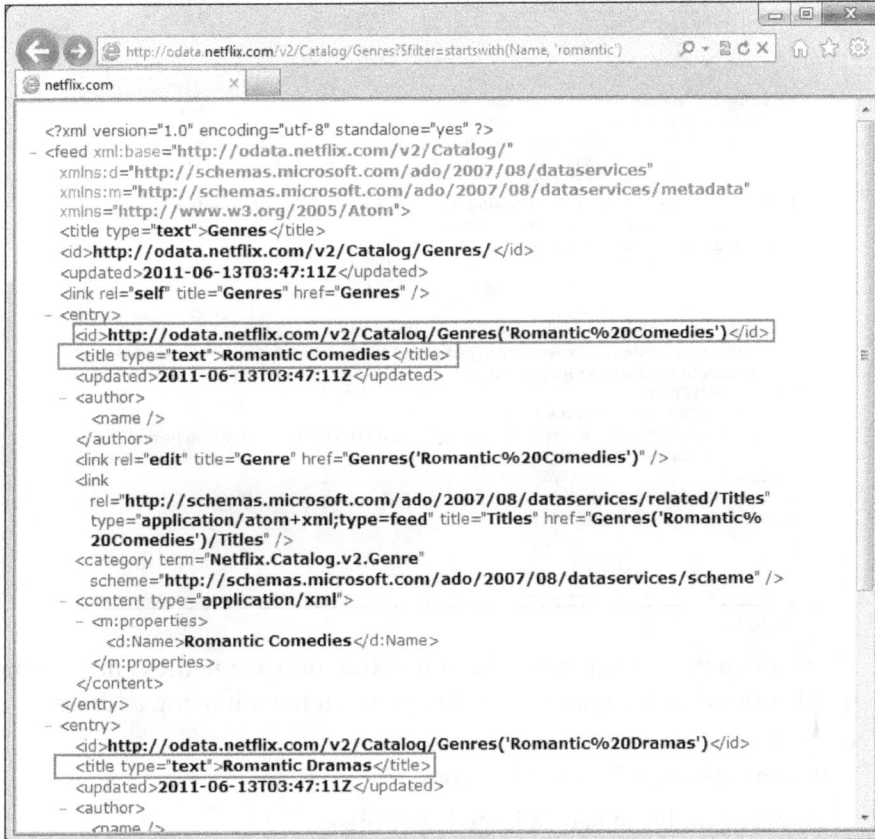

9. Navigate to the **Romantic Comedies** entity by passing the unique ID into the genres entity set at the following address:

```
http://odata.netflix.com/v2/Catalog/Genres
('Romantic%20Comedies')
```

10. The data for that individual entity should be displayed, similar to the following screenshot. There are two attributes in this entity with **\<link rel.../\>**. These show you that the URIs that can be used for additional operations on this entity. The edit URI is the endpoint that should be used when using an HTTP Put to edit the entity. However, we do not have appropriate permissions on this service to update the entity. The second link named **Titles** is more interesting as it is the link that shows us the child entities of this genre:

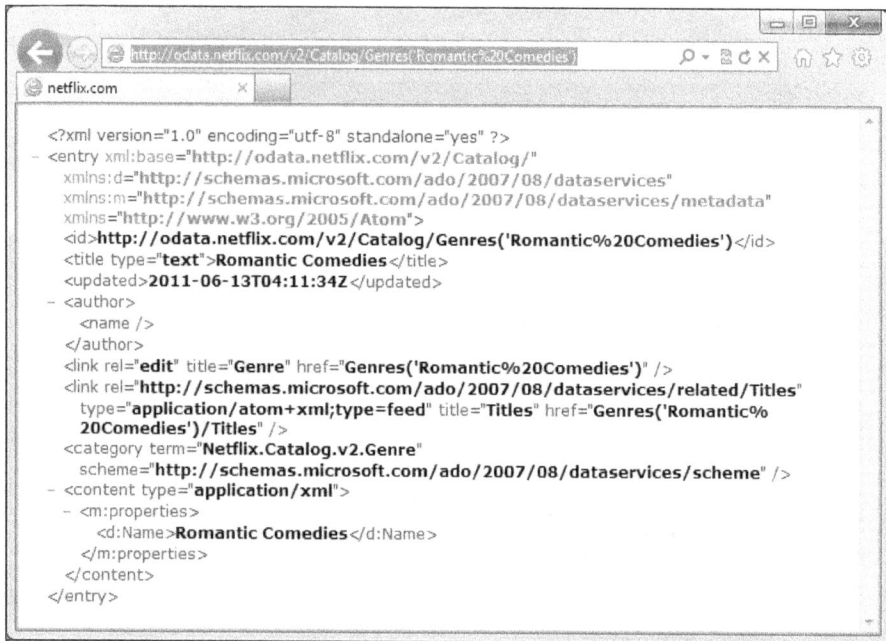

11. Navigate to the `titles` property of the **Romantic Comedies** entity to display all the titles that are available for this genre at the following address:

```
http://odata.netflix.com/v2/Catalog/Genres
('Romantic%20Comedies')/Titles
```

12. This will again bring back a large list of titles.

13. Filter the **Romantic Comedy** titles, so that only the wedding movies are returned at the following address:

```
http://odata.netflix.com/v2/Catalog/Genres
('Romantic%20Comedies')/Titles?$filter=substringof
('wedding',Name)
```

14. Select a movie that you wish to see more details about and write down the unique URI of the entity. **The Wedding Singer** will be used in this example which has a unique title ID of **1EGz3**.

15. There are two possible URIs that could be used at this point, that is, we could continue to chain the commands along our URI and append the title ID as follows:

    ```
    http://odata.netflix.com/v2/Catalog/Genres
    ('Romantic%20Comedies')/Titles('1EGz3')
    ```

    Alternatively, the unique URI of the entity could be used which was returned in the search results as follows:

    ```
    http://odata.netflix.com/v2/Catalog/Titles('1EGz3')
    ```

16. Both the URIs will show the entity details for the movie as shown in the following screenshot:

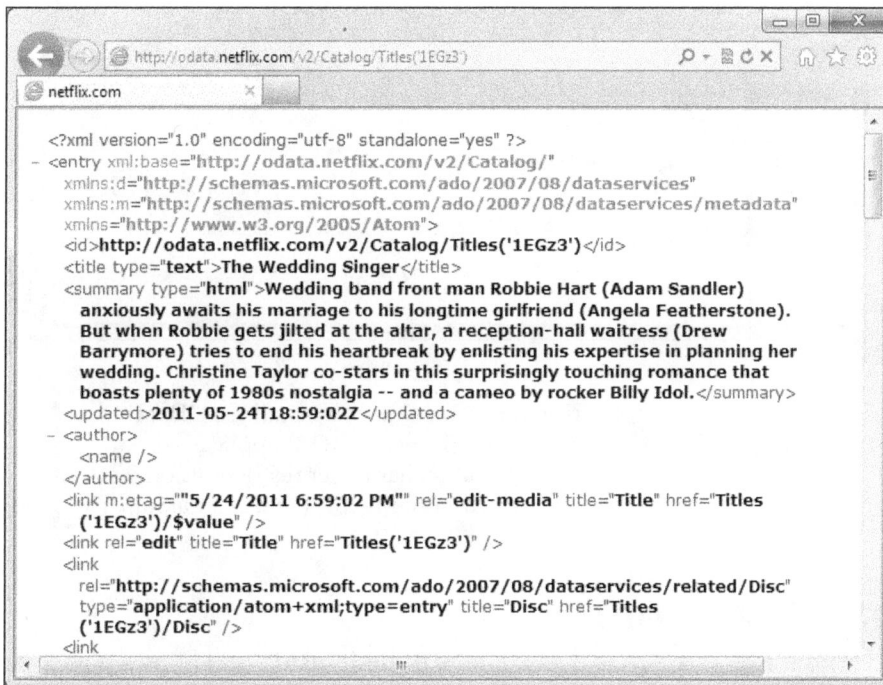

17. The `Title` entity has a lot more **<link rel .../>** attributes that link to more related entities of this title. Some examples are **Cast**, **Directors**, **Screen Formats**, and **AudioFormats**.

18. The `Cast` entity set of the movie title will return all of the actors that appeared in the movie. Navigate to the following address:

    `http://odata.netflix.com/v2/Catalog/Titles('1EGz3')/Cast`

    You can see that *Adam Sandler* starred in the movie.

OData Explorer

The OData Explorer is a handy utility to browse through the entity sets and help in building search queries. It can be found at the following URL:

`http://www.silverlight.net/content/samples/odataexplorer/`

The following screenshot shows the OData Explorer being used to query Netflix for romantic genres:

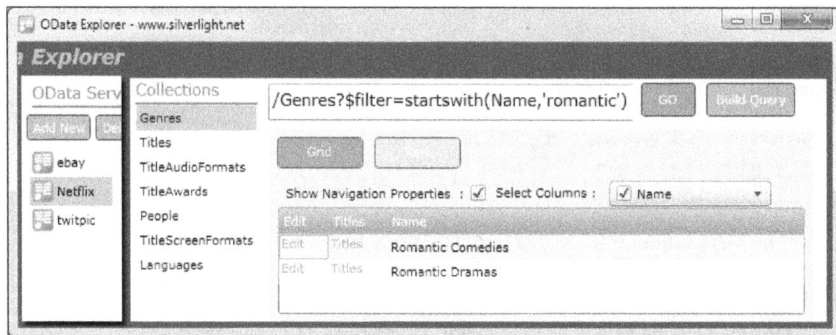

> It is highly recommended that you install the OData explorer as an **Out Of Browser** (**OOB**) application. An OOB-installed application has fewer restrictions on the network usage, which can be helpful in this situation.

Using Silverlight

The Silverlight framework has the OData SDK built inside it. It allows developers to write LINQ queries against an OData service that will be resolved down to a URI. This exercise will build a simple Silverlight application that uses the Netflix OData service. We do this as follows:

1. In Visual Studio 2010, create a new Silverlight application. Name the project as **NetflixClientExercise**, as shown in the following screenshot. Leave the default settings when it asks whether the application should be hosted in an ASP.Net website, and so on:

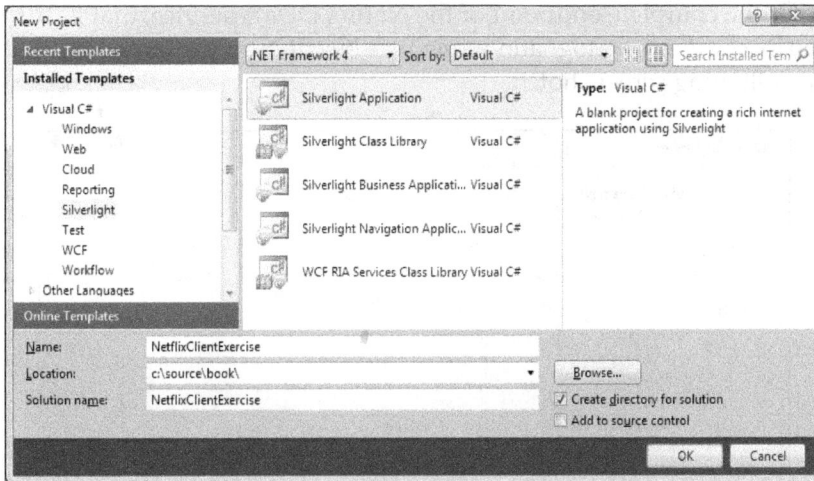

2. Right-click on **NetflixClientExercise** Silverlight project and select **Add Service Reference** as shown in the following screenshot:

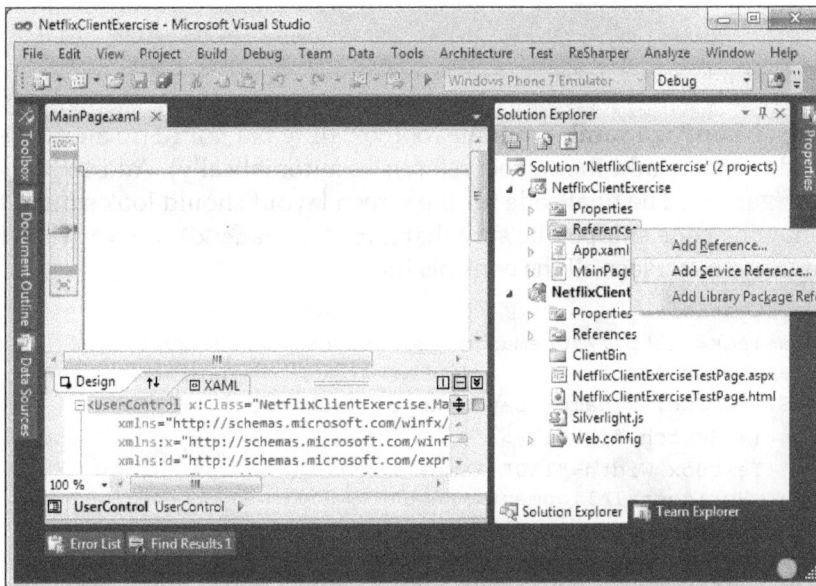

3. Enter the complete endpoint of the Netflix OData service, that is, **http://odata. netflix.com/v2/Catalog/** and name it as **NetflixServiceReference** as shown in the following screenshot:

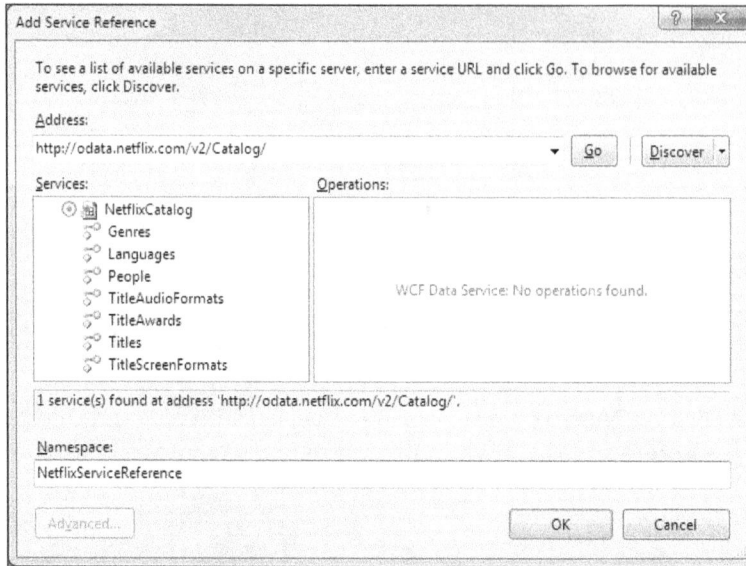

4. Open **MainPage.xaml**. From the toolbox, drag `DataGrid` (to allow Visual Studio 2010 to add the correct references automatically). Add `TextBox` and `Button`. The final code for the screen layout should look similar to the following code snippet. Be sure that `AutoGenerateColumns="True"` is set on `DataGrid`. Place all the controls into `StackPanel`:

```xml
<UserControl>
xmlns:sdk="http://schemas.microsoft.com/winfx/2006/xaml/
presentation/sdk">
  <StackPanel x:Name="LayoutRoot" Background="White">
    <!--Search filter-->
    <TextBox Width="150" Name="textBox1"
      HorizontalAlignment="Left" />
    <!--Search Button-->
    <Button Content="Search" Name="searchButton"
      Click="SearchButtonClick" />
    <!--The DataGrid-->
    <sdk:DataGrid AutoGenerateColumns="True" Name="
      titlesDataGrid" MinHeight="100" />
  </StackPanel>
</UserControl>
```

5. Open the **MainPage.xaml.cs** code behind the file. Start by creating two new properties. The first will hold a reference to the Netflix catalog OData service. The second is a special collection that can handle the tracking of entities and continuation tokens from a service. Also, include the `using` statements for the following steps:

```
using System;
using System.Data.Services.Client;
using System.Linq;
using System.Windows;
using System.Windows.Controls;
using NetflixClientExercise.NetflixServiceReference;
namespace NetflixClientExercise
{
  public partial class MainPage : UserControl
  {
    public NetflixCatalog NetflixService { get; set; }
    public DataServiceCollection<Title> TitlesCollection { get;
      set; }
  }
}
```

6. Inside the constructor, `NetflixService` will be initialized with the address of the OData service. The constructor then initializes `TitlesCollection` and passes it in `NetflixService`, so that it can interact with it when required. `TitlesCollection` then has a `LoadCompleted` event connected to it. Finally, `titlesDataGrid` is bound to `TitlesCollection`:

```
public MainPage()
{
  InitializeComponent();
  // Create the OData client and specify the service base.
  NetflixService = new NetflixCatalog(new
    Uri("http://odata.netflix.com/v2/Catalog/"));
  // Create a DataServiceCollection that can handle
    continuation tokens
  TitlesCollection = new
    DataServiceCollection<Title>(NetflixService);
  TitlesCollection.LoadCompleted += TitlesCollectionLoadCompleted;
  titlesDataGrid.ItemsSource = TitlesCollection;
}
```

7. Next, add the event handler for the search button. First, a query is created that selects `Titles` and orders them by their `AverageRating` out of five stars. Next, if the user has typed a search term that the titles should be filtered by, then that search term is chained on top of the query. As Netflix has thousands and thousands of results, a limit is imposed on the results to only return the top 100 results. Finally, the query is passed into `TitlesCollection` which will execute the load request asynchronously:

```
private void SearchButtonClick(object sender, RoutedEventArgs e)
{
    IQueryable<Title> results =
    from title in NetflixService.Titles
    orderby title.AverageRating descending
    select title;
    // Apply the filter if one exists
    if (string.IsNullOrWhiteSpace(textBox1.Text) == false)
    {
        results = from r in results
        where r.Name.Contains(textBox1.Text)
        select r;
    }
    // Limit the result set! There are thousands and thousands of
        results
    results = results.Take(100);
    TitlesCollection.LoadAsync(results);
}
```

8. The final code required is an event handler for the `LoadCompleted` event. The handler will check the `Error` property that displays any error found to the user. If the load was successful, the continuation token is checked. If there are more results to be returned, `TitlesCollection` will automatically request the next batch. In this exercise, the grid will automatically display the results as each of the batches is returned from the data service. However, if you were executing a business logic that required all the results to be loaded into the memory before continuing, the `else` block is the one where you would implement this logic as follows:

```
void TitlesCollectionLoadCompleted(object sender,
    LoadCompletedEventArgs e)
{
    if (e.Error == null)
    {
        // The server can only send a limited payload each time
        // If there are more results to return, then load the next
            portion
```

```
    if (TitlesCollection.Continuation != null)
    {
        TitlesCollection.LoadNextPartialSetAsync();
    }
    else
    {
        // All of the data has been loaded.
        // This is where you would place logic if you required the
            entire result set to be loaded first before continuing.
    }
}
else
{
    MessageBox.Show(e.Error.Message);
}
}
```

9. Press *F5* to compile and run the application.

10. Type **wedding** into the filter textbox and click on **Search**. Be patient as it may take a few seconds for the data to appear. The results should look similar to the one shown in the following screenshot:

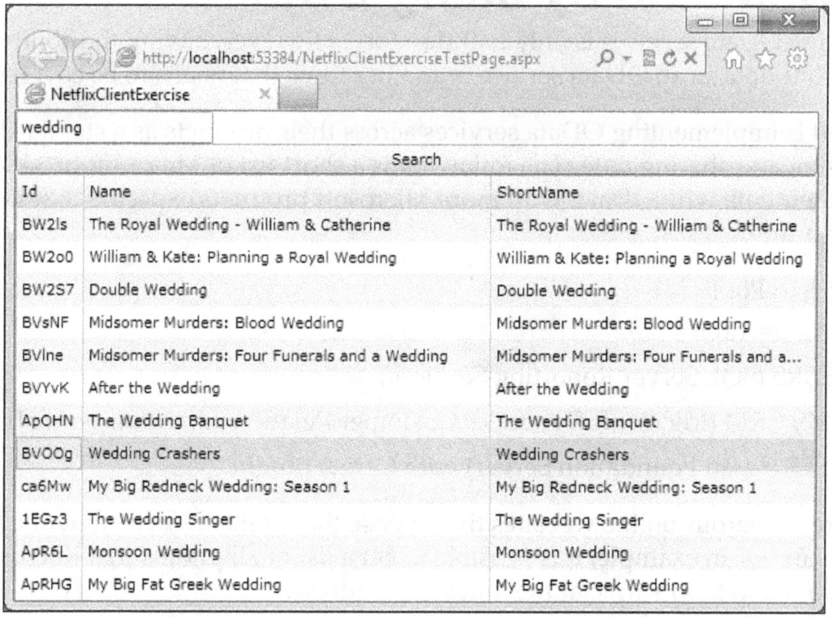

11. To see the continuation token working, change the LINQ statement and take 1,100 items instead of 100. The Netflix service returns 500 results at a time. Place a breakpoint in the `LoadCompleted` method, and you will see that it automatically retrieves the additional batches until they are all loaded.

This exercise was a quick demonstration of how to consume an OData service in a read-only situation. The OData libraries built into Silverlight allow for the tracking of an entity change, similar to what is done while using RIA Services. This cannot be demonstrated here as the Netflix service is a read-only service.

Consuming OData on other platforms

Three examples were just given on how to consume OData through a web browser, the OData Explorer, and through your own code in Silverlight. OData is an open web protocol that allows any platform to consume it. Refer to the OData page in the SDKs for more information on consuming the OData from the other platforms such as iPhone, Android, and so on at the following address:

```
http://odata.org/developers/odata-sdk
```

Sharing data by using OData

Consuming OData services is only half the story. However, having the ability to expose your data as an OData service is another topic that needs to be covered.

Microsoft is implementing OData services across their products as a standard way of exposing and sharing data. The following is a short list of Microsoft products that expose their data with OData, with more Microsoft products expected to follow in the near future:

- SharePoint
- Azure Tables
- SSRS (SQL Server Reporting Services)
- MS CRM (Microsoft Dynamics Customer Relationship Management)
- TFS (Team Foundation Server) with OData plugin

There are numerous online websites that expose their data, allowing anyone to query them. As an example, it is possible to get a list of all photos that Microsoft has uploaded to the Twitpic at the following address:

```
http://odata.twitpic.com/Users('Microsoft')/Images
```

The following is a short list of sites that support the protocol:

- **EBay** at `http://ebayodata.cloudapp.net`
- **Netflix** at `http://odata.netflix.com`
- **Twitpic** at `http://odata.twitpic.com`
- **Windows Azure data market** at `https://datamarket.azure.com`

The Windows Azure data market has a list of commercial data that can be consumed. There are data feeds from NASA, the American government, and so on, that can be utilized in your own applications.

More examples of products and websites that expose OData services can be found on the following OData website:

`http://www.odata.org/producers`

Creating your own OData services

The .Net framework provides a way to create OData services through the use of **WCF Data Services**. In some instances, creating an OData service can be as easy as writing two lines of code. Passing an Entity Framework model as a generic parameter into the class of WCF Data Services is enough to get started.

RIA Services also support exposing your domain service with an OData endpoint. This is usually the best approach, as it gives you a way to have a deep integration with Silverlight, while supporting the other software clients as well.

RIA Services domain service with Entity Framework and SQL Azure

The easiest way to update an existing domain service to expose an OData endpoint is to simply place the attribute `[Query(IsDefault = true)]` on the methods. This exercise will walk through the steps of creating a new OData service with RIA Services by using the wizards.

This exercise assumes that you have already created the database from *Chapter 7, Relational Data with SQL Azure and Entity Framework*. We do this as follows:

1. Open Visual Studio 2010, and create a new **Windows Azure Project** named **RiaOdataExercise** as shown in the following screenshot:

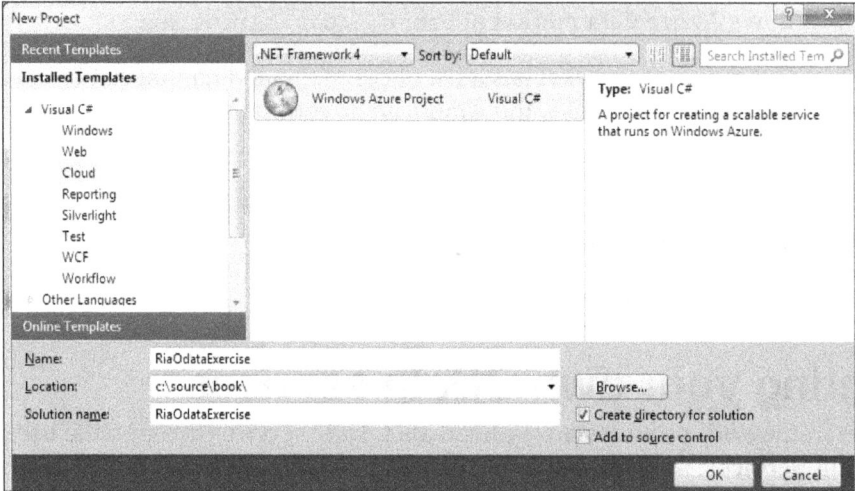

2. Add a single **Silverlight Business Application** role named **BusinessApplication** to the project and click on **OK**:

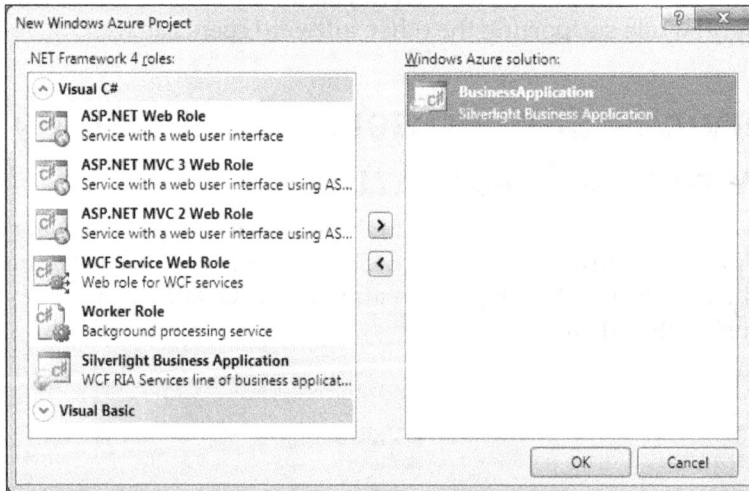

3. From the **BusinessApplication.Web** project, right-click on the **Models** folder, and select **Add | New Item** as shown in the following screenshot:

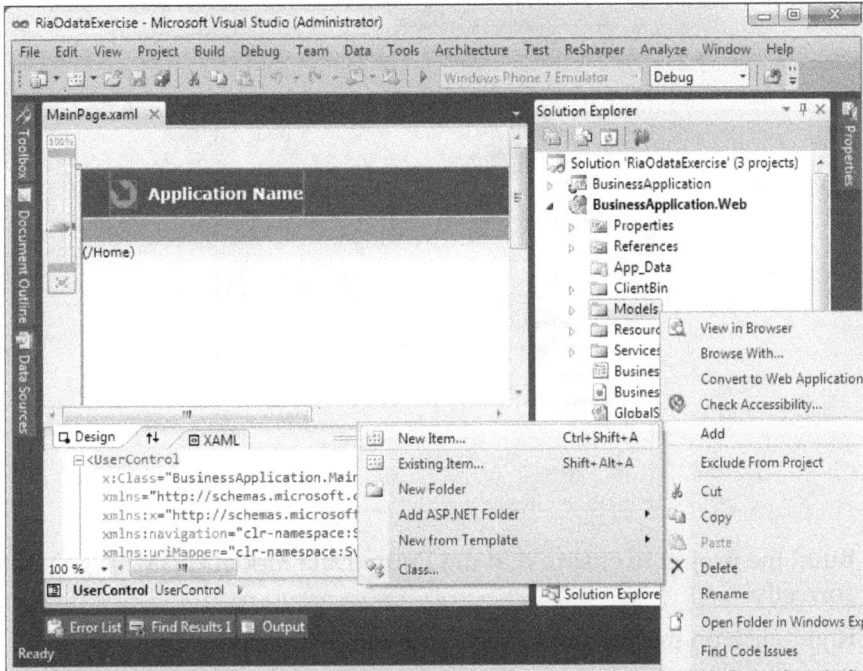

4. Add a new **ADO.NET Entity Data Model** and name it as **WorkplaceModel.edmx**.

5. The **Entity Data Model Wizard** will start automatically. Select the option to generate a model from an existing database. Enter the details of your existing SQL Azure database.

6. Select the tables that should be included in the model. The following screenshot shows the database of the workplace being used by selecting **Divisions (dbo)** and **Employees (dbo)** tables :

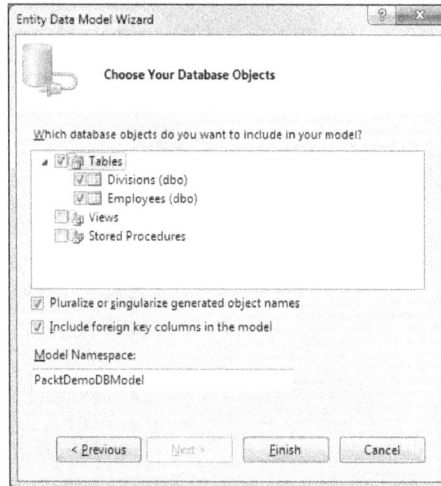

7. Build the project to ensure that the Entity Data Model (EDM) is generated correctly.

8. Right-click on the **Services** folder and add a new item.

9. Click on **Add New Domain Service Class** and name it as **WorkplaceDomainService**.

10. Select the entities **Division** and **Employee**. Click on the **Enable editing** checkboxes to enable editing. Be sure that you click on the checkbox **Expose OData endpoint**, as shown in the following screenshot:

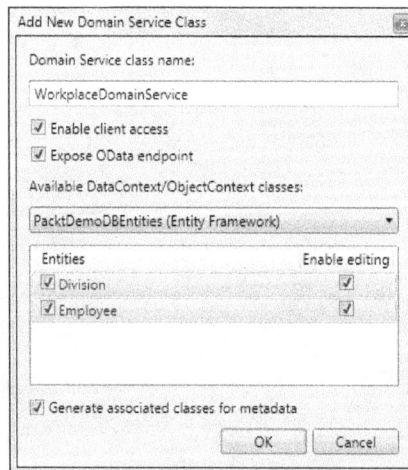

11. The domain service will be code generated for you. Notice that the method has the attribute `[Query(IsDefault = true)]` on it that exposes the method to OData as shown in the following screenshot:

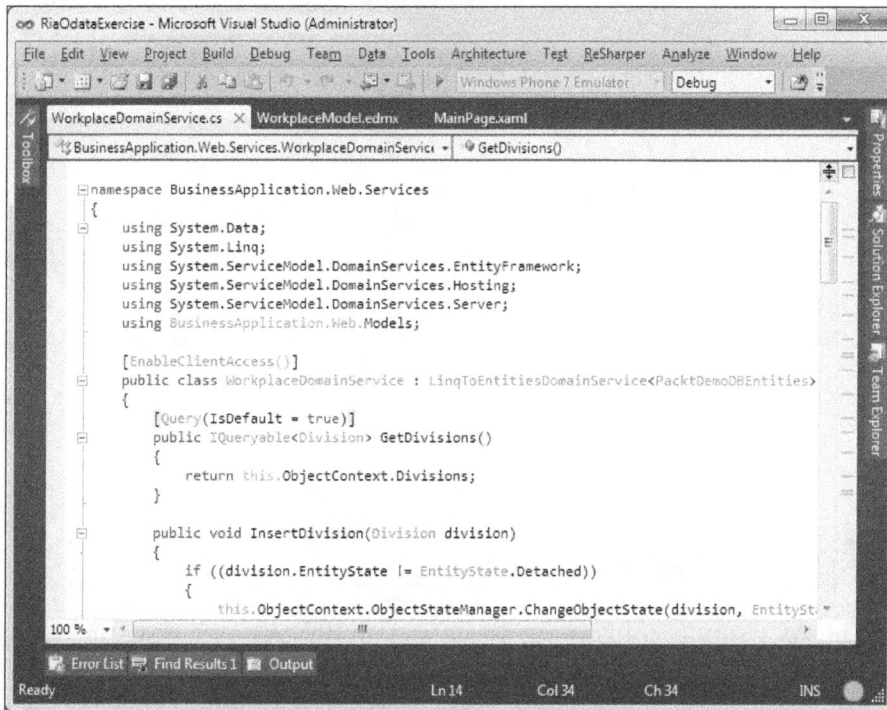

12. Press *F5* to compile and run the application.

13. The endpoint URI is generated automatically from the fully qualified name of the domain service. Take the full name as `BusinessApplication.Web.Services.WorkplaceDomainService` and replace `'.'` with `'-'`. This will result in a URI similar to the following: `http://127.0.0.1:81/BusinessApplication-Web-Services-WorkplaceDomainService.svc`.

14. The port number may vary on your machine. The following screenshot shows the generic WCF endpoint when you navigate to it:

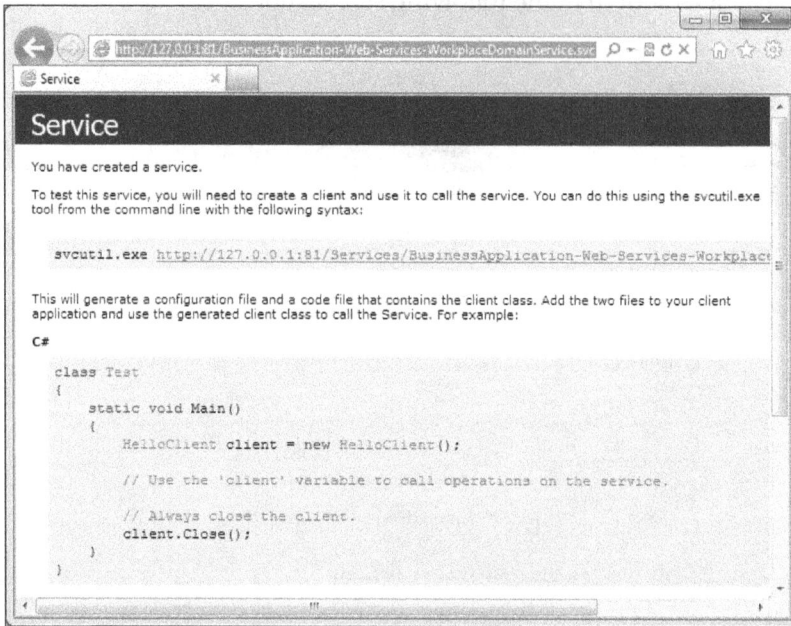

15. The WCF service is exposing the data as an RIA Services endpoint, ready for Silverlight consumption. At the same time, it is also exposing an OData endpoint. The OData endpoint can be navigated by adding /OData/ to the end of the service. The trailing / is required, otherwise you will just get an error. Navigate to:

```
http://127.0.0.1:81/BusinessApplication-Web-Services-
WorkplaceDomainService.svc/OData/
```

16. It will display the OData service as shown in the following screenshot:

17. The OData service now works as normal. Navigating to entity sets is possible through the normal means: navigating to `http://127.0.0.1:81/BusinessApplication-Web-Services-WorkplaceDomainService.svc/OData/DivisionSet` will display the divisions as shown in the following screenshot:

With the OData service exposed, any client can now consume it through the normal means. The steps that were followed in the preceding exercise to add an OData endpoint can be applied here to consume the feed within Silverlight.

WCF Data Services with SQL Azure

In certain situations, you may want to just expose an OData service without using the RIA Services. You can instead use the base WCF Data Service class directly in your code. This simply requires an Entity Framework Data Model to be passed in as a generic parameter. We do this as follows:

1. Open Visual Studio 2010 and create a new **Windows Azure Project** named as **WcfOdataExercise**.

2. Add a single ASP.Net web role into the project and click on **OK**.

3. Add a new **ADO.NET Entity Data Model** and name it **WorkplaceModel.edmx**.

4. The **Entity Data Model Wizard** will start automatically. Select the option to generate a model from an existing database. Enter the details of your existing SQL Azure database.

5. Select the tables that should be included in the model. The following screenshot shows the database of the workplace. Make sure you select the **Division (dbo)** and the **Employee (dbo)** tables:

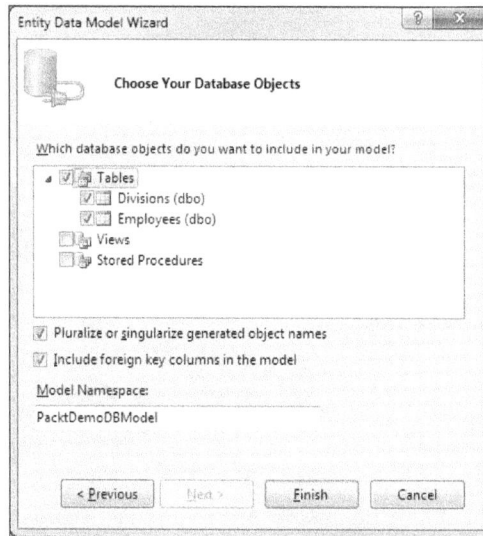

6. Build the project to ensure that the EDM is generated correctly.

7. Add a new WCF Data Service and name it **WorkplaceDataService.svc** as shown in the following screenshot:

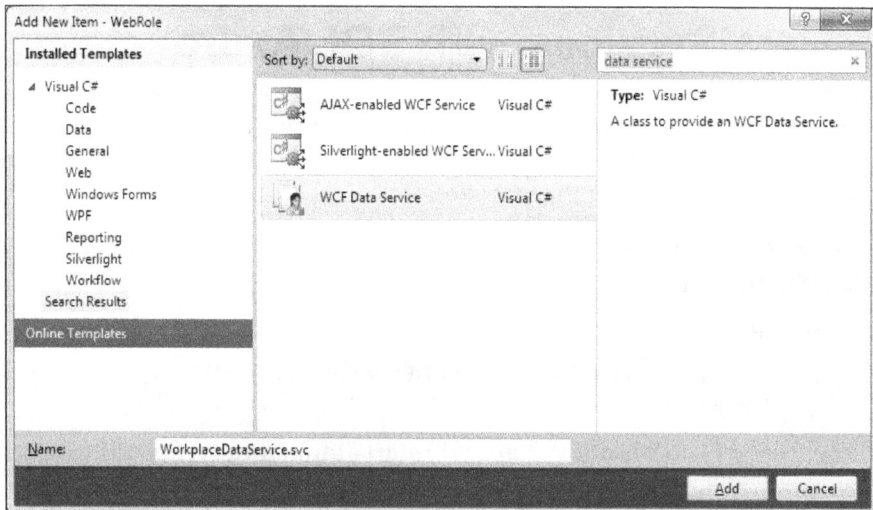

8. The WCF Data Service will be code generated for you, which is not more than four lines of code. The result should be similar to the one shown in the following screenshot:

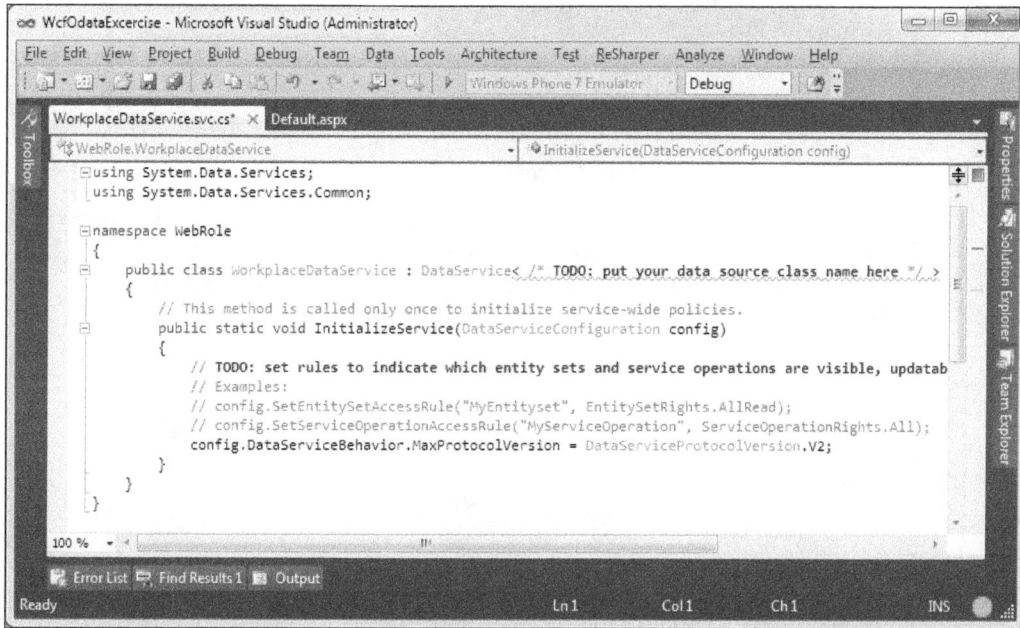

9. In the class definition, `DataService` is expecting the EDM class to be entered. Replace the inline comment with your model as follows:

```
public class WorkplaceDataService : DataService
    <PacktDemoDBEntities>
```

10. The `DataService` class now knows about the model, but by default, none of the entity sets are exposed for security reasons. You are required to manually expose each entity set and the operation. Modify the `InitializeService` class, so that the `Employees` can be written to, but `Divisions` are all read-only as follows:

```
public static void InitializeService(DataServiceConfiguration
config)
{
  config.SetEntitySetAccessRule("Employees",
    EntitySetRights.AllWrite);
  config.SetEntitySetAccessRule("Divisions",
    EntitySetRights.AllRead);
  config.DataServiceBehavior.MaxProtocolVersion =
    DataServiceProtocolVersion.V2;
}
```

> **WCF Data Services Configuration**
>
> More details on different security options and configuration settings can be found on MSDN at the following URL:
>
> `http://msdn.microsoft.com/en-us/library/ee358710.aspx`

11. Press *F5* to compile and run the service.

12. As this is a WCF service that is being exposed, you can navigate to the SVC file directly to access the endpoint. Navigate to `http://127.0.0.1:81/WorkplaceDataService.svc/` to see the OData service as shown in the following screenshot:

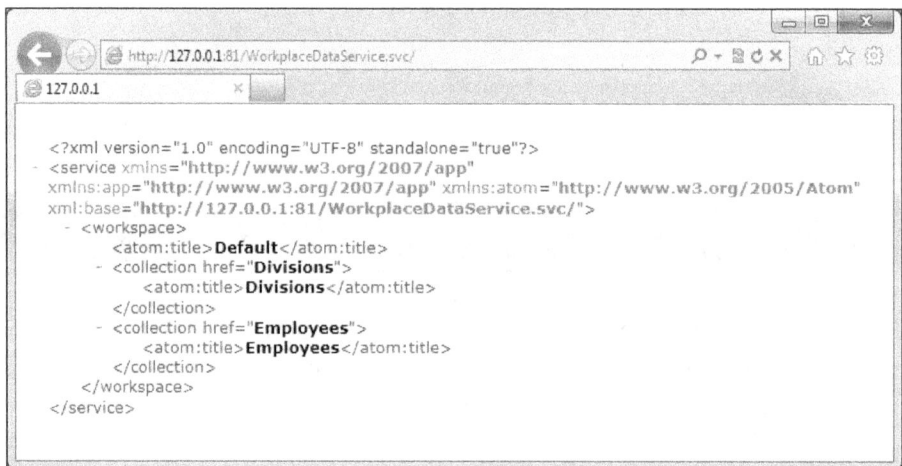

With the OData service exposed, it can now be consumed through the client of your choice. The service can be consumed in a Silverlight application easily by following the preceding exercise in this chapter, but using the URI of the service you just created.

Summary

This chapter showed that OData can be easily consumed and exposed within multiple applications. OData is a great way to have data interoperability across an enterprise.

The following chapter will discuss how worker roles can be used to assist in the scaling of Azure applications.

10
Web-scale Considerations

This chapter explores a few non-Silverlight specific concepts around the ways to scale your applications. These are useful techniques that can be applied to all the cloud applications, and they help to create the global applications with clean architectures. Architecting for the cloud has some subtle differences from creating the traditional applications. This chapter covers the following topics:

- Asynchronous processing and componentization
- CQRS (Command Query Responsibility Segregation)
- Globalizing your applications

Asynchronous processing and componentization

The ability of an application to scale in the cloud is vital when it comes to building large Internet applications. One way to ensure that an application is able to scale efficiently is by breaking it down into smaller, independent components, which operate asynchronously with each other.

Breaking a large application into functionally separate modules can have a number of benefits for the architecture of your application. They are as follows:

- It allows the components to be scaled independently.
- It reduces **coupling** within the application (when constructed with the messages and the interfaces). The components can then be updated separately.
- It reduces the complexity by reducing the contact points to the business logic. The interactions must be explicit rather than a simple method call.

Having the components operate asynchronously with each other means the following:

- The users and the **User Interface** (**UI**) are not being held up, waiting for the work to complete
- The resources are not tied up with the blocking calls
- The work can be queued and buffered

Putting the concepts of **componentization** and **asynchrony** together allows us to build applications that can handle the spikes in the usage and instead smooth out the required computing resources.

By splitting an application into the components, you can divide the tasks that require immediate responses (web roles: displaying a page, returning files such as media), and tasks that need to be processed asynchronously (worker role: tasks that have a delay, such as saving large volumes of data, processing video files, calling external resources).

To give a more in-depth look as to how these concepts can be used within the architecture of a cloud application, we will investigate a fictitious website named **AzureTube**.

AzureTube is a website that enables the users to upload video content, and allows the videos to be hosted online. When users upload video content, the video needs to be re-encoded into different codecs and bit rates.

The web application has a few key functions:

- It accepts the videos uploaded by the users and converts them into a number of formats
- It allows the users to browse the videos
- It allows the users to play the videos

Two examples will be given: a naive implementation, and a website that was built to scale with Azure.

Naive website example

A naive website may try to handle all the functions at once, and also tries to scale by throwing more servers at it.

An example workflow for a naive implementation is as follows:

- The user uploads a video. The server immediately begins to transcode the video.
- The user browses the videos. The server then returns the list of the available videos.
- The user plays a video. The server starts streaming the file to the user.

The problem with this approach is that all the functions are being handled simultaneously by the same servers. If there is a significant number of videos uploaded at once, which are then transcoded simultaneously, it could have performance impacts on the other functions of the website (video listings and streaming).

Another issue with this implementation is the lack of **buffering** work to be done. Any incoming video would be processed immediately on the thread that handles the request of the user. This leads to massive spikes in the required computing resources.

Scaling would also become an issue, as each additional server added would need to handle all the functions of the application. It could be difficult to determine if the performance issues are coming from a high user load (browsing and streaming videos), or from the servers that are currently encoding the videos.

The following diagram shows how a traditional website architecture and user load may look similar, with the same set of servers handling the video uploads and the user requests:

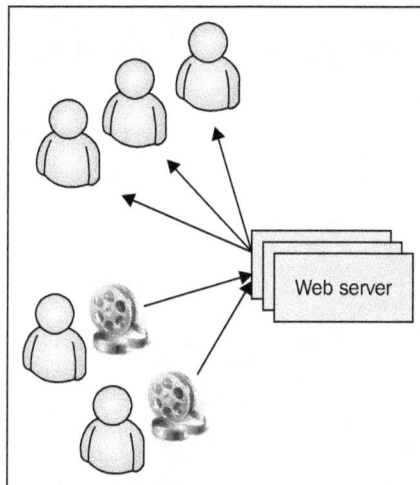

Asynchronous website example

Instead of containing all the application code in one piece, the units of work will
be divided into components. There are multiple ways that the segregation could
happen. An initial splitting can be based on the expected response time of the user,
as follows:

- Immediate response
    - ° Video listings
    - ° Video streaming
    - ° General website functions (registration, browsing, and so on)
- Delay acceptable
    - ° Video transcoding

Some functionalities require an immediate response while the other tasks can
wait. For example, a video that is being transcoded can be delayed, as it is not an
interactive command. Taking 20 minutes to process a video instead of 15 minutes
would not annoy most of the users. However, users will be very vocal about the
listing of the available videos taking longer than five seconds to load or if there are
delays while playing a video.

This first segregation of functions gives us a good place to start architecting the new
structure of the application. There can now be web roles handling the immediate
response items, and worker roles to handle the work that can be done asynchronously.

The following diagram shows a high-level concept of how the new architecture
could work:

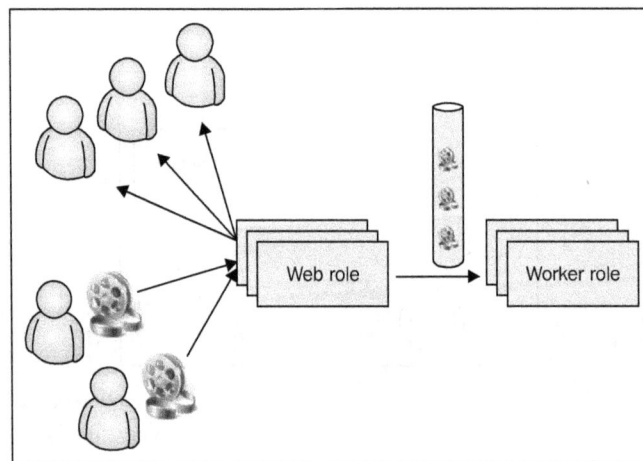

The frontend web roles handle the listing of the videos and accepting the uploading of the videos. However, instead of processing the videos immediately, the web roles can pass the work to the worker roles by adding the videos to a **queue** of work that needs to be done. The worker roles can then pick up a job from the queue of work, and process the videos one at a time.

The two roles that make the application are now working asynchronously and independently. From a performance perspective, the components can now be scaled independently and easily with Windows Azure. If there is a spike of users watching the videos (due to a video going viral), then the number of web roles handling the users can be scaled up and down as the demand dictates. With the worker roles, if there are only a few videos uploaded each hour, then a single worker role can sit there, processing the videos one after the other. However, if the queue of work to be done starts to get too lengthy, additional worker roles can be brought online that help to bring the number of videos back in the queue down to a more manageable level. Once the queue has become shorter again, then the number of worker roles can be scaled back down.

The following diagram shows how the conceptual architecture could be implemented with Windows Azure. As a real-world example, **Pixar** uses the render farms of Azure workers to process their videos, which valid can be found at the following address:

```
http://www.istartedsomething.com/20110831/green-button-makes-pixars-
renderman-concept-on-windows-azure-a-reality/
```

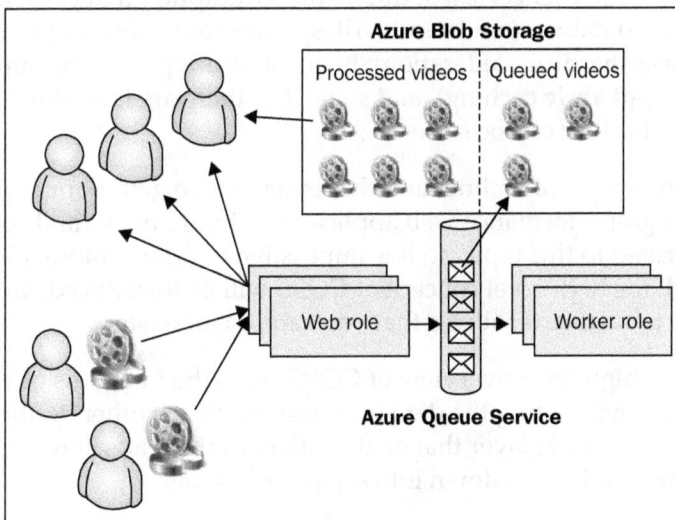

In this new architecture with Azure technologies, the user again uploads a video. The video is then stored in a temporary folder in the **Azure Blob storage**. A message is added to the Azure queue to indicate that a video needs to be processed. The message holds the URI to the video being held in the Blob storage. The worker role then takes a message off the queue, reads the address of the video to be processed, processes the video, and places the processed video back into the Blob storage. The users are still able to browse the listings of the videos through the web roles, but the videos are loaded from the Blob storage.

The preceding example can be further optimized through the use of the **Azure CDN** (**Content Delivery Network**) that was covered in *Chapter 5, Accessing Azure Blob Storage from Silverlight*. The video files can be pushed to the edge servers that are geographically closer to the users watching the videos, which can reduce the latency and increase the bandwidth.

CQRS (Command Query Responsibility Segregation)

Most of this book has focussed on the reading and writing of data within a standard "three-tier architecture", with a database, database access or a business logic layer, and a UI. This has been generally mapped to the **SQL Azure**, **RIA Services**, and **Silverlight**. All reads and writes in this configuration are done to the "business logic database". Depending on how you scale your application, this can eventually lead to performance bottlenecks, just due to the assumption that everything is done against that single database (reads and writes). There are many ways to mitigate this, by using **database sharding** (federation), by incorporating more caching into the system (**Azure AppFabric** caching), and so on. but there are limitations to how far a traditional architecture can be scaled.

CQRS is a different style of architecture that is starting to gain popularity among the creators of high-performance web applications. Entire books and conferences have been dedicated to this topic, so it is impossible to fully explore it within a single chapter. Instead, the high-level concept of CQRS will be introduced, and will be backed by links to further resources that you can research later.

A very simplistic, high-level overview of CQRS splits the functions of writing the data (commands) and reading the data (queries) from each other. Rather than having a single database and logic layer that deals with both the reads and the writes at once, they are instead broken down into separate systems.

The following diagram shows a high-level architecture of CQRS:

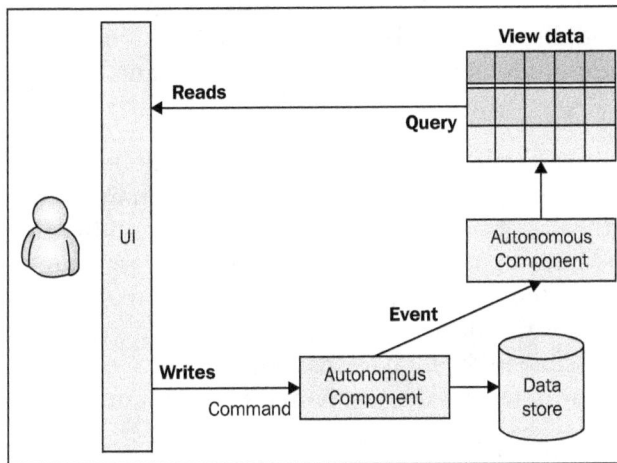

There are two main reasons why CQRS splits these functions into separate components. They are **concurrency** and **query speed**.

When an application simultaneously reads and writes against a single database, there is an issue of concurrency. Two users may be looking at the same screen, that is, user A then updates the data, while user B is still working with the stale data on their respective screens. When user B submits the changes, most of the systems will just flag that there was a concurrency issue and refresh the screen, forcing the user to input all the data again (unless there is complex logic on how to handle a concurrency conflict). CQRS handles this through the concept of commands. Each command should say what is being done to the data, such as adding five to the number of units sold. This can help to reduce the occurrence of concurrency issues as it models the intent, rather than what the final values should be.

While reading the data from a database, the traditional flow of data results in the performance of many transformations as follows:

- The data is held in the relational database in a normalized format
- The data is returned as a dataset
- The dataset is transformed into the database objects (LINQ to SQL, Entity Framework)
- There may be a need to perform an additional business logic on the objects
- There may be a need to transform the database objects into **Data Transfer Objects (DTO)** in order to send it to the client
- The client then takes the DTOs and transforms them into a view-specific format (**view model**)

Depending on the system, there may be fewer or more steps than the preceding ones that are outlined . This can be seen as much additional overhead just to get some data to the client and display it on the screen. What if there was a way to store the data in the final view model form, ready to be returned and displayed immediately to the client?

CQRS separates the reads and the writes so that the redundant transformation of data through the traditional layers can be reduced. The commands to change the data are submitted by the user. The main business logic and the data are held in a relational database, with all the rules and the validation happening on that single "source of truth". Once the main data store has been updated, an event can then be raised and another background worker can write the data in a denormalized form that is as close as possible to the final format required by the UI. The UI can then simply query the view data, and display it on the screen immediately.

Additional resources

Again, CQRS is a long and complicated topic, which we cannot do justice to in such a short section. If you do find the concept to be interesting, then here are some resources to help you in your research.

Udi Dahan is one of the main proponents of CQRS. He regularly talks at conferences and user groups on the topic. He also travels the world internationally, delivering a training course on the topic. His blog is the best starting place to find out more on this subject. There are also recordings of some of his previous talks available online that you can take advantage of. If Udi does come to your city and is providing training, I highly recommend you to pester your boss and get along to one of his courses as follows:

- The blog post, *Clarified CQRS,* is found at the following address:

  `http://www.udidahan.com/2009/12/09/clarified-cqrs/`

- The CQRS talk that Udi did at a user group is found at the following address:

  `http://vimeo.com/8944337`

- The cloud architecture CQRS series on MSDN is found at the following address:

  `http://blogs.msdn.com/b/brunoterkaly/archive/2012/02/07/cloud-architecture-series-cqrs-command-query-responsibility-segrega-tion-part-01.aspx`

- The asynchronous systems architecture for the Web (the embedded video works) is found at the following address:

  `http://skillsmatter.com/podcast/open-source-dot-net/asynchro-nous-systems-architecture-for-the-web/js-1417`

MSDN magazine provides a good introductory article on how to implement CQRS in Windows Azure with **ASP.NET MVC2** at the following address:

`http://msdn.microsoft.com/en-us/magazine/gg983487.aspx`.

There are a number of CQRS frameworks that can be used to assist the development. However, many of them rely heavily on knowing the concepts such as **DDD** (**Domain Driven Design**), and can be very heavyweight in the required additional code infrastructure. I recommend that you research the concepts of CQRS yourself, and also implement the basic structure to ensure that you fully understand how the entire system works. However, the following are some popular frameworks that can be investigated:

- **NCQRS**: It is to be found at the following address:

  `http://ncqrs.org/`

- **Lokad.CQRS**: It is found at the following URL:

  `http://lokad.github.com/lokad-cqrs/`

- **Lokad.CQRS NuGet package**: It is found at the following address:

  `http://nuget.org/List/Packages/Lokad.CQRS`

Implementing CQRS with Azure

To assist your research, here is a brief guide on how a CQRS architecture could be implemented with Windows Azure technologies. The following diagram shows how the components could be mapped to Azure offerings:

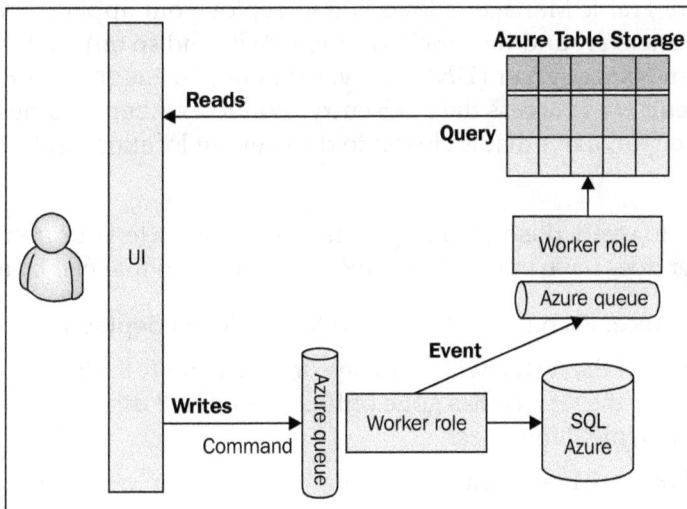

In the diagram, the UI could be either a web role, or a Silverlight talking to a web role. The commands are put into an Azure queue. The worker roles then process the commands one at a time, and update the SQL Azure database. One worker role then places a new message on another queue, while another worker role then picks it up from the queue, and updates the denormalized data held in the Azure Table storage.

If you are going to do any serious work by using the queues as a message medium between the roles, then I highly recommend to use **nServiceBus** instead of the communication. It further simplifies working with the messages, as follows:

- nServiceBus homepage is found at the following address:

  `http://www.nservicebus.com`

- The blog of *Goeleven Yves* (one of the developers of Azure support in nServiceBus) is found at the following URL:

- `http://cloudshaper.wordpress.com`

Globalizing your applications

In *Chapter 6, Storing Data in Azure Table Storage from Silverlight*, it was shown that files could be pushed out through a CDN (Content Delivery Network) to be geographically closer to the end users. The computing resources can also be pushed out to be geographically closer to your global customers in Europe, Asia, and America.

Windows Azure has a product called **Windows Azure Traffic Manager** that can help you to distribute the computing power across a number of datacenters globally. Windows Azure Traffic Manager allows you to deploy your application onto the multiple datacenters around the world (Europe, Asia, and so on), and then create a single **Domain Name Server** (DNS) entry, for example, `<suffix>.trafficmgr.com`). When clients try to access the DNS entry, Windows Azure Traffic Manager will detect the deployment that is closest to the client in location, and redirect them to use it.

This is one way to easily push your application to be closer to your users. But the Traffic Manager does have many other modes of operation that can be useful:

- **Performance**: Each request is routed to the closest deployment.
- **Failover**: All the traffic will go to one deployment. If the Traffic Manager detects that the service has gone offline, then it will direct the traffic to the next deployment in the list.
- **Round robin**: These requests are sent out to the deployments equally, one at a time.

The performance mode is what helps your application to be geographically distributed. However, this can lead to unequal usage patterns. You may find that the datacenter in Europe requires more instances to handle the load, as it gets more users routed to it than the Asian instances.

The failover option allows an application to be deployed onto the two different datacenters to increase the uptime due to unexpected outages. There have been a handful of outages in both the Azure and the Amazon datacenters in the past, which brought some applications offline. Applications that were hosted in the other datacenters were not affected, so this is one way to mitigate any potential, unscheduled downtime. However, a more cost-effective solution may be the last option.

With round robin, traffic is split up evenly across each of the deployments. If a service goes down, then the traffic will just not be routed to it.

A side effect of having multiple deployments is that each of them requires their own local data source such as SQL Azure. This means that the databases get out of sync very quickly. One way to keep all of the databases in sync is to use **SQL Azure Data Sync**.The following are a number of links to the resources that can provide you with more information on Windows Azure Traffic Manager and how to implement it in your own applications:

- **Traffic Manager home page**: It is found at the following address:

  `http://www.microsoft.com/windowsazure/features/virtualnetwork`

- **Windows Azure training course–Traffic Manager:** It is found at the following address:

  `http://msdn.microsoft.com/en-us/WAZPlatformTrainingCourse_Win-dowsAzureTrafficManager`

- The video from **Microsoft MIX 2011** that shows how to combine Traffic Manager and SQL Azure Sync (22mins) is found at the following URL:

  `http://channel9.msdn.com/Events/MIX/MIX11/SVC05`

Summary

It is important to keep yourself aware of the different architectures and patterns that are available while architecting for the cloud. This chapter showed that the asynchronous components are essential while trying to create the scalable applications. By creating independent components, you are able to spot the performance problems and scale the components individually.

CQRS was then introduced as an alternative architecture for creating cloud applications. It is slightly more complex, but can result in massive scalability improvements. The links provided in the chapter can be explored before you begin with your project. Dedicate an hour to watch the introductory video Udi did at the **Victoria.NET** user group before making any decisions.

Finally, Windows Azure Traffic Manager was presented as a way to distribute your application globally. CDNs are useful for pushing the static data out to your clients, but Traffic Manager is useful for pushing the computing resources closer to your clients.

11
Application Authentication

This chapter will look at the different ways an application can be secured to allow access only to the authorized users.

There are two main ways in which an application can be secured: **Windows Identity Foundation** and **ASP.NET providers**.

This chapter will cover the following topics:

- Windows Identity Foundation and Azure Access Control service
- ASP.NET providers
- Using the SQL Azure provider
- Using the Azure Storage provider
- Windows authentication

Windows Identity Foundation and Azure Access Control Service

Windows Identity Foundation (WIF) is a new framework from Microsoft that assists in creating applications that use **Federated Authentication**. It is a new technique that is gaining popularity for creating the enterprise applications that are hosted outside the corporate firewall. While hosting an application in the cloud, it is difficult to have the user log on with their active directory credentials as the Azure roles are not joined to the domain.

By using **Windows Identity Foundation** and **Azure Access Control Service (ACS)**, it is possible to federate the authentication of the users to an on-premise active directory. Azure ACS handles the authentication of users to the remote user directories, and passes a valid security token to your application. The Azure ACS can also be used to federate the authentication to not just an active directory of a single corporation, but to multiple corporations if enabled correctly. This allows a single application to service the users from multiple companies.

Azure ACS is the recommended way of creating enterprise applications that require authorization to the active directory of an enterprise. Unfortunately, the support of WIF for Silverlight is lacking at the current time. Currently, the best approach involves in securing access to all the resources on the web server (Silverlight, XAP files, web services, and so on) and enabling **passive federation** within the Silverlight application.

The best way to learn more about securing your application with Azure ACS is by checking the latest guidance in the **Identity Developer Training Kit** at the following address:

```
http://www.microsoft.com/download/en/details.aspx?id=14347
```

ASP.NET providers

If Azure ACS does not cover your needs, then the traditional ASP.NET methods are still available for use. ASP.NET membership providers have offered developers an easy way to integrate the user stores into an application. Other capabilities such as session state, roles, and so on are all core to the ASP.NET provider model.

When a user clicks on the **Login** button in a silverlight RIA Services application, it is actually using the built-in ASP.NET membership providers under the covers. This allows Silverlight the same flexibility that ASP.NET has in selecting a provider, based on the desired backing stores.

The providers grant features to an application such as membership (username and passwords), session state, roles, and so on.

> **Session state**
>
> While session state can be stored in SQL Azure or Azure Storage, be aware that it can also be stored in AppFabric caching. Depending on the load your application experiences, you may find a benefit in using one over the other. Refer to *Chapter 12, Using Azure AppFabric Caching to Improve Performance*, for more information on caching.

The ASP.NET providers offer a consistent interface that can be used to create the users, check whether a user is logged in, has been granted a particular role, and so on. By using different providers, you are able to use different data stores, such as SQL Azure or Azure Storage.

> **SQL Azure or Azure Storage?**
>
> For a majority of the applications, SQL Azure will be the preferred option for ASP.NET membership as SQL membership providers are well understood. Azure Storage is mainly used as a fallback solution if SQL Azure is not a part of your architecture.

Once one of the providers has been enabled, then you can continue to secure your application with the same techniques that you are familiar with.

Using the SQL Azure provider

The original **ASP.NET SQL providers** were built only to work with standard **SQL Server** and **SQL Server Express**. Some of the required capabilities of SQL Server that the ASP.NET SQL providers rely on are not available in SQL Azure. Some of the features that will not work are session state and the creation of the required tables through the ASPNET_REGSQL tool. There are some workarounds that can be found online, such as the updated SQL scripts for table creation at `http://support.microsoft.com/kb/2006191`. However, there is a better way to get this working.

Microsoft released a new provider called the **ASP.NET Universal Providers**, which resolves these issues. The universal providers will work with SQL compact, SQL Server Express, SQL Server, and SQL Azure. This makes development easier as the same provider will work against a local SQL Server on the machine of a developer, and can then work with the SQL Azure database with just a connection string modification. The next version of ASP.NET will include the new provider, but for the moment they are available from Microsoft as a **NuGet package**.

This exercise will show how to create a Silverlight RIA services application quickly that uses the ASP.NET Universal Providers to use SQL Azure as the backing store. Create a new SQL Azure database, or use an existing one, as follows:

1. Open Visual Studio 2010 and create a new **Windows Azure Project** named `SqlAzureMembershipExercise`, as shown in the following screenshot:

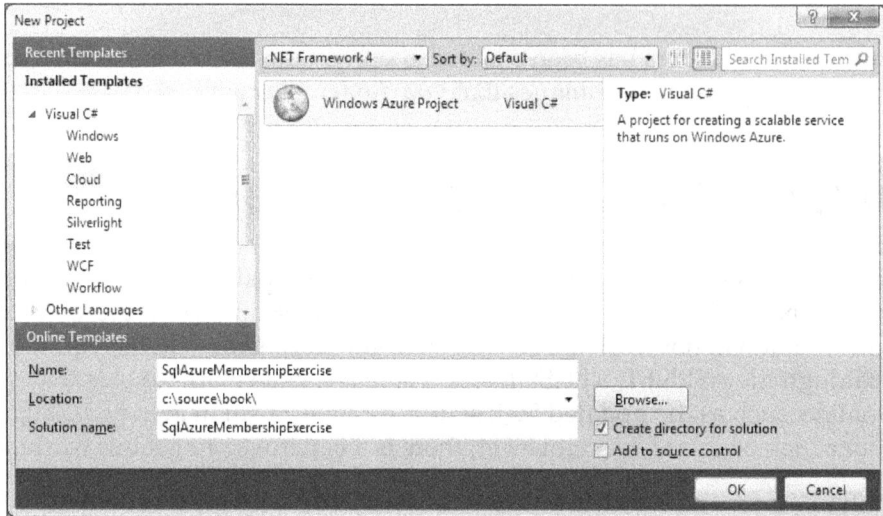

2. Add a single **Silverlight Business Application** role to the project named `BusinessApplication`, as shown in the following screenshot, and click on **OK**:

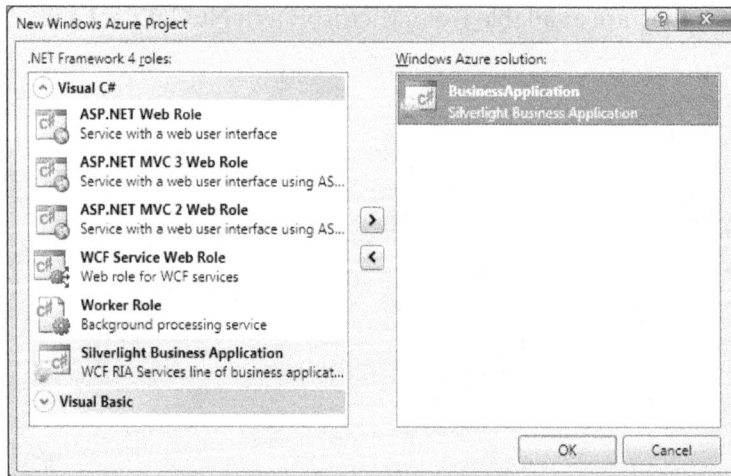

3. Once the solution is created, add the NuGet reference. In the web project, right-click on **References,** and click on **Manage NuGet Packages**, as shown in the following screenshot:

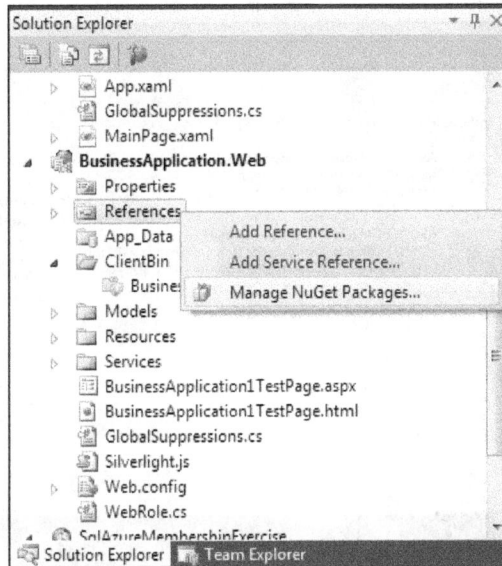

NuGet

If you do not have the NuGet menu option, then install the Microsoft NuGet extension from the following address:

`http://NuGet.org`

4. Search for `System.Web.Providers`, and install the **ASP.NET Universal Providers for SqlExpress**, as shown in the following screenshot. For an unknown reason, the latest release of the package had its name changed to include SqlExpress in the name, but it works with all the versions of SQL Server:

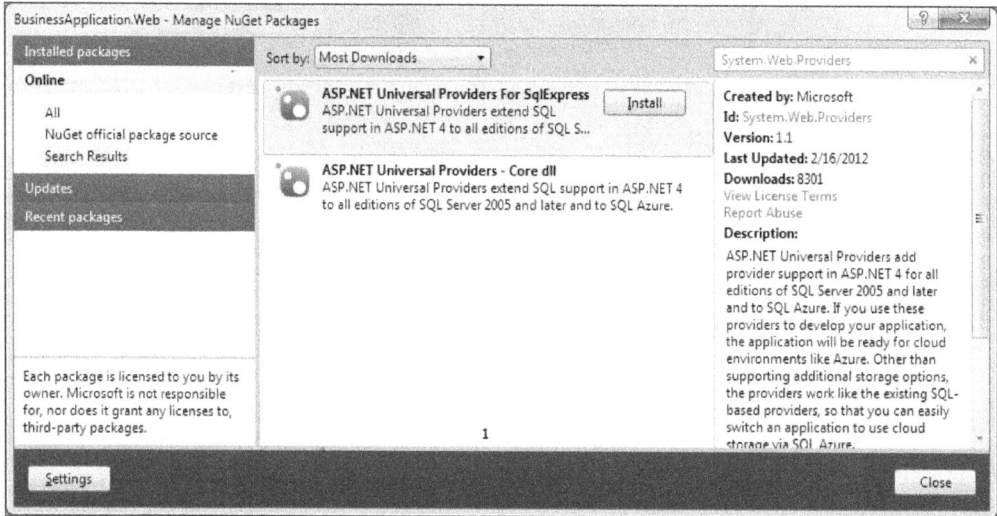

5. Once the ASP.NET Universal Providers NuGet package is installed, it will automatically add the correct assembly references to the application. The `web.config` file will also be automatically updated with the required configuration settings to enable the universal providers and set them as the application defaults.

6. The `web.config` file now needs to have two settings changed before it is ready to be used. The connection string to the database needs to be set to the SQL Azure instance and the membership provider needs to store the hashed passwords, rather than just plain text. Modify the `DefaultConnection` connection string so that it is connecting to your SQL Azure instance:

```
<connectionStrings>
  <add name="DefaultConnection"
    connectionString="data
      source=[SqlAzureName].database.windows.net;
    Initial Catalog=[database];
    User ID=[username];
    Password=[password];
    Encrypt=true;
    Trusted_Connection=false;
    MultipleActiveResultSets=True"
```

```
        providerName="System.Data.SqlClient" />
</connectionStrings>
```

7. Find the membership provider named `DefaultMembershipProvider` and add the `passwordFormat` attribute to it:

```
<membership defaultProvider="DefaultMembershipProvider">
  <providers>
    <add name="DefaultMembershipProvider"
      type="System.Web.Providers.DefaultMembershipProvider"
        connectionStringName="DefaultConnection"
    passwordFormat="Hashed" />
  </providers>
</membership>
```

8. Ensure that the Azure project is set as the default project.

9. Press *F5* to compile and run the application.

> **Application name**
>
> The application will be automatically configured to have the application name set as the default `applicationName="/"`. It is possible to go through it and change all the instances of application name in code, and provide a new name for the application to identify itself as in the SQL Azure Applications table.

10. Click on **Login** and then click on **Register Now**. Fill out the form similar to the one in the following screenshot:

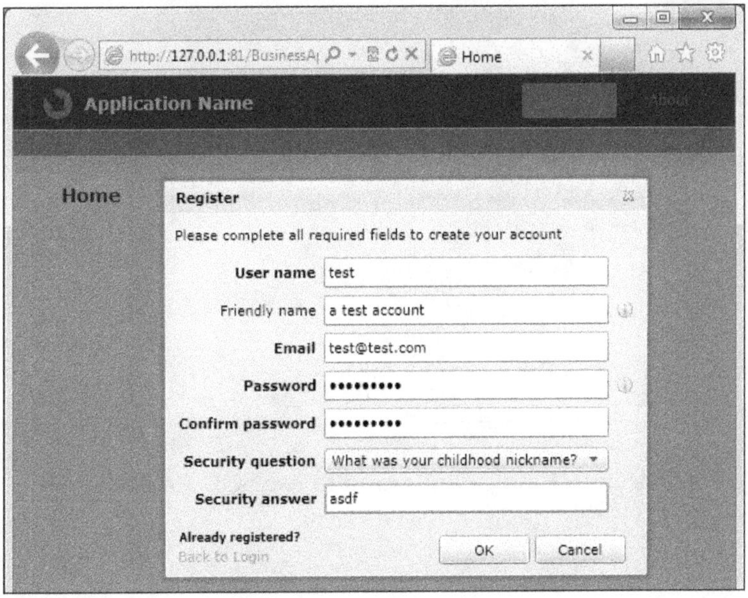

11. Once you click on the **OK** button, the ASP.NET Universal Provider will inspect the database. If this is running for the first time, the required tables will be automatically created (application, memberships, sessions, users, and so on). The user will then be created. Now, the user logs in, as shown in the following screenshot:

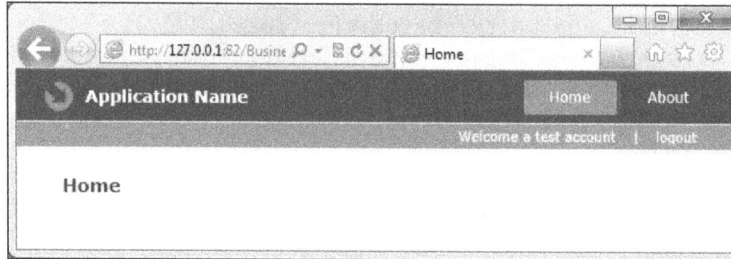

12. Opening SQL Server Management Studio and connecting to the database will allow you to see the tables that were automatically created. The following screenshot shows the `test` user that was created in the preceding step:

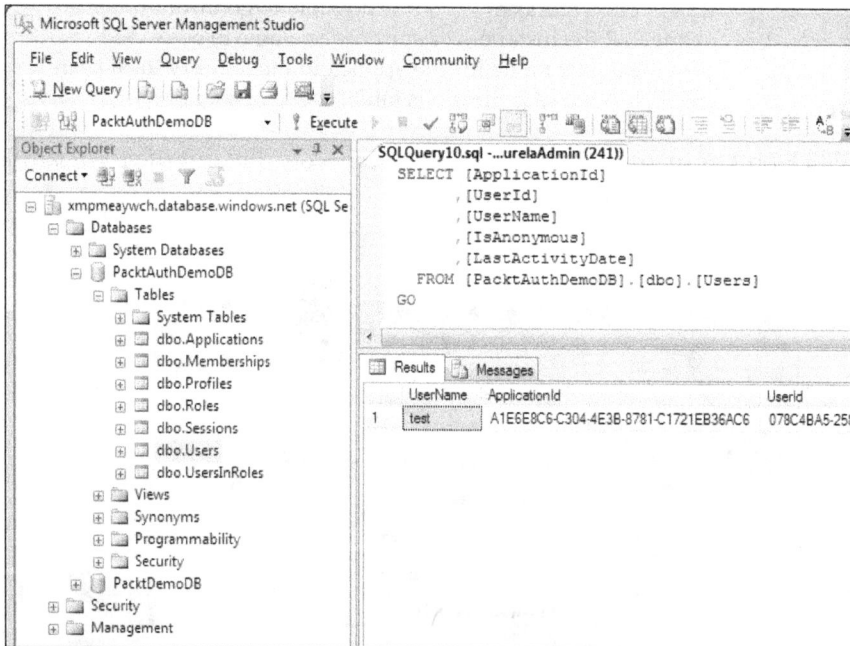

The Silverlight application is now configured to use SQL Azure with the universal providers.

Using the Azure Storage provider

The majority of applications, SQL Azure will be the preferred option for storing ASP. NET membership, session state, and so on. If the architecture of your application does not require SQL Azure, then falling back to using Azure Storage is a possibility.

Microsoft has released a code sample that contains the code required to enable the ASP.NET Azure Storage provider. This provider will store the user details (e-mail, username, password hash, and so on) in Table storage and store the customizable profile details (friendly name) in Blob storage in a text file per user.

Enabling the Azure Storage provider requires a few more manual steps than the universal provider did in the preceding exercise. This is because the NuGet package automatically configures many parts of the `web.config` file for us:

1. Go to the Microsoft code sample site for Windows Azure and download the **Windows Azure ASP.NET Providers Sample**. The direct link to the sample is `http://code.msdn.microsoft.com/windowsazure/Windows-Azure-ASPNET-03d5dc14`; but if the link no longer works, go to `http://code.msdn.microsoft.com/windowsazure` and search for the latest version.

2. Once downloaded, extract the sample ZIP file to a folder on your computer. Open the folder and browse to `AspProviders\bin\Debug` and locate `AspProviders.dll`.

3. Open Visual Studio 2010 and create a new **Windows Azure Project** named `AzureStorageProviderExercise`, as shown in the following screenshot:

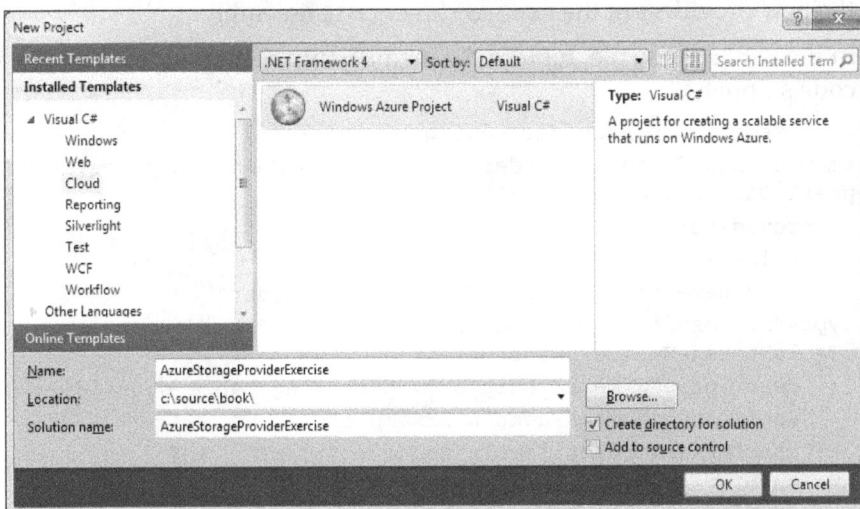

4. Add a single **Silverlight Business Application** role to the project named BusinessApplication, as shown in the following screenshot, and click on **OK**:

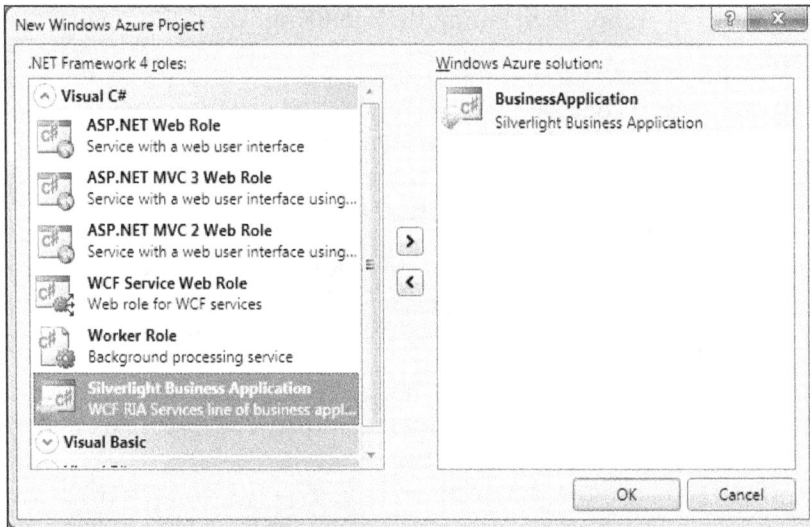

5. Once the solution is created, add a reference to AspProviders.dll that was downloaded in the preceding steps. In the web project, right-click on **References** and click on **Add Reference**. Browse to the location where AspProviders.dll is located and select it.

6. Open the web.config file. The application needs to be configured to use the new providers in the AspProviders.dll assembly.

7. In the web.config file, replace the membership section with the following code snippet:

```
<!-- Membership Provider Configuration -->
<membership defaultProvider="TableStorageMembershipProvider"
userIsOnlineTimeWindow="20">
  <providers>
    <clear/>
    <add name="TableStorageMembershipProvider"
type="Microsoft.Samples.ServiceHosting.AspProviders
.TableStorageMe mbershipProvider"
    description="Membership provider using table storage"
    applicationName="PacktAuthExample"
    enablePasswordRetrieval="false"
    enablePasswordReset="true"
    requiresQuestionAndAnswer="false"
```

```
    minRequiredPasswordLength="6"
    minRequiredNonalphanumericCharacters="0"
    requiresUniqueEmail="true"
    passwordFormat="Hashed"/>
  </providers>
</membership>
```

8. Replace the role manager section with the following code snippet

```
<!--RoleManager Provider Configuration -->
<roleManager enabled="true"
  defaultProvider="TableStorageRoleProvider"
  cacheRolesInCookie="true"
  cookieName=".ASPXROLES"
  cookieTimeout="30"
  cookiePath="/"
  cookieRequireSSL="false"
  cookieSlidingExpiration="true"
  cookieProtection="All">
  <providers>
  <clear/>
  <add name="TableStorageRoleProvider"
type="Microsoft.Samples.ServiceHosting.AspProviders.
TableStorageRo leProvider"
  description="Role provider using table storage"
  applicationName="PacktAuthExample" />
  </providers>
</roleManager>
```

9. Replace the profile manager section with the following code snippet

```
<!-- Profile Manager Provider Configuration -->
<profile enabled="true"
defaultProvider="TableStorageProfileProvider" >
<providers>
  <clear/>
  <add name="TableStorageProfileProvider"
type="Microsoft.Samples.ServiceHosting.AspProviders.
TableStorageProfileProvider"
  description="Profile provider using structured storage"
  applicationName="PacktAuthExample" />
</providers>
<properties>
  <add name="FriendlyName"/>
</properties>
</profile>
```

10. Before the application can be run, the Azure Storage credentials need to be configured. In the Azure project, under `Roles`, right-click on **BusinessApplication.Web** and select **Properties**. Go to the **Settings** tab and click on **Add Setting**. Name the connection as `DataConnectionString` and configure your credentials to point to your Azure Storage service, similar to what is shown in the following screenshot. The local development storage emulator will also work fine for this exercise:

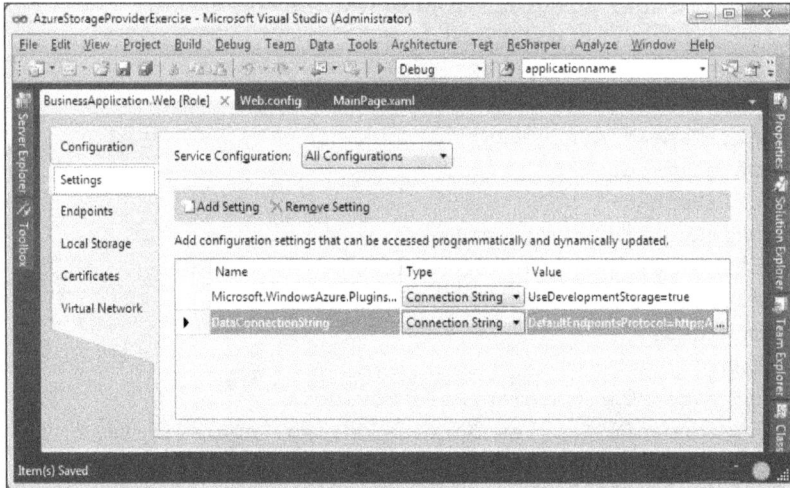

11. Ensure that the Azure project is set as the startup project.

12. Press *F5* to compile and run the application.

13. Click on **Login** and then click on **Register Now**. Fill out the form similar to the following screenshot:

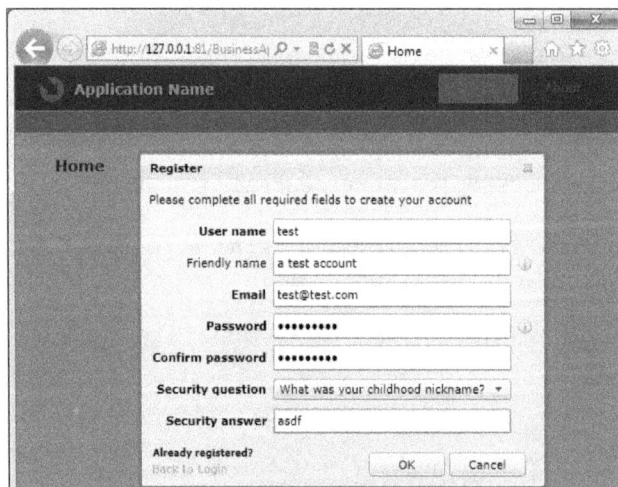

14. When you click on **OK**, if this is the first time it is running, the required tables and the files will be created in Azure Storage to support it. The application will then automatically log you in and display the friendly name at the top right of the screen:

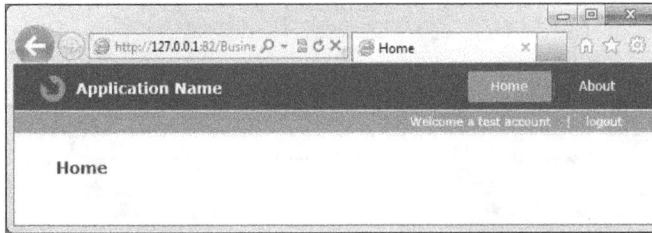

15. Opening Azure Storage Explorer and connecting to the storage account will allow you to see the tables and the files that were created. The following screenshot shows the user record in the Table storage:

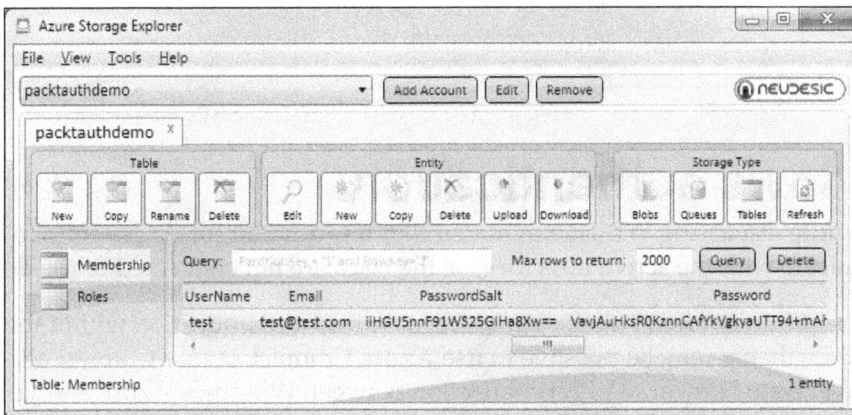

The following screenshot shows the additional information that is being stored in the Blob storage for the user accounts:

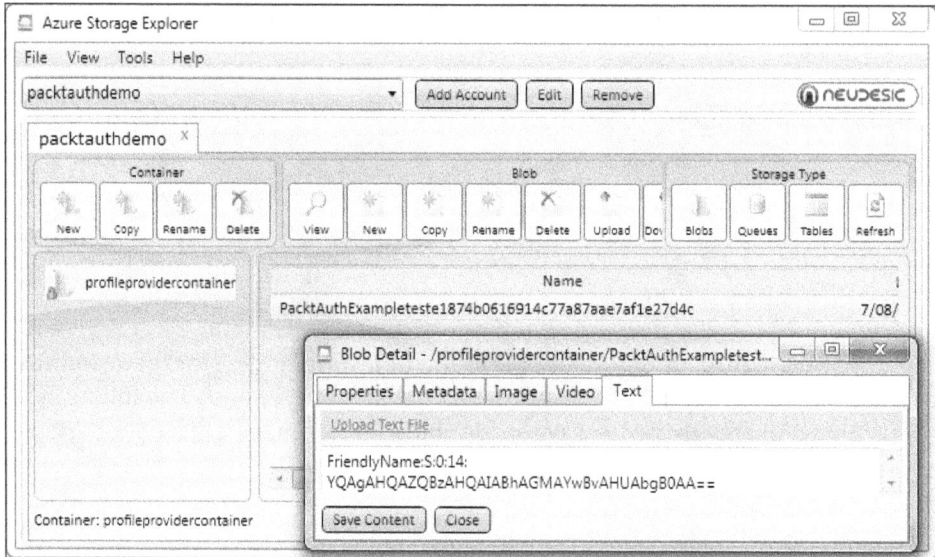

Windows authentication

Earlier while discussing WIF, it was stated that it is difficult for Azure roles to communicate with the active directory, as the roles are not connected to the domain.

If it is a requirement that you use standard windows authentication within the application, then it may be possible to use **Azure Connect**. Azure Connect allows a Virtual Private Network (VPN) connection between Windows Azure and your corporate environment. It will also allow you to connect the roles to your domain. There is not much guidance to support this scenario, but a good place to start researching is on the Azure Connect team blog at the following address:

http://blogs.msdn.com/b/windows_azure_connect_team_blog/

However, it is highly recommended that you research using Azure ACS first, as the Azure Connect solution has limitations, such as it also requires the users to be within the corporate network or connected to the VPN.

Summary

This chapter looked at a variety of options for enabling user authentication within your application.

Using WIF and Azure ACS is the preferred solution, however, the limited support for Silverlight may be a hindrance to their adoption.

When WIF is not an option, the ASP.NET provider model allows a developer to easily configure where user credentials and other information is stored. SQL Azure and Azure Storage were both offered as different solutions, with SQL Azure as the preferred option, as it is the one supported by Microsoft through the use of the universal providers. It was also noted that while SQL Azure is able to hold the session state, that AppFabric caching may be a better solution and should be explored.

The final chapter will introduce the use of **Azure AppFabric caching** to improve the application's performance.

12
Using Azure AppFabric Caching to Improve Performance

Caching is an essential part of the tool that enables applications to scale in order to handle a large number of concurrent requests. This chapter will explore what data caching is and how it can improve the performance of your application. A sample application will be created that adds an **AppFabric cache** to **RIA Services**.

The topics covered will be as follows:

- Data caching
- Azure AppFabric caching
- Caching raw data in AppFabric
- ASP.NET session caching

Data caching

Data caching is used to improve the performance of applications. The performance gains are achieved by creating a copy of the master data and storing it in a location that the consumer can access faster than the original data (for example, holding it in the memory rather than fetching it from a database). Caching is typically done on the data that is accessed frequently (such as lookup tables) or is expensive to obtain (long request times, data calculations, and so on.)

Using data caching can bring a number of benefits to the architecture of your application as follows:

- **Quicker response times**: The requests from the clients can be processed quicker, as the required data can be retrieved quicker.

- **Reduction of requests to data source**: Sending fewer requests to your SQL Azure instance will allow your application to handle more concurrent users.

- **Reduction of data processing**: There is no need to use resources to calculate values on the fly as results in each Azure instance are able to handle more load.

- **Reduction of data transfer costs**: It reduces the cost of data transfer.

The main types of data that will be stored in the cache are the raw data and the processed data, explained as follows:

- **Raw data**: The values are retrieved directly from a data source (SQL Azure, Azure tables, and so on). It reduces the requests and the load on the data source.

- **Processed data**: It comprises the data that can be expensive to calculate, such as monthly totals, statistical averages, and so on. It reduces the computational load, which results in high concurrent usage.

Caching lifecycle

The lifecycle of a cache typically goes in the order as illustrated in the following diagram:

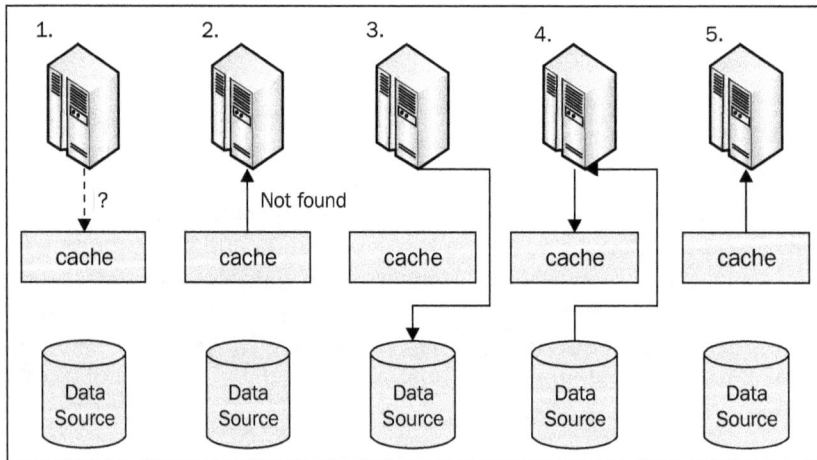

Check the cache for the required data:

1. The cache reports that the data is not stored.
2. The data is then requested from the data source.
3. Once the data has been retrieved, a copy is stored in the cache.
4. Later, when the data is requested from the cache, the cache can immediately return the data.
5. The values stored in the cache expire, either through a trigger or an elapsed time, and are removed from the cache. The next time the values are requested, it will start from step one again.

Caching issues

While caching data, it is important to consider the consequences of where the cache is stored as well as how long the data is cached for.

While scaling an Azure application, multiple web role instances are created to distribute the load evenly. If a request from a user is handled by one instance and the results are cached locally on that instance, and later when the next request from the user is handled by a different instance, different results may be returned to the user. It is important that only the data that does not need to be shared across the instances is cached at machine-level (similar to the one in ASP.Net in-memory caching).

It is also important to realize that if an instance restarts, any cache that was being held locally will be lost. If the data takes a long time to prepare before being cached (for example, the yearly totals), then there may be a delay before the data can be calculated and the instance can be ready to handle the requests.

The expiry time of data is another important consideration. If the data is quickly changing (for example, the stock prices), then the caching may result in showing stale data to the users. Slowly changing data should be stored in the cache, with appropriate lifetimes allocated. A list of countries could be cached for days, while the list of products sold may only be cached for an hour.

If the data has become stale earlier than expected, then the values stored in Azure AppFabric cache can be easily overwritten.

Azure AppFabric caching

Azure AppFabric caching is a **distributed in-memory caching service**, which is provided as a provisionable service that can be consumed. What it means by "in-memory" is that the servers that are hosting the AppFabric caching service hold all the cached values in the memory. This allows the caching servers to return the cached results rapidly, rather than retrieving the values from the disk. The **distributed** part of the name refers to the fact that the cache is distributed over a number of AppFabric servers to ensure the durability of the data.

A typical scenario for using the caching service is to cache data that is retrieved from an SQL Azure Database, or an Azure Table storage. This can reduce the load on the data stores, and also improve the response time by quickly retrieving the cached values. The following diagram shows an example of this scenario. Each of the Azure web or worker role instances retrieve their values from the AppFabric cache. As explained in the preceding part, if there is a cache missed due to the values not being stored, then one of the instances will retrieve the data from the data store and store it in the AppFabric cache, ready for the other instances to retrieve it, as follows:

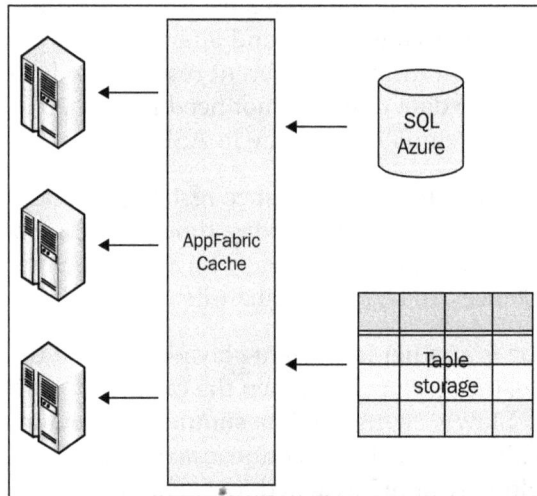

The AppFabric caching servers are able to handle requests and return the data very quicky due to the values being held in the memory. However, there is still a delay in communicating over the network between the web role and the AppFabric servers.

To reduce the network latency, it is possible to use some of the memory on the Azure web and worker role instances to cache values that are retrieved from the AppFabric server locally on the machine. The first request for the data will incur a network delay. However, subsequent requests will be handled by the the local copy.

This can be achieved automatically through a single configuration setting while creating the connection. The role instance will automatically check its local memory first. If the value is not there, then it will hit the AppFabric cache to retrieve the value. It will then store the value locally in the memory for future requests. The following diagram shows the role instances accessing their local cache first, which holds a copy of a small section of the full AppFabric cache:

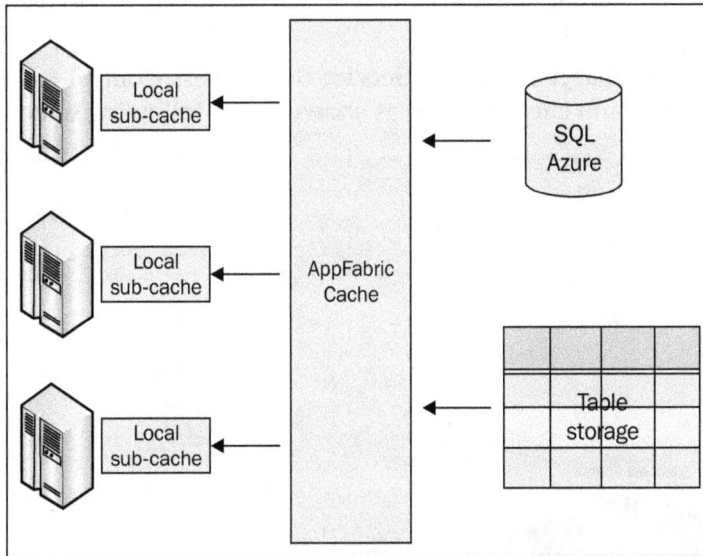

The pricing for the Azure AppFabric caching service can be found on the AppFabric website http://www.microsoft.com/windowsazure/features/caching/.

Caching raw data in AppFabric

This exercise will demonstrate a method to quickly integrate Azure AppFabric caching with the cached raw data from an SQL Azure Database.

A Silverlight or RIA Services application will be built that interacts with the SQL Azure Database. To improve the performance of the application, the slowly changing data will be cached in an AppFabric cache. The exercise will use the same workplace that SQL Azure Database has used in the preceding exercises.

Provisioning the AppFabric cache service

In order to use Azure AppFabric Caching in your application, an AppFabric Caching Service first needs to be provisioned. Once the AppFabric cache has been created, the Azure Management Portal provides many configuration settings that need to be added to your application in order to interact with it, as follows:

1. Start by navigating to `http://Azure.com` and logging in to the Azure Management Portal.

2. From the sidebar menu, select **Service Bus, Access Control & Caching**. Then select **Cache** and click on **New**, as shown in the following screenshot:

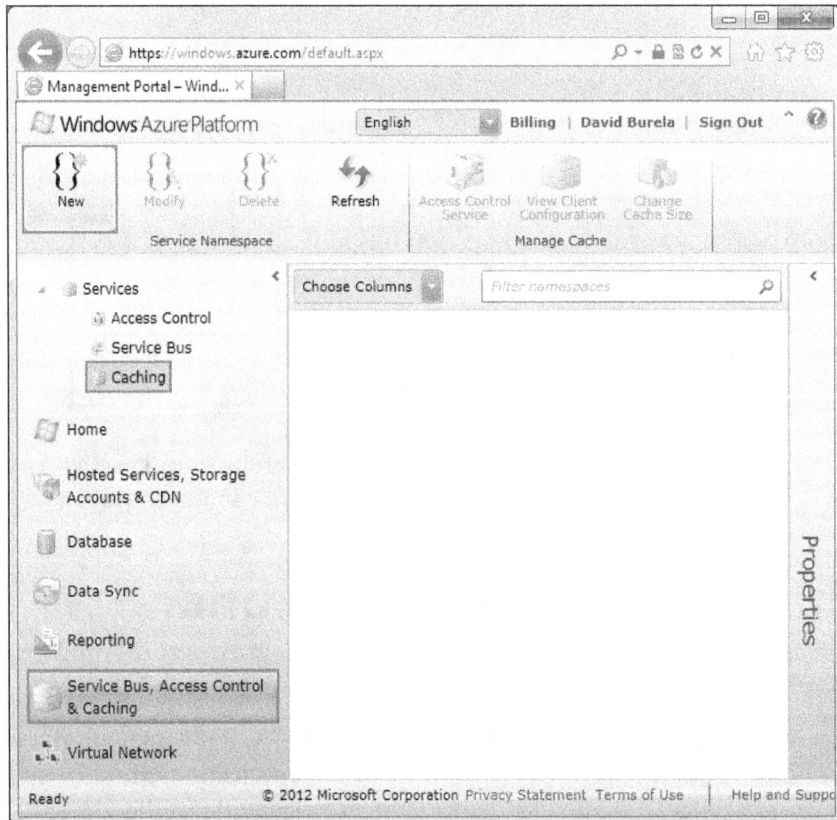

3. In the **Create a new Service Namespace** dialog, give the cache a namespace that will be used. Select the desired cache size. The following screenshot shows an example of a configured cache. Be sure to select the same region as the Azure compute instances that will be hosting the application, as follows:

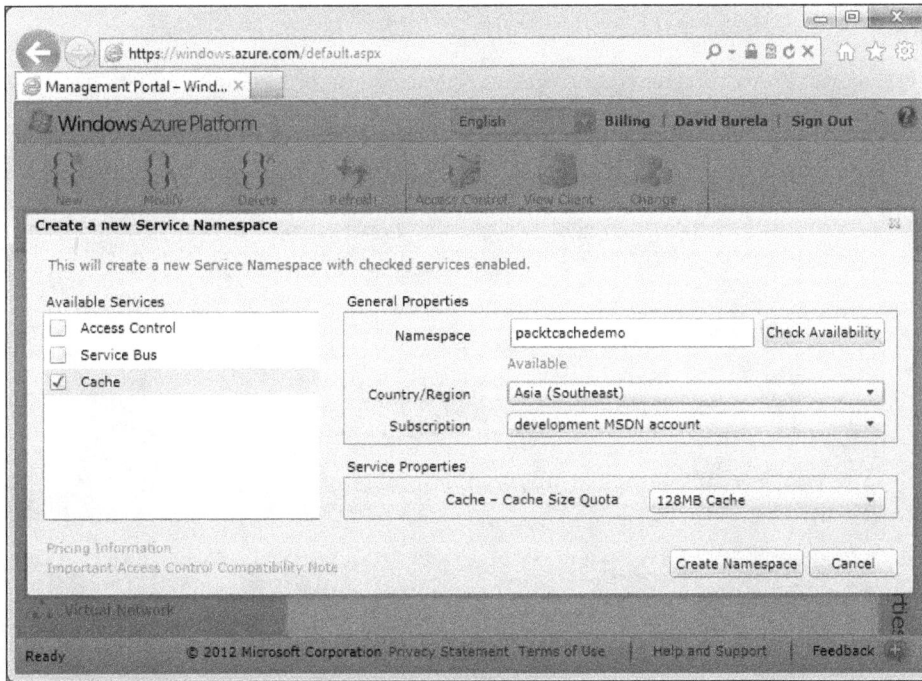

Cache region

It is essential that you locate the cache in the same location as the compute instances of your application. Having the hosted service and cache in different regions can introduce a great deal of **latency** into the requests.

4. Once the cache has been created, click on **View Client Configuration**. The pop up will show configuration settings that can be added to the `web.config` of your application. The following screenshot shows an example of the configuration settings:

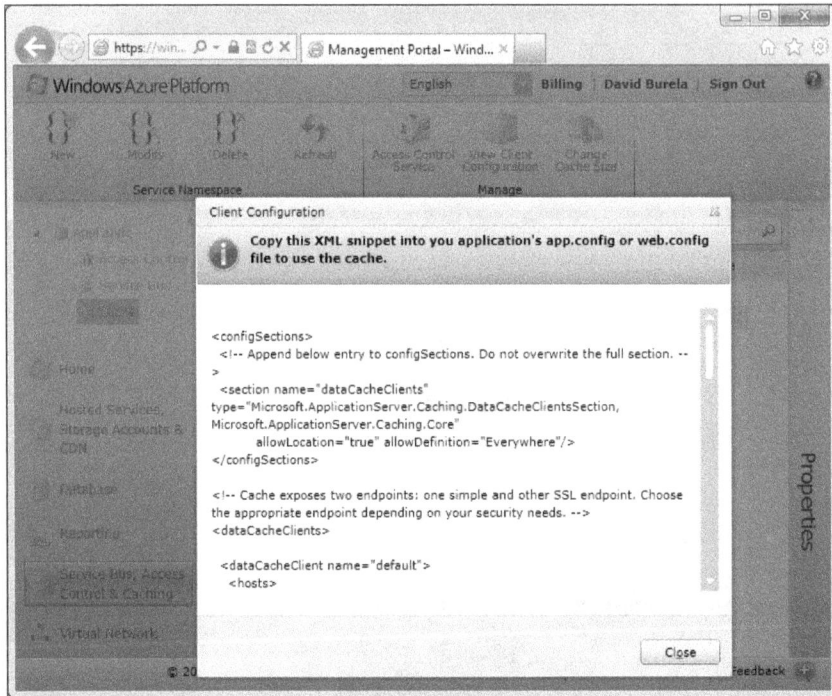

5. Select all of the configuration settings and save them locally somewhere on your computer for the steps that we will discuss later.

Creating the RIA Services application

With the AppFabric Caching Service provisioned, the Silverlight RIA Services application can now be created to consume it. The Silverlight client will not be consuming the AppFabric cache service directly. Instead, the RIA Domain Services will utilize the AppFabric cache to hold results from the database queries. These steps are the same as the ones discussed in *Chapter 7, Relational Data with SQL Azure and Entity Framework*:

1. In Visual Studio 2010, create a new **Windows Azure Project** named `AppFabricCacheExercise`.

2. Add a **Silverlight Business Application** to the project. Rename the role to `CachingBusinessApplication`. Click on **OK** to create the application.

3. Inside the ASP.Net **CachingBusinessApplication.web** project, right-click on the `Models` folder and click on **Add | New Item**.

4. In the search box, search for **entity**. Create a new **ADO.Net Entity Data Model**, and call it `WorkplaceModel.edmx`, as shown in the following screenshot:

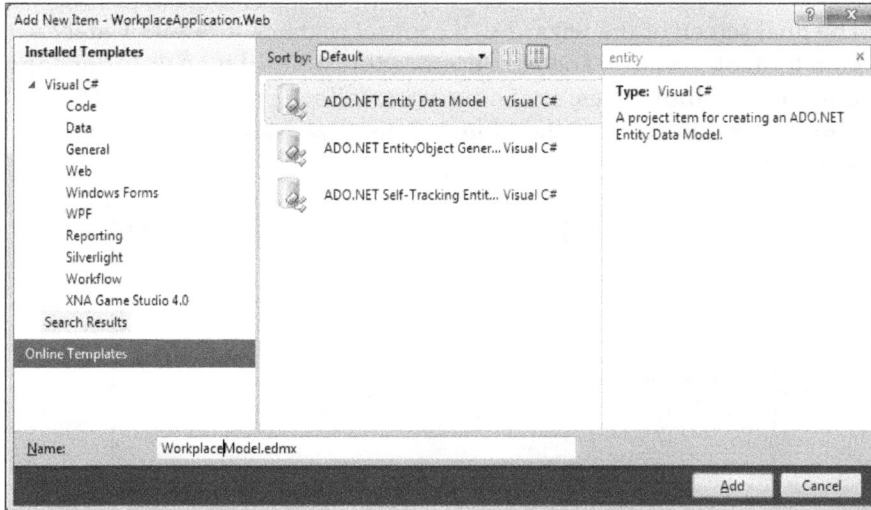

5. A wizard will open, allowing you to reverse engineer an existing database (database first), or to start from an empty model (model-first). This time, select **Generate from database**, and click on **Next**, as shown in the following screenshot:

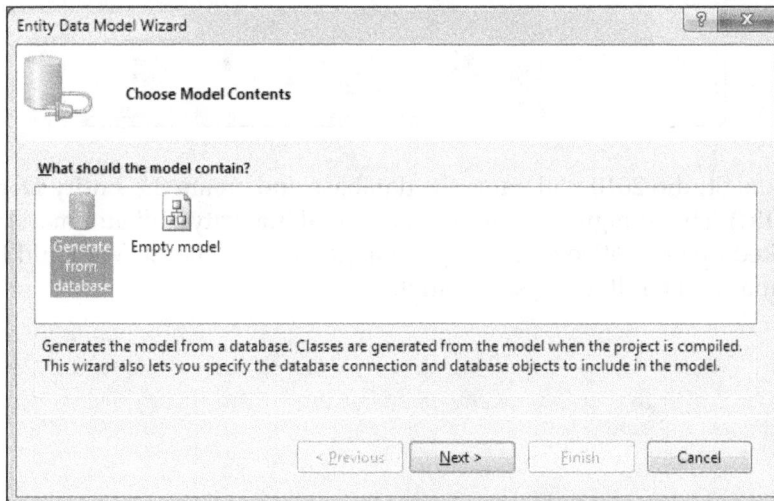

6. The next step of the wizard will ask for your SQL Azure credentials. Visual Studio 2010 should still have your SQL Azure connection string cached from the preceding exercise. If it does not, then click on **New Connection** and enter your SQL Azure server name and login credentials.

7. Once the connection has been selected, select to save all the details in the `web.config` file, then click on **Next**.

8. The final screen of the wizard will connect to the SQL Azure Database and scan for tables, views, and stored procedures. Select the **Divisions (dbo)** and **Employees (dbo)** tables, as shown in the following screenshot. Then click on **Finish**. For this exercise, the **Model Namespace** of `PacktDemoDBModel` will be used:

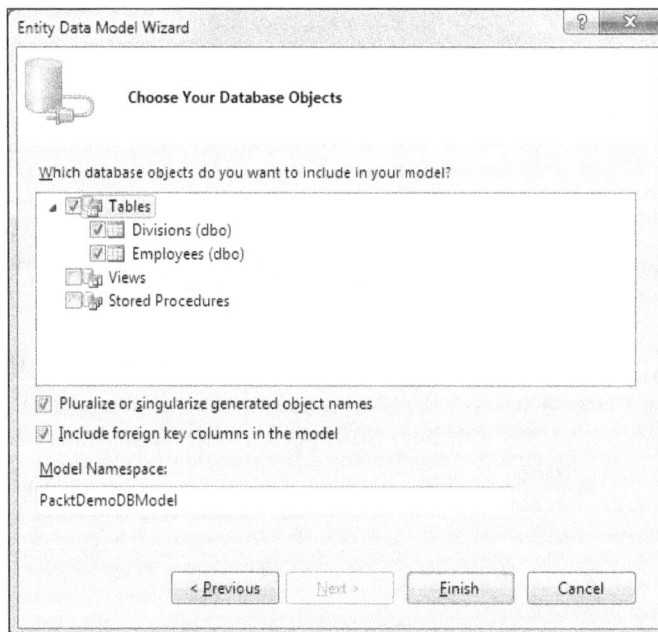

9. Visual Studio 2010 will parse the database and create the **Entity Data Model (EDM)**. The foreign key and the referential integrity will automatically be picked up and reflected in the generated entities. The EDM should look similar to the following screenshot:

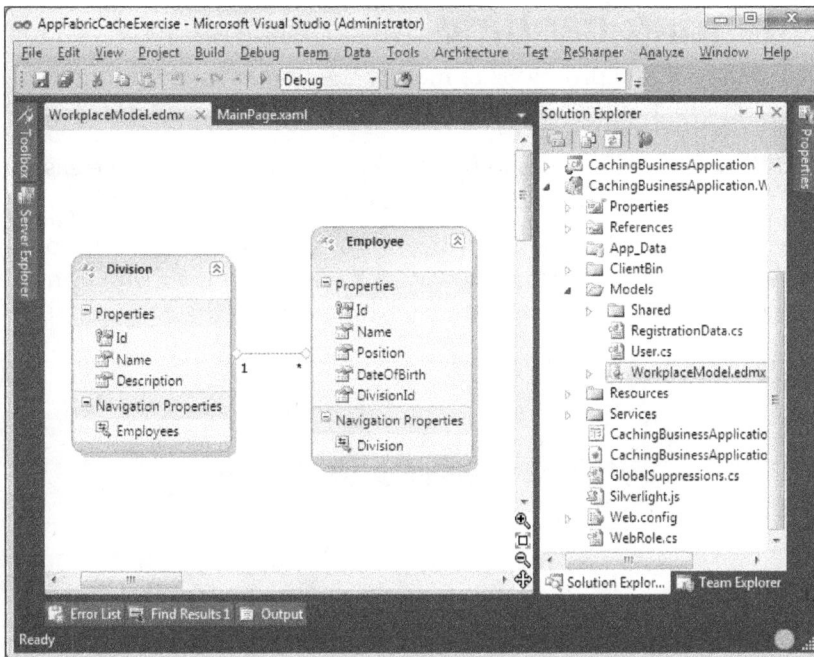

10. The EDM that was just created will help to generate the domain service. Build the project to ensure that the EDM has been compiled.

11. Inside the **CachingBusinessApplication.Web** project, right-click on the **Services** folder and click on **Add | New item**.

12. Create a new domain service class and name it `WorkplaceDomainService.cs`.

13. In the drop-down menu, select your EDM.

> **Why are my entities not appearing in the drop down?**
>
> If your EDM is not appearing in the drop down of the available `DataContext` classes, then you may not have built your project recently. After adding a new EDM, you need to build the project so that the entities are generated.

14. Click on the checkboxes next to **Division** and **Employee**. Click on **OK** to enable Visual Studio 2010 to generate the domain service.

15. The code generator will create a basic `WorkplaceDomainService` class. The `GetDivisions` and `GetEmployees` methods that are generated will simply return all the rows in those tables. These methods can be configured to cache the results for a period of time.

Implementing caching

The following stage of the process is to modify the domain service so that the results are cached for a period of time, as follows:

1. Start by adding references to the AppFabric caching SDK. The easiest way to do this is to use **NuGet** to add the AppFabric caching package.

2. From the **CachingBusinessApplication.Web** project, right-click on **References** and select **Manage NuGet Packages**. If the menu option does not appear, then install NuGet from `http://NuGet.org`:

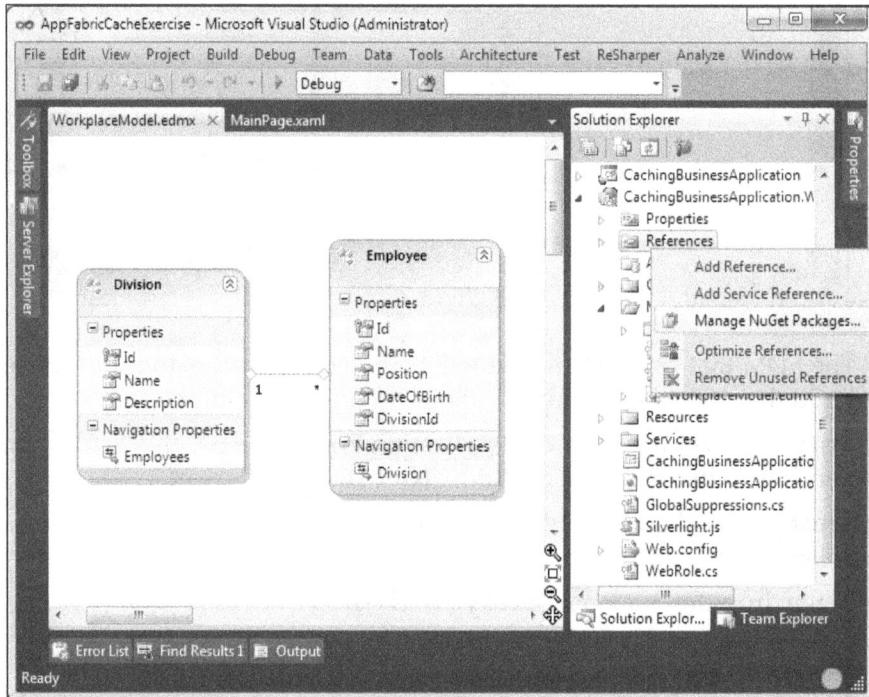

3. From within the **Manage NuGet Packages** window, search for **Windows Azure.Caching** and install the package, as shown in the following screenshot. This will add the AppFabric caching assemblies, as well as the placeholders into the `web.config` file:

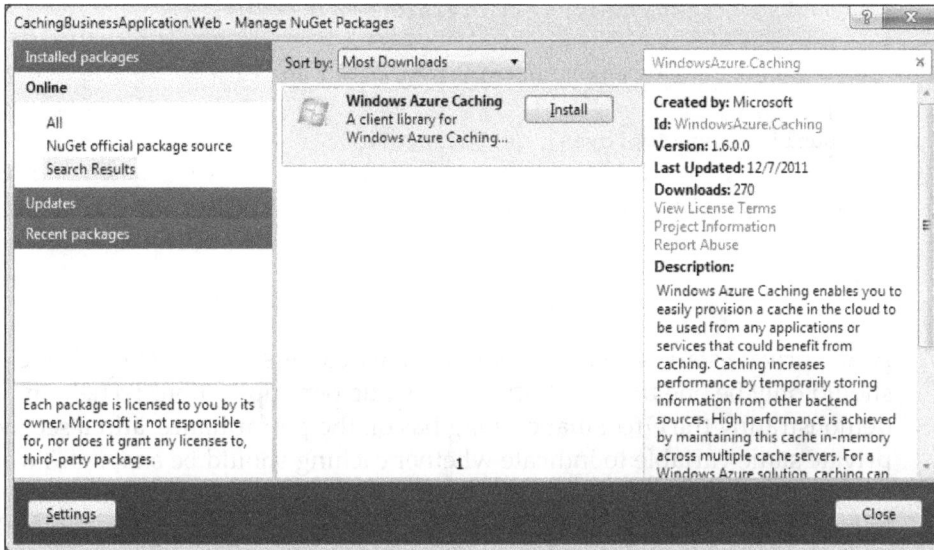

4. Open the `web.config` file **CachingBusinessApplication.Web**. Find the `<dataCacheClients>` section and replace it with the `<dataCacheClients>` configuration settings that were copied from the Azure Management Portal earlier.

5. Open the `WorkplaceDomainService.cs` class. Add all the using statements, as shown in the following code snippet to ensure that the namespaces are ready for the steps to follow:

```
namespace CachingBusinessApplication.Web.Services
{
    using System;
    using System.Collections.Generic;
    using System.Data;
    using System.Linq;
    using System.ServiceModel.DomainServices.EntityFramework;
    using System.ServiceModel.DomainServices.Hosting;
    using System.ServiceModel.DomainServices.Server;
    using Models;
    using Microsoft.ApplicationServer.Caching;
```

6. Change the method signatures of the `Get` entity methods so that they return `List<>`. We will be storing `Divisions` as a lookup table in the memory:

```
[EnableClientAccess()]
public class WorkplaceDomainService :
    LinqToEntitiesDomainService<PacktDemoDBEntities>
{
```

```
      public List<Division> GetDivisions()
      {
        return this.ObjectContext.Divisions.ToList();
      }
      public List<Employee> GetEmployees()
      {
        return this.ObjectContext.Employees.ToList();
      }
    }
  }
```

7. Add a private static variable to hold the DataCacheFactory value. There should only be one DataCacheFactory value per application. To help in demonstrating the effect that caching has on the performance, add a second private static variable to indicate whether caching should be enabled. Two new methods will also be added. One sets the _isCacheEnabled Boolean to false, while the other method sets it to true and also instantiates a default DataCacheFactory value, as follows:

```
private static DataCacheFactory _cacheFactory = new
  DataCacheFactory();
private static bool _isCacheEnabled = false;
[Invoke]
public void TurnCacheOff()
{
  _isCacheEnabled = false;
}
[Invoke]
public void TurnRemoteCacheOn()
{
  _isCacheEnabled = true;
  _cacheFactory = new DataCacheFactory();
}
```

8. Add a third method to the class. This method will also set the _isCacheEnabled Boolean to true. However, it will also configure the DataCacheFactory instance to enable the Azure instance to use a part of the memory within it to locally cache a subsection of the AppFabric cache to improve the performance. The DataCacheLocalCacheProperties object is set to cache 2,000 objects for a default period of 30 minutes, as shown in the following code snippet:

```
[Invoke]
public void TurnLocalCacheOn()
{
```

```
    _isCacheEnabled = true;
    var localCacheConfig = new DataCacheLocalCacheProperties(2000,
      new TimeSpan(0, 0, 30),
        DataCacheLocalCacheInvalidationPolicy.TimeoutBased);
    var factoryConfig = new DataCacheFactoryConfiguration();
    factoryConfig.LocalCacheProperties = localCacheConfig;
    _cacheFactory = new DataCacheFactory(factoryConfig);
}
```

9. Modify the `GetDivisions()` method. It should check whether the caching is enabled or not. If the caching is enabled, it should get a handle to the `DataCache` and attempt to get the data of the cached `divisions`. If the `divisions` data was found in the cache, then return it. If it was not, then use Entity Framework to query for the data, store it in the cache, then return the data. If caching is not enabled, then use Entity Framework to return the data. When the `dataCache.Get("divisions")` method is executed, it will automatically check the local server memory to see whether the `DataCacheFactory` was configured to use the local cache, as shown in the following code snippet. There is no need to query differently:

```
public List<Division> GetDivisions()
{
  if (_isCacheEnabled)
  {
    try
    {
      var dataCache = _cacheFactory.GetDefaultCache();
      var divisions = dataCache.Get("divisions") as
        List<Division>;
      if (divisions != null)
      {
        // the divisions were in the cache. Return them now
        return divisions;
      }
      // the divisions were not in the cache, query for them
      divisions =
        this.ObjectContext.Divisions.Include("Employees").ToList();
      dataCache.Add("divisions", divisions,
        TimeSpan.FromSeconds(30));
      return divisions;
    }
    catch (DataCacheException ex)
    {
      // ignore temporary failures
```

```
    if (ex.ErrorCode != DataCacheErrorCode.RetryLater)
    {
      throw;
    }
  }
}
var a = this.ObjectContext.Divisions.Include("Employees");
return a.ToList();
}
```

10. Open `Home.xaml`.

11. Drag a `DataGrid` from the toolbox onto the designer to enable Visual Studio 2010 to automatically add the references required to use the `DataGrid`.

12. To the screen, add a `DataGrid` to display the Divisions, a `TextBlock` to display the status of the caching service, and another one to display the time it takes the service to return the data. Then add four `Buttons`. The first will refresh the `DataGrid` based on the current settings. The other three buttons will invoke the domain service method to change the cache settings as follows:

```
<navigation:Page …
xmlns:sdk="http://schemas.microsoft.com/winfx/2006/xaml/
presentation/sdk">
  <Grid x:Name="LayoutRoot">
    <ScrollViewer x:Name="PageScrollViewer" Style="{StaticResource
      PageScrollViewerStyle}">
      <StackPanel x:Name="ContentStackPanel"
        Style="{StaticResource ContentStackPanelStyle}">
        <sdk:DataGrid Name="divisionDataGrid"
         Name="divisionDataGrid"
        AutoGenerateColumns="True" Height="150" />
        <TextBlock Name="cacheSettingsTextBlock" Text="Cache: Off"
          />
        <TextBlock Name="timeTakenTextBlock" />
        <Button Content="Refresh" Height="23" Width="180"
          Click="RefreshButton_Click" />
        <Button Content="Disable cache" Height="23" Width="180"
          Click=" DisableCache_Click" />
        <Button Content="Enable cache" Height="23" Width="180"
          Click=" EnableRemoteCache_Click" />
        <Button Content="Enable cache &amp; local cache"
          Height="23" Width="180"
          Click=" EnableLocalCache_Click" />
      </StackPanel>
    </ScrollViewer>
  </Grid>
</navigation:Page>
```

13. Open `Home.xaml.cs`. Add the event handler for the `RefreshButton`. The method clears the `DataGrid` and creates an instance of the `WorkplaceDomainContext`. The domain context is then queried and the results are placed into the DataGrid. The current time is captured just before and after the request is made. The difference between these two values is displayed to the user as the time taken:

```
private void RefreshButton_Click(object sender,
  System.Windows.RoutedEventArgs e)
{
  // clear the DataGrid before continuing
  divisionDataGrid.ItemsSource = null;
  var context = new Web.Services.WorkplaceDomainContext();
  var query = context.GetDivisionsQuery();
  // get the time just before the Load method is called
  var start = DateTime.Now.Ticks;
  context.Load(query, callback =>
  {
    // immediately get the time that the data was returned
    var stop = DateTime.Now.Ticks;
    var timeTaken = new TimeSpan(stop - start);
    timeTakenTextBlock.Text = "Elapsed time: " +
      timeTaken.TotalMilliseconds;
    divisionDataGrid.ItemsSource = callback.Entities;
  }, null);
}
```

14. Add the event handlers for the remaining three buttons. These invoke the domain service to turn the cache off, on, or on with the local cache on the Azure instance also enabled, as shown in the following code snippet:

```
private void DisableCache_Click (object sender,
  System.Windows.RoutedEventArgs e)
{
  var context = new Web.Services.WorkplaceDomainContext();
  context.TurnCacheOff();
  cacheSettingsTextBlock.Text = "Cache: Off";
}
private void EnableRemoteCache_Click (object sender,
  System.Windows.RoutedEventArgs e)
{
  var context = new Web.Services.WorkplaceDomainContext();
  context.TurnRemoteCacheOn();
  cacheSettingsTextBlock.Text = "Cache: Appfabric caching
    enabled";
}
```

```
private void EnableLocalCache_Click (object sender,
  System.Windows.RoutedEventArgs e)
{
  var context = new Web.Services.WorkplaceDomainContext();
  context.TurnLocalCacheOn();
  cacheSettingsTextBlock.Text = "Cache: Appfabric caching & local
    server cache enabled";
}
```

15. Make sure that the Azure project is set as the startup project and press *F5* to compile and run. Click on a button to turn the cache on or off, then click on **Refresh** multiple times. The first request will usually take much longer as connections are established. So only pay attention to the time taken on subsequent requests.

16. After ensuring that the application works, deploy it to Azure. The following references in the web project need to be set to `Copy Local=true`: `System.ServiceModel.DomainServices.EntityFramework`, `System.ServiceModel.DomainServices.Hosting`, and `System.ServiceModel.DomainServices.Server`. This is required as the Azure servers only have the .Net framework installed without any additional frameworks. All the external assemblies need to be deployed with the application.

17. Once deployed, check the time it takes to return the data to the Silverlight client with cache disabled, enabled in AppFabric, and enabled in AppFabric with the Azure instance also using its spare memory to cache.

When run on my computer in Australia, with the project being hosted in the Azure datacentre in South East Asia, the results were as follows. Your results may vary, and the following results should only be used to see the relative sizing differences between the three options:

AppFabric cache status	Time
AppFabric cache disabled	210ms
AppFabric cache enabled	170ms
AppFabric cache enabled with instance memory caching	150ms

In the previous example, there is only a slight difference between accessing directly from the SQL Azure Database and utilizing the cache. However, this was a simple query with only eight rows of data being returned directly from the database. The difference between the three times would be larger if it was a more complex SQL Query with multiple joins and filters on a larger dataset, if more results were being cached, or if the application was under significant load.

You may find that in some instances, SQL Azure can return individual results faster than AppFabric (without instance caching). Be sure to consider what the effect would be if you had hundreds of clients querying at the same time though. The performance of SQL Azure would quickly degrade, while AppFabric would continue to return the data quickly.

ASP.NET session caching

There may be scenarios where it is desirable to use the ASP.NET session state to store user data. But, by default, this data would be stored on each individual role instance, which can quickly cause inconsistencies in the data.

AppFabric caching can be utilized to resolve this issue by storing the session data in the shared AppFabric cache where each instance can access it. A project can be enabled to use AppFabric to store session state through a single configuration entry on the `web.config` file. Once the AppFabric `<dataCacheClients>` configuration section has been inserted into the `web.config`, then one additional entry needs to be added to `<configSections>`. Following is the code snippet that is provided by the management portal:

```
<configSections>
  <!-- Append below entry to configSections. Do not overwrite the
    full section. -->
  <section name="dataCacheClients" type="Microsoft.ApplicationServer.
   Caching.DataCacheClientsSection,
    Microsoft.ApplicationServer.Caching.Core"
  allowLocation="true" allowDefinition="Everywhere"/>
</configSections>
```

Summary

This chapter introduced the concept of caching to improve application performance. AppFabric was shown to be a distributed cache that can be accessed by Azure role instances to quickly access the frequently used data. It is important to remember that only slowly changing data should be stored in the cache or you risk working with stale data. An example application was built to show how easily caching can be added to an application with a few configuration settings and a single query.

Index

W

[PACKT] PUBLISHING   enterprise ❁
professional expertise distilled

Thank you for buying
Microsoft Silverlight 5 and Windows Azure Enterprise Integration

About Packt Publishing

Packt, pronounced 'packed', published its first book "Mastering phpMyAdmin for Effective MySQL Management" in April 2004 and subsequently continued to specialize in publishing highly focused books on specific technologies and solutions.

Our books and publications share the experiences of your fellow IT professionals in adapting and customizing today's systems, applications, and frameworks. Our solution based books give you the knowledge and power to customize the software and technologies you're using to get the job done. Packt books are more specific and less general than the IT books you have seen in the past. Our unique business model allows us to bring you more focused information, giving you more of what you need to know, and less of what you don't.

Packt is a modern, yet unique publishing company, which focuses on producing quality, cutting-edge books for communities of developers, administrators, and newbies alike. For more information, please visit our website: www.packtpub.com.

About Packt Enterprise

In 2010, Packt launched two new brands, Packt Enterprise and Packt Open Source, in order to continue its focus on specialization. This book is part of the Packt Enterprise brand, home to books published on enterprise software – software created by major vendors, including (but not limited to) IBM, Microsoft and Oracle, often for use in other corporations. Its titles will offer information relevant to a range of users of this software, including administrators, developers, architects, and end users.

Writing for Packt

We welcome all inquiries from people who are interested in authoring. Book proposals should be sent to author@packtpub.com. If your book idea is still at an early stage and you would like to discuss it first before writing a formal book proposal, contact us; one of our commissioning editors will get in touch with you.

We're not just looking for published authors; if you have strong technical skills but no writing experience, our experienced editors can help you develop a writing career, or simply get some additional reward for your expertise.

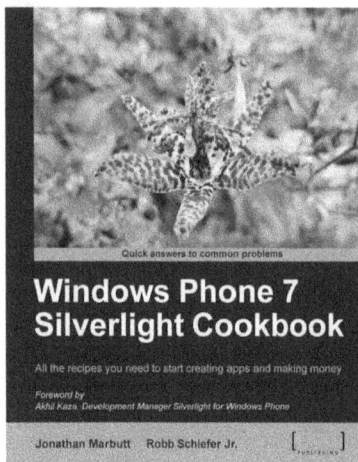

Windows Phone 7 Silverlight Cookbook

ISBN: 978-1-84969-116-1   Paperback: 304 pages

All the recipes you need to start creating apps and making money

1. Build sophisticated Windows Phone apps with clean, optimized code.

2. Perform easy to follow recipes to create practical apps.

3. Master the entire workflow from designing your app to publishing it.

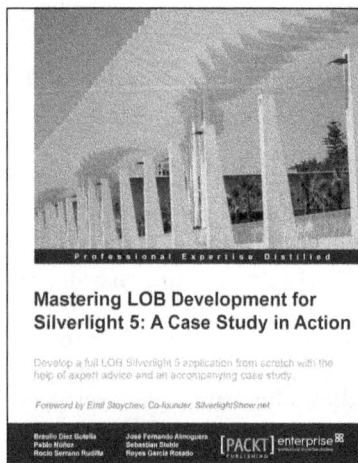

Mastering LOB Development for Silverlight 5: A Case Study in Action

ISBN: 978-1-84968-354-8   Paperback: 430 pages

Develop a full LOB Silverlight 5 application from scratch with the help of expert advice and an accompanying case study

1. Dive straight into Silverlight 5 with the advanced techniques in this expert guide

2. Fully up-to-date content for Silverlight 5 and RIA Services SP2

3. Complete your knowledge with a gradually built upon case study with this book and e-book

Please check **www.PacktPub.com** for information on our titles

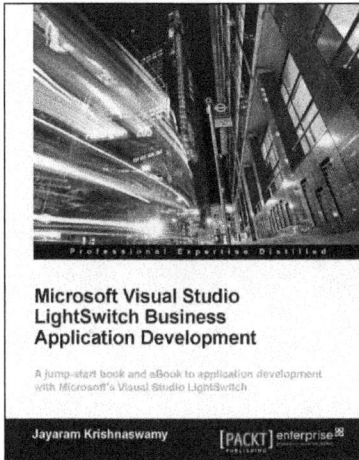

Microsoft Visual Studio LightSwitch Business Application Development

ISBN: 978-1-84968-286-2   Paperback: 384 pages

A jump-start guide to application development with Microsoft's Visual Studio LightSwitch

1. A hands-on guide, packed with screenshots and step-by-step instructions and relevant background information — making it easy to build your own application with this book and ebook

2. Easily connect to various data sources with practical examples and easy-to-follow instructions

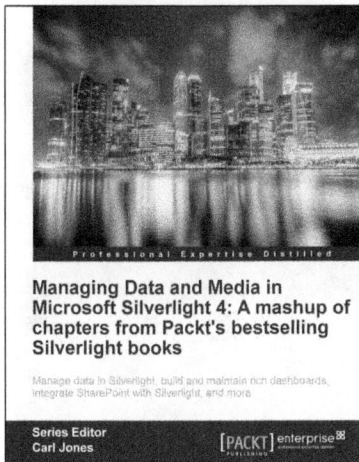

Managing Data and Media in Microsoft Silverlight 4: A mashup of chapters from Packt's bestselling Silverlight books

ISBN: 978-1-84968-564-1   Paperback: 530 pages

Manage data in Silverlight, build and maintain rich dashboards, integrate SharePoint with Silverlight, and more

1. A mashup book from expert Silverlight professionals, from 6 Packt donor titles - professional expertise distilled in a true sense starting at just $19.99

2. Packed with practical, hands-on examples, illustrating techniques to solve particular data problems effectively within your Silverlight business applications

Please check **www.PacktPub.com** for information on our titles